Naomi's Story

First published in 1999

Allen & Unwin Pty Ltd
9 Atchison Street
St Leonards, NSW 1590, Australia
Phone: (61 2) 8425 0100
Fax: (61 2) 9906 2218
E-mail: frontdesk@allen-unwin.com.au
Web: http://www.allen-unwin.com.au

National Library of Australia
Cataloguing-in-Publication entry:
Casimir, Jon.
Naomi's story: a baby's journey. A father's diary.

ISBN 186508 152 3.

1. Casimir, Naomi—Birth. 2. Fathers and infants. 3.
Fathers—Biography. 4. Pregnancy. 5. Fathers and
daughters. I. Title.

306.8742092

Designed by Ruth Grüner
Typeset by Midland Typesetters
Printed by Australian Print Group, Maryborough, Victoria

1 3 5 7 9 10 8 6 4 2

A Baby's Journey
A Father's Diary

JON CASIMIR

ALLEN & UNWIN

January

January 10

9.46 pm. Just impregnated your mother. Feeling good. Off to the pub to brag about it to my friends ... Okay, none of this is strictly true (I have no friends), but it seems like a good way to start.

January 11

My father makes things with his hands. At the foot of the bed is a chest he gave me fifteen years ago, when I left home to go to university; his way of wishing me luck. It's a memory chest now, crammed with letters, school report cards and souvenirs—fragments of other places and times.

When Helen and I decided to try the pregnancy thing, I wanted to create something special for you, my as yet unborn, and possibly unconceived, child. But your father makes nothing. To the best of my knowledge, and I'm sure medical science will back me up on this, the home handyman gene skips generations. I live in fear of the dripping tap and the squeaky gate, because I know they have my measure. My hands are good for two things: sock puppetry and typing. There's not a lot of call for the former these days, so I've made a career from the latter.

This diary, then, is the best I can offer you. It came about because I kept thinking, wouldn't it be good if you knew how things were when you were born, if you had some idea of your parents, not when they were old, but when they only felt old? Wouldn't it be good if you knew how you came into the world?

So this is a picture of life as you can't remember it, a prebiography (no, hang on, it's a premoir). Here's how it began ...

JANUARY 12

Blood. And the lack of it. This is what I spend my time thinking about. Waiting. Watching. Asking. It's the first thing that comes to mind as I lever the sleep dust from my eyelids in the morning, and the last before those lids clamp shut at night. I try not to sound too interested, too hopeful—that would somehow be uncool, or just bad karma—but I can't stop myself from checking with Helen three or four times a day.

'How's the flow?' I ask over breakfast.

'Non-existent,' she says, without even looking up from her muesli. It's a scene that's been replaying itself for days.

The arrival of Helen's period has always been a good sign in our relationship. It has represented a potential difficulty averted, a question unasked, a problem that will not have to be faced. But after years of willing the blood to arrive, I'm now praying for it to stay away.

Helen is a week late. This in itself is not unusual, so we're acting as if it's not important. But I think it is. I believe you're in there. Helen doesn't. Or if she does, she's playing it down, refusing to acknowledge the possibility until it goes before a medical jury.

She may be right. A week ago, she had the kind of mood swing that would suggest it's menstrual business as usual. It was more a mood playground: not just the swing, but the monkey bars, seesaw and slippery dip. For five days, everything I did was wrong, every move I made a mistake, every word I uttered further evidence of my tragic flaws. For five days, I wondered if a posting to Antarctica might not be a bad idea. I like the cold.

Then we thought her period had come, but it was just a spot. The tiniest of trickles. And now nothing. We wait and wonder. Was that spot significant? Women often spot when they are pregnant. Has she missed a period? The PMT has crested and fallen—Helen's back to a calm state. But her breasts are still swollen. Her glands are up.

There are little, nervous butterflies in my stomach. I buy a home pregnancy test kit. 'Accurate. Results in as little as two minutes. Use any time of day.' These testers are a landmark of modern design, with their Easy Grip™ handle, attractive Result Window™ and Absorbent Strip™. If you believe the back of the box, they're 99 per cent accurate in lab testing. How well they work at home is another question.

The directions are straightforward. Hold one end of the icecream-stick-shaped tester in your urine stream (and doesn't that sound like a place beside which you'd want to picnic?) for ten seconds, then wait for the result. The tester works by detecting the presence of the pregnancy hormone hCG (human Chorionic Gonadotrophin). If the hCG is there, two pink lines show up in the Result Window™. If not, only one.

Late in the afternoon, I wander into the bathroom and find a tester in the wastebasket. I see the two pink lines, one strong and one faint, but definitely two. Helen is having a nap. When she comes to, blearily dragging herself down the hall, I ask why she didn't show me the results.

'It wasn't clear,' she says blithely. 'I have to do another one. I didn't want to get you all excited. I know you— you get carried away. I have to do one later.'

Later comes when we're watching a video. Right at the movie's climax, Helen stops the tape and cheerfully announces that her bladder is telling her to excuse herself.

'It's the same as the first,' she says on her return, brandishing an indicator on which there are quite clearly two pink lines. 'It's inconclusive. There's one line but the second one is too faint.' She shrugs and drops the packet into the bin. I say nothing, but in my mind I'm thinking of a phrase a friend once used, 'She's swimming the Egyptian river.' In denial.

As we're undressing for bed, Helen reminds me of an earlier, unfinished conversation: 'You started to say something before, something about if I was pregnant, you would ...'

'I can't remember.'

'Damn, I was hoping it involved jewellery.'

JANUARY 13

Still no blood. I guess here's as good a place as any to make a couple of notes. We're both journalists—we work for the same paper. I'm 32, Helen's 38. We've been together three years. We're not married. That's not my fault. Every time I bring the subject up, she says, 'Been there, done that.'

I reckon that if Helen is pregnant, the conception date would have been around 21 December. Don't ask me how I know, I just know. That would mean your due date, if you are gestating already, is in mid-September.

'Damn!' says Helen when I tell her. 'A Virgo.' From her point of view, this is shorthand for fussy, vain and difficult. 'Still,' she says, 'it would be pretty.'

If egg and sperm have met, your heart will already be beating. Your lungs will be starting to form. The placenta will be there working for you. You will have a head, with the tiniest evidence of eyes and ears. All of this will have taken place if Helen is pregnant. But take her word for it—she's not.

'Feel my breasts,' she says indignantly. 'Go on, feel them. They're not sore. They're not sore at all. So I'm not pregnant.'

I humour her. Playing with her breasts is not how I usually spend my day, but for a matter as important as this, I'm prepared to make the sacrifice. They seem to be growing. As I take my hands away, there's a long pause.

'It's a pity I'm not,' Helen says. 'I want to be pregnant now. I've decided.'

A Web site I check says that if Helen were pregnant (which—have I mentioned this?—she is not) she would be fatigued, hormonally crazy and as thirsty as a camel after eight weeks of sand duty. Even she admits that she is all of these things. But she doesn't think it's worth seeing a doctor yet and cancels an appointment I asked her to make.

JANUARY 14

No blood, but Helen's still swimming upriver.

'I'm hot. I'm cold. I'm hot again. Now I'm really hot.' She changes clothes twice before leaving for work. Her metabolism is haywire. Every time I look, I see another symptom.

We've been trying to get pregnant for about six weeks now. We made the decision halfway through last year and then left if for a few months to see if we'd go cool on the idea. By November we were still sure. What we were not sure of was how long it would take. We had a feeling that if the time was right, it would just happen. And in some way we can't quite explain, it seems to both of us that our bodies have been actually asking for it.

I wonder if Helen is holding out on me in the hope that if she is not pregnant, I will have to go and have a sperm count done. When we started trying, she jokingly said that if she didn't get pregnant within three cycles, I'd have to have my equipment checked out. I think, in the nicest, most loving way, she relishes the image of my embarrassment at having to provide the sample. Somehow, I don't think she's going to get her wish.

JANUARY 16

No blood. 'I'm not pregnant, you know,' she insists, standing over me and pointing at her chest. 'My breasts are going down. They're getting smaller.'

Selflessly, I feel her breasts again.

'You may be right, but what about those two tests?'

'You can get strange hormones during the lead-up to your period,' she says, stomping off to the bathroom.

Later, I offer what I think is a brilliant solution.

'How about we buy another pair of tests? You piss on

one and I'll piss on the other and we'll see what happens. I can be the non-pregnant control group.'

No response.

At dinnertime, she exclaims, 'I want tomato soup.' Let the record show, we have seen Craving Number One.

JANUARY 17

No blood. Helen relents and agrees to see a doctor. Not because she thinks she is pregnant, but because we need to make decisions on our yearly holidays. We're keen to sneak in a short overseas trip. After pointing out, yet again, that she couldn't possibly be, you know, in the family way, she says she feels tired and queasy (is it morning already?) and retires to bed for most of the day.

JANUARY 19

This is going to sound really dumb, but it's true. Today I sit on the beach (we're spending the weekend with our friend Ruth at her sand-handy wonderpad), my toes pushing through the orange sand, the breeze riffling through the pines at the edge of the parking lot. The tide line is dotted with kids in sunsuits, building castles as teenage surfers wobble in on half-hearted waves. Helen and Ruth are out in the waves too, but I'd much rather look at the water than be in it, so I'm happy to sit. Helen tells me later that I looked like a faithful dog, waiting patiently for them to come out.

Anyway, I sit there feeling the wind on my face and thinking it's a new year and work has found an even keel and everything seems to be laid out in front of me and

Helen is pregnant (no matter what she says). And you know what? I feel content. I feel calm. Happy. How often can you say you feel happy? How often do you catch yourself, in perfect silence, and realise how lucky you are?

JANUARY 20

No blood. I once asked my mother how you could possibly know when it was the right time to have children. Everyone I know always has excuses: 'Oh, we don't have enough money yet.' 'We haven't got the right house.' 'We haven't got the right clothes.' 'We really just want a puppy.'

I must have been eighteen or nineteen when I asked. My mother stopped and thought, then gave what seemed an inscrutable answer. 'You wake up one morning and everything you have is not enough.' It floats back to me now. It took years to understand what she meant, perhaps because it's not there to be understood. It's there to be felt.

In bed, Helen arrives at her best non-pregnancy excuse yet. Her breasts are hurting, tender, making it hard for her to sleep.

'Maybe I have cancer,' she says, gingerly examining them.

'No, babe, you have Virgo.'

JANUARY 22

Helen calls from a phone box. I've been spending the day in a parade of pointless meetings and by the time she rings, I am so distracted that I have somehow forgotten she had a doctor's appointment.

'It's very, very positive,' she says excitedly.

It takes a second or two for me to work out what she means, then the grin spreads across my face. I can feel the heat in my cheeks. I turn towards the wall so no-one in the office will see. When she makes it back to work, I ask if she's happy.

'I guess so,' is the reply, 'but what do I do, where do I go, what's going to happen? How do I buy clothes? What size do I get? I just saw a stretchy skirt, 38 or 55?'

The due date, it seems, is pretty close to our reckoning, somewhere between the 9th and 16th of September. Being at work at this moment just seems so wrong. I drag Helen into the stairwell and give her a big hug, lifting her off her feet and squeezing her. 'Careful of the breasts,' comes the small voice from my armpit.

'Are you sure you want this?' she asks, but she can see on my face what I'm thinking, and I can see it on hers. There's a lot of kissing going on.

'You're going to be a daddy,' she announces, her hand flattened on my chest, over my heart. 'You're going to be a daddy, and I'm going to be ... out of it pretty much.'

Hello you.

January 23

No blood ... hard to kick the habit. Helen wakes up very queasy. She now admits how unwell she's been feeling lately. Her doctor told her to exercise gently but she finds it hard enough just getting out of bed. Standing in the kitchen in her nightie, hair dishevelled, holding a precious cup of tea, she looks as if she might fall over at any second.

We're not telling anybody about you. We've decided that we want to wait, for a number of reasons:

1. There are tests to go through
2. It seems as if it would jinx it to tell everyone so early, as if something would almost certainly go wrong
3. We want to share it with each other for a while, to get used to the idea before we have to share it with the world
4. We want to put off being deluged with friendly advice from family and friends for as long as possible
5. It takes twelve weeks to get through the miscarriage woods.

I have to keep telling Helen she is pregnant—she asks me to remind her. We don't really know what it means— our sense of it is abstract, romantic. Even if we did, Helen's too busy with the nitty gritty of watching her body go into revolt to take much notice of the bigger, brighter picture. Her happiness is filtered through tiredness, vagueness and a nausea that seems constant already.

I feel the surge of biology, the DNA-encoded protective- ness rising in me. I look into Helen's eyes and tell her I love her. She knows this, and I know she knows it, but it seems important to me to reassure her that I'm not going anywhere. Only 24 hours into the official pregnancy, I'm feeling like a useless male, trying to over-compensate. What is my role? If this were a previous century, I could bang my jug of mead on the table, declare, 'My work is done', and bugger off to the Crusades for a couple of decades, returning home in time to see my adult son knock off his first peasant. Perhaps I should buy some of those how-to books.

JANUARY 24

I spend the afternoon perusing the shelves of various bookshops for guidance. I can't find much of interest or use, which suggests to me that: a) there's a pregnancy epidemic and all the good stuff has been bought; b) there just isn't any good stuff; or c) I'm in the wrong kind of bookshops. (I should have realised when I saw the blow-up dolls by the door.)

Having failed in that task, I buy Helen a ring from Tiffany's. It's a plain silver band with a pinhead-sized ruby (hey, I'm not rich) and costs me a couple of hundred dollars. Something to commemorate or celebrate or whatever. Walking back to the car, I notice that women are stopping to open doors for me. It must be the Tiffany's bag. The first time I tell myself it's a coincidence. By the third, I'm certain it isn't. The woman looks at my face, at the bag, at my face again and then takes two or three steps out of her way to hold a door.

JANUARY 25

Helen is slowing down. After a morning of shopping and running errands, she collapses onto the couch, fatigued and nauseous. Something in her lunch, she says, is performing gymnastic routines in her stomach. Purity is now her number one food concern. Everything must be fresh and unprocessed. Simple, unfussy, good. Anything else upsets her hypersensitive balance and leaves her like this, moaning to herself and watching bad TV.

JANUARY 27

My friend David and I are out for the day, watching rock bands in the sun, never a pretty sight. I want to tell him about you, but I can't. I've never been good at keeping secrets. I wonder how long I'll hold out. When I get home, Helen says she has been exhausted. The issue of purity now seems to be extending to her personal space—she no longer has much interest in being near me. She says she doesn't like the way I smell any more.

She's vaguely nauseous all the time. Her senses are heightened, particularly those of smell and sound. She says the doctor told her she would be permanently exhausted, but she didn't think it would be like this, 'like living inside a fog'.

'Can I make you a cup of tea?' I ask.

'No.'

'Can I come over and give you a kiss?'

She scrunches up her face, looks like a sucked lemon.

'Yeah, that's right,' I say. 'You've used me, taken my sperm and now you're rejecting me. That's some weird biology you've got there, some weird animal mother behaviour.'

'Hey, it could have been worse,' she says. 'I could have eaten you.'

JANUARY 28

Enough of the feel-good celebration. A week has passed since the news. It's time to get down to it. I make a list of things I have to do in the next eight months or so:

1. Take whole thing seriously (hard)
2. Buy those books that tell me what the hell is happening (easy)
3. Be kind to Helen (easy)
4. Choose baby name (hard)
5. Begin program of sleep deprivation as practice for inevitable (hard)
6. Come up with novel way to explain to you that yes, we are your parents (hard)
7. Get over fears of responsibility and commitment (easy)
8. Get stonkingly huge pay rise (easy)
9. Buy new house and car (easy)
10. Learn Spanish (hard)
11. Take washing to laundromat (easy)
12. Grow up (hard)
13. Stop making lists I will forget or lose (hard).

January 30

I realise my list doesn't include anything practical such as 'Organise birth' and decide not to show it to Helen. Not that she'd be able to read it. Yesterday she slept, worked for half an hour, slept, worked for half an hour, slept, and so on. Whenever I saw her, she was groaning and clutching her stomach. She looked drugged.

The cravings have hit like a meteor. I thought they came much later in the pregnancy—apparently not. Eggs. Cheese on toast (and she's always been a lactophobe!). Yoghurt. Fruit. And fruit juice. Endless fruit juice.

Her desire not to be touched is growing stronger. Basically, she'd rather cuddle roadkill than me. I don't know why that is—it's not as if I got her pregnant or anything. She sometimes comes over for a quick hug, but I can hear her holding her breath. I'm hoping this rejection is just a first trimester thing.

JANUARY 31

Off to the obstetrician. Dr Andrew, a middle-aged man of Hungarian extraction, speaks slowly and delightfully dryly. He says our suspected conception date of about December 21 is believable. And if it's true, then yes, the due date is September 15 or thereabouts. This would mean that today, the pregnancy is about seven and a half weeks in.

Dr Andrew nominates two possible obstacles in front of Helen, her family history of diabetes and her age. For the former, there will be a glucose tolerance test at about twenty weeks. For the latter, various other types of screenings. There will be antenatal tests, blood tests, including an HIV test, if she doesn't mind. And, of course, an ultrasound, as soon as possible.

The genetic specialists, he says, will offer us two screening alternatives, amniocentesis and chorionic villus biopsy. Both detect chromosomal and developmental abnormalities. The chorio is done early, at ten weeks. The amnio wouldn't happen until thirteen weeks. We want to know as soon as possible. We have already decided what will happen if there's a problem—we won't go through with it.

Meanwhile, Helen has to watch her diet (when doesn't she?) and avoid fat and carbohydrates. She tells Dr Andrew she is feeling seriously sick.

'The good news,' he replies, 'is that it will go. If you do what most people do, it will go in about three weeks.'

The examination. Helen undresses and lies down behind a screen. The doctor checks her breasts (I feel a pang of loss at my job being taken away) and her abdomen before casually announcing, 'It appears to be a normal pregnancy, I can feel an enlarged uterus.' Who would have thought that those words, 'enlarged uterus', could sound reassuring?

Helen adds that beyond sick, she is falling-over tired.

'Well, the tiredness will continue forever [a little obstetrician humour there]. It's not going to improve.'

The doctor explains that he will have to see Helen every four weeks until week 28, then every two weeks until week 36, then every week. Because he works at Royal Prince Alfred in Sydney's inner west, Helen will have her baby at the King George V maternity hospital, part of the sprawling campus.

He says it's okay for us to make travel plans, as long as we do so before the 32nd week of the pregnancy, after which airlines refuse to fly mothers-to-be. He tells us we should book a room at King George V. Yes, this early. And that's it for our first meeting.

What are the biggest mistakes we could make? I ask before we go.

'Taking drugs,' is the very quick reply. He says alcohol is not a problem as long as Helen is not bingeing or getting smashed. He also recommends that she avoids saunas and checks any drug with him. For the nausea, he suggests a cup of tea and a biscuit in bed in the morning.

February

February 1

The drink and dry biscuit trick helps, at least a little. Helen feels better all day. Of course, it could be the placebo effect. Not that it matters—whatever works, works.

One of my listed tasks is completed today. We buy a new car, watching all those Ferrari dreams evaporate as we opt for something sensible with four doors and enough room for a baby seat. In all honesty, petrol-head Helen has more snazzy-car inclination than I do, but it still feels sober and grown-up to consider a vehicle based on criteria such as 'Is there air-conditioning?' and 'How much luggage space?'.

Tonight, I find Helen sitting at the table eating brown rice (which I have never seen her eat before, never, no way, no hippie stuff) and tomato sauce.

'It's not like it's a craving,' she says. 'I just know exactly what I want to eat right now.'

'And what's a craving then?'

'Not that.'

February 2

The extra-sensory properties of the pregnancy are starting to unnerve me. Helen can smell dinner cooking up and down the street. If she gets any better, she'll be up for a job sniffing luggage at the airport.

'I'm sure this smell thing is about self-preservation,' she muses, 'my body helping me to pick things which might not be good for it, but I do think it's gone a bit overboard. I mean, I'm not stupid. I could smell a dead body from twenty paces and know not to eat it. This is way over the top.'

FEBRUARY 4

After days of wariness, I convince Helen that we should have a bit of a cuddle. It takes some arguing. The pregnancy has made her disappear into herself—her skin is now a wall. At a time when I'm feeling very warm and emotional, she doesn't want to be touched. She's submerged in her body, dealing with its changes, talking to her organs in a language I will never understand. And though I can see what is happening, it still feels like there's a void in the middle of our relationship. It's as if she is cheating on me with the embryo. With you.

While I'm showering, Helen stomps into the bathroom waving a piece of paper. 'The rip-off starts here,' she announces. 'I have to pay $250 for an ultrasound which will tell me I'm pregnant, which I already know, and for genetic counselling, which will tell me that there are two tests I can take and what they are, when I've already decided what I want to do anyway.'

Meanwhile, she is eating at two-hour intervals.

'I feel like one of those geese being stuffed for fois gras.'

FEBRUARY 5

Helen has her blood tested in the morning, a procedure requiring six vials of the stuff to be removed. Though she has slender veins, the whole process apparently goes easily. I can't be there. As she describes the events to me later, I feel light-headed and consider letting my stomach turn over. I am going to be *sooo* useful during labour.

February 7

The ultrasound. Helen is on her back on the trolley bed with her dress hiked up. The operator asks a set list of questions about previous pregnancies, operations, medical histories. Today's procedure, she explains, is a dating scan, which will tell us how many weeks old you are (eight weeks and three days) and whether your heart is beating.

Gel is squeezed onto Helen's stomach and the hand-held ultrasonic 'camera' is pressed onto it. In the middle of the screen is a dark circle. And in that dark circle is a sort of peanut-shaped thing, which we realise is you. A little growing you. Your heart is pointed out, fluttering fast, a hummingbird's wing of a thing. This, I imagine, is how it will beat on your first date.

I am thinking two things as I look at you. One, how happy I am that there *is* a you. And two, that for your first television effort, it's not great. Don't count on getting a lot of callbacks from this audition tape.

We stare, though frankly, there isn't much to stare at. No brothers or sisters. Just you, 1.8 centimetres long, surrounded by the amniotic sac. I ask for a photo to take home and one is printed out. Hey, Peanut, I can keep you in my wallet, even if it is a pretty blurry shot, like one of those grainy, blown-up pics of the Kennedy assassination that people wave at you saying, 'See, there's the second gunman.' In the waiting room afterwards, I look at the picture. Helen says, 'You know, I don't connect with it [you]. They say it happens when it starts to move, but I'm not feeling it yet. Then again, I'm not connecting with anything at the moment.'

In the counselling part of the appointment, Dr Jock, the

Scottish specialist (his beard and compact frame give him a slight terrier air), drags out a chart. He shows us that, given Helen's advancing age (she describes herself as 'gynaecologically dead'), the odds of you having Down's Syndrome are one in 165. The odds of you having other chromosomal abnormalities are probably one in 90. The chart is one of the scariest things I have ever seen. The numbers are irrelevantly high for younger women. Past 35, they go into freefall.

Dr Jock explains how the tests are done. The risk of error with the chorio is one in 4000. With the amnio, it's one in 12,000. The risk of miscarriage in chorio is one in 100–130. The risk with the amnio, which is three weeks later, is one in 300–400. To take the cell sample they need for the chorio, they use a catheter or push a needle through the abdominal wall. The latter is more common. Of course, he says, there are other things to worry about—birth defects caused by trauma, viral or parasitical infection, loss of oxygen to the foetus or congenital reasons—but let's start by ruling out what can be ruled out.

February 8

Lunch with Helen's sister, Michelle, and mother, Janina, in Melbourne. Michelle is pregnant with her third. (Grant is a little past his first birthday, Nicola is four and a bit.) As the meal goes on, I sense that Helen is not going to tell her family. I wait for eye contact and raise an eyebrow. She shakes her head slowly and looks away. People are talking about other things. The kids are occupying everybody's attention. It doesn't seem like the right time. Though we predicted we would not be able to contain ourselves, we end up sticking to the original plan to keep quiet.

After some discussion of how we could possibly reintroduce intimacy into our lives, I go shopping for odourless deodorant in an attempt to change my smell. Most shop assistants I ask eyeball me oddly and wait for me to leave. Then finally, at one of those organic bath salts and shampoo boutiques, the ones where everything sounds like it could be spread on toast (banana marmalade exfoliant), I strike lucky. The kindly sales assistant, to whom I have explained the bare bones of my plight, scampers over to a shelf and returns with a white, quartzlike seashell, small enough to sit snugly in the palm of my hand. And what do I do with this, I enquire? 'Oh,' she says, 'you just wet it and rub it under your arm.' A lot of 'the girls' are apparently using them.

Later, I stand in the bathroom, one hand raised, the other rubbing a small, hard Japanese seashell all over my armpit. For some reason, Helen finds this incredibly funny and keeps sticking her head around the door to point and giggle.

February 9

We repeat yesterday's lunch performance with my brother Tim and his wife Aleks. The words stay locked away. I suppose we want to keep you to ourselves a while longer. I'm not sure why. The tests have not been done, but there is more to it than that—most people we know told their families instantly. I guess it gives us time to come to terms with this thing, which is still strange and new. Maybe our own curious disbelief makes us unable to think we can sell it to others.

FEBRUARY 10

Blood. Jesus, blood. On the hotel sheet, brilliant red and
fresh. I close my eyes and there it is, burning into my memory.
Just a few drops, but enough to make my knees turn to
rubber. Helen comes out of the shower and tells me there's
been something else, some kind of clot. She calls Dr Andrew,
who says nothing more than a few calming words and that
she should book in for an ultrasound as soon as possible.
The booking is made for 9.15 tomorrow morning. She hugs
me. We stand quietly in the centre of the room.

We are scared. I feel sick, hollow and distracted, but
it's a work day. I have interviews to do for an article I'm
writing. Later, I play the tapes and hear myself fading in
and out of the conversation, unfocused, short on concentration. I ring Helen in the afternoon. She's at her sister's
house, so can't talk openly. I ask her how it is. She just
says, 'It's a worry', which means that the bleeding has not
stopped. I go for a walk and listen to my lungs tighten.
The bleeding stops by late afternoon. I'm still panicked
and upset, but I try not to show it. I know Helen can see
it though, because she keeps resting her hand on my
forearm on the flight home.

FEBRUARY 11
Tuesday, Nine weeks

Sleep is a wading pool. I paddle about, making the odd
splash but never getting my head under. At the clinic in
the morning, Helen walks in while I drive around the
block a few times looking for a parking spot, growing
frantic at the thought of missing what's going on. When

I finally make it through the door, Helen is already on the trolley bed.

'Everything is fine,' the operator says. 'Good heartbeat, right shape and size.' On the screen, I can see that the sac and foetus look intact. Bigger than only four days previous, your little arms and legs already starting to form. We are told that when the foetus buries itself into the wall of the uterus, the lining often sloughs. It's quite common. Nothing to worry about. Hey, thanks for telling us earlier.

FEBRUARY 15

Morning house hunting. There's an amazing number of pregnant women out looking. Most seem to have left it until they're ready to drop the child, struggling through doorways and up and down stairs. On the way to one house, we discuss how we're going to afford to have you. I suggest we try to live on my wage and use Helen's for child care. The conversation peters out. I think we both realise we have no idea, no sense of the reality we're heading towards, no way to plan. Until we do, it's all just play-acting, just words.

FEBRUARY 17

I find Helen peering at her breasts in the bathroom mirror, poking at them, pulling the skin. She explains that she is looking for stretch marks as they swell. Later, we make a dinner date with friends. I listen to Helen on the phone weaving together an excuse for eating early in a town where everyone wants to eat late (there's no way she'll make it past 10 pm without falling into the dessert).

'It would be good to be able to tell people,' she says afterwards. 'Then I could just say, "Sorry, I'm pregnant and if I'm not in bed in 12 minutes, I'll go into a coma."'

FEBRUARY 18
Tuesday, 10 weeks

I'm watching one of those television medical dramas. Traumatic childbirth, pain, blood, a woman screaming and eventually a Caesarean. I don't know whether I'm just being pathetic or not, but I find myself paying extra attention, scrunching up nervously in my chair. My reactions now seem raw, more sensitised. Tears are easily coaxed.

FEBRUARY 20

While out driving, Helen says she wants to know what sex you are. She explains that the old wives' tales dictate that the more knocked around she is by the pregnancy, the more likely it is that you are male. She says she wants to know, so that she can have an excuse for feeling so bad.

Her smell/food/sleep/nausea problems make planning for the holiday difficult. We're thinking one month, with a week each in Los Angeles, New York, London and Paris (Helen refers to it as 'the perfume bottle tour'). We don't want to take any tough, long-haul flights—I think about fourteen hours is the most Helen could cope with. One airline is offering a ticket for $2800, or we can get another for $2000 that has the same stops but is on an airline that still has smoking sections.

February 22

Look, you might at this stage be wondering why it's me who's keeping this diary. I mean, the father? Kind of stupid, isn't it? It's not as if I'm the one actually going through anything here. And don't believe for a second that I don't have guilt about that. But think about the alternative. Imagine if it were Helen keeping this, with all her brain-dead, animalistic simplicity:

8 am: open eyes
8.05 am: eat cracker and drink apple juice
8.10 am: ablute
8.11 am: consider going back to bed
8.14 am: surf first wave of dizziness
8.15 am: shower
8.20 am: look for new stretch marks in bathroom mirror
8.25 am: forget what I should be doing today
8.30 am: eat
8.36 am: wonder who that guy on other side of breakfast table is
8.45 am: experience moment of lucidity and plan entire day
8.47 am: descend into fog ...

February 25
Tuesday, 11 weeks

Things I Worry About Part 37: though I try to be optimistic, pretty much everything. When I think about this pregnancy, I think in terms of what could go wrong. I don't dare visualise what could go right. That seems as if it would be putting down a welcome mat for bad luck to wipe its feet on. What's interesting about this is that I've always thought of myself as a duck's back. Worries just slide off. Now I feel like Mr Anxiety. Woody Allen will play me in the movie version. I am the worrier. Helen is the one who passes out on the couch. I try to talk to her about this. In between moments of unconsciousness, she says she is aware of it.

'That's why I'm so calm,' she says, 'because you're doing the worrying for both of us. That and the fact that any time I try to think about anything at all, I get distracted by this sickening feeling.'

FEBRUARY 27

Chorio day. Dr Jock is an hour late. I suspect this will not be the last time in the next few months that I will sit in a waiting room leafing through six-month old women's magazines that offer beauty tips such as 'Rub a lemon on your elbows and heels'. I show this to Helen and say how dumb I would feel if I had to do that. The only thing I could imagine that would make me feel dumber would be having to rub a seashell in my armpit. She shoots me a look of pity.

Eventually we're shown into a room with Dr Jock and his lovely assistant Fiona (sorry, their costumes give them the air of a magic act). She asks me to put on a pair of sky-blue elastic bootie covers (shower caps for shoes). I cough slightly, just to see if thousands of germs are coming out of my mouth. No-one seems worried. Apparently my feet are the greatest threat. Helen has the gel rubbed on her stomach and as the ultrasound scanner presses down, the doctor decides to follow the usual path and go in from the top.

'So you're not going in through the vagina?' Helen confirms. He explains that it's easier to go this way, through the abdominal wall.

'But don't worry,' he coos. 'I'm not going to use a needle. I'll just use a thin, sharp instrument.'

Neither of us is good with needles. As the doctor invites me to move a little closer, I wonder if I could actually get away with the reverse. Helen's belly is painted redbrown with iodine.

'Is this going to hurt?' she asks in a voice that is meant to sound casual, but doesn't.

'They tell me it's like getting your ears pierced,' Dr Jock says.

'Great,' Helen moans. 'That really hurt.'

He administers a local anaesthetic and pushes the needle in. My stomach expands and contracts; I try not to let my face show my queasiness. Helen winces as the tip pushes through. I put a hand on her shoulder.

'You'll feel it moving now, but there shouldn't be any pain,' the doc says.

On the screen, we can see a lot of movement in the sac. This, apparently, is normal. The doctor explains that he has to jiggle the needle around to knock cells off the walls and into the fluid he is collecting. You don't seem bothered by any of this. Dr Jock gently removes the needle, looking very pleased with himself, and strides across the room to the microscope.

We sigh with relief that it is over. The results, we are told, will take around fourteen days. Dr Jock asks if we'd like to see the tissue sample under the microscope. It lies there in the liquid like seaweed, its fronds gently rolling with the currents. Helen checks the sample and the paperwork, initialling both to verify that they are hers.

'That went well,' Dr Jock says brightly. 'There's a good sample. It was very simple to get and I would be very disappointed if there are any problems. Now it's just ...' He crosses his fingers.

March

MARCH 5
Wednesday, 12 weeks and one day

Brad and Sharon, two friends from the UK, are staying. Great. More people we can't talk to. Sometimes I feel like a spy, undercover in my own life. We conjure up excuses for Helen feeling unwell, concoct reasons for eating early, pretend that we normally do these things.

Last night, I did finally crack and tell someone about you. David and I were saying goodbye at the end of a barbecue. He promised to ring me next week and I said, 'Good, I'll have a secret to tell you then.' A couple of minutes later, in the driveway, he pulled me aside and said, 'So she's pregnant?' And I said, 'Nearly three months.' He gave me a big hug. 'That's great, great news. That's brilliant.' I can't tell you how good it felt to finally try out the words.

MARCH 6

David rings to congratulate me again. Helen reveals she has told a friend, Caroline, too. The pair were out walking and when Helen said she had been going to bed early, the friend guessed. Helen refused to confirm or deny which, as any conspiracy theorist knows, is proof of guilt.

Meanwhile, I've been setting up a family company to deal with the freelance work that Helen and I sometimes undertake. We've decided to call it Peanut Media. Twenty years from now, when our public offering rakes in a few billion on the stock exchange (with a name like that, the big guys will never see us coming), you'll know how and why it started.

MARCH 8

More of the interminable house hunting. As with the car shopping, I find myself asking dad-to-be questions. 'How will a baby cope with stairs?' 'Is the yard big enough to play in?' 'Where would we sleep a newborn?' 'How far is the kitchen from the bedrooms?' (I'm thinking about the dangers involved in blindly stumbling around at 3 am preparing bottle feeds.) No luck again. We must have seen 50 places already this year.

MARCH 10

A visit to King George V to book your arrival. The once-grand building is about to undergo a major overhaul and needs it. It has little of the glamour of the hospitals we see on TV all the time. Where are the millions of shiny machines? The glistening corridors? The military bustle? KGV looks more like the hospitals in films with titles like *Carry On Matron*. The woman in the Parent Education Centre talks us into taking baby classes, which surprises us both. I would not have picked us as likely class candidates—too self-reliant, too book-reliant.

MARCH 11
Tuesday, 13 weeks

I hear a note of nervousness in Helen's voice. 'Why haven't they rung about the chorio results?' she asks, a rhetorical question, almost (but not quite) an absent-minded one. These have been quiet weeks. The worst of the first trimester appears to be over. I'm at home in the daytime, ploughing through a book about the Net I have to finish by early next month. Helen's at work, trying to take things slowly, fighting all the same bodily demons, but winning more often. On Saturdays we look at houses. On Sundays we collapse.

MARCH 12

6.30 pm. I spoke too soon about Helen winning. She's in the bathroom throwing up—lunch hasn't met with digestive approval. Back in the lounge-room armchair, she has that sick person's look of disgust with their own body, sort of 'How could it do this desperately uncool thing to me?' It's funny how when someone is sick—and I guess when they're pregnant—they develop a mind/body split, a them-and-us relationship.

MARCH 14

Appointment with Dr Andrew. 'G'day, how are you?' he says as we plant ourselves on the seats opposite his desk.

'You don't want to know,' Helen groans.

'Yes I do, or I wouldn't ask you.'

He works out that the pregnancy is thirteen to fourteen weeks in. He says it is unusual, but not impossible, that she should still be nauseous at this point and that we shouldn't see it as sinister. The blood test results are back. Helen's blood group is O positive, there are no abnormal antibodies, the blood count is normal and there's no sign of hepatitis, syphilis or HIV. The chorio results have not returned yet. There will be a blood test for spina bifida in a couple of weeks.

'You should feel better soon,' he assures. 'It's very rare to feel this uncomfortable for the rest of the pregnancy.'

As for the tiredness, he explains: 'Your blood volume is up 50 per cent during pregnancy. Your heart rate is up 50 per cent. It's like being on the track for the whole day. So you have to find time to rest. There is a perfectly logical reason for you to be tired.'

Helen weighs in at 49 kilos. Dr Andrew checks her blood pressure (fine) and feels her tummy. He says the uterus is no longer retroverted. I nod as if I know what he's talking about.

MARCH 17

I find Helen pushing two fingers into her upper abdomen, just below the rib cage. 'It's getting firm here. It never has been.' As she stretches, I can see that the pregnancy is becoming an oval area, her whole abdomen beginning to push forward.

MARCH 18
Tuesday, 14 weeks

It's been nearly three weeks since the chorio, so I ring to ask about the results. The receptionist says, 'Yes we have them, it's a normal female.' On one hand I am relieved. On the other, I am angry. I really didn't want to know what sex you are. I didn't ask to know and the receptionist should have dealt with enough parents-to-be to know she should be more circumspect. Helen says I should complain. She also says I should keep the knowledge of your sex to myself for as long as possible. Dr Jock is not there when I call back. I feel deflated and disappointed. They have taken away some of the magic.

MARCH 20

I finally get through to the doctor. He is angry too. The situation cannot be fixed, but I'm reassured that it might not happen to someone else now. Helen asks what I said to him and my reply is, 'Well, I explained that I asked the receptionist for the test results and she said, "Yes, it's a normal female" and ...'

Oh dear, now I've told her. My stupid gland is being overactive again. When Helen points out exactly how overactive, I tell her she is being unfair. How could I be expected not to crack when she wheedled it out of me so cunningly? She says she wanted a boy and that she was counting on my gene pool to provide one. I come from a family of boys, she from a family of girls. For the same reason, I wanted a girl. Truly, though, I don't think we care either way—those are just detached notions.

Helen's latest culinary kicks are honey and cornflakes. Cornflakes. I have never seen her eat any form of packaged cereal before. Only hand-cut, hand-rolled, hand-sifted, hand-collected muesli.

MARCH 21

The positives are beginning to sink in. Now that I've stopped being steamy about knowing you're a girl, the word that keeps coming back to me is 'normal'. For the first time, I can feel myself relaxing about this whole business.

MARCH 22

Lying in bed in the morning, I ask Helen whose surname you should have. (Christian name is easy: Peanut.)

'Whose do you want?' she asks, half awake and half interested, not even lifting her head from a book.

'Well, mine of course,' I reply. 'After all, it's a dynasty thing.'

'God,' she laughs, 'you're so primeval sometimes, so tragic. Well, I figure she gets your surname and my religion.'

It feels like time to blab. I tell Helen that I'm going to ring my parents, since my brother Paul is coming over later in the day. The burden of not telling has finally tipped the scales. It's been harder and harder to make the excuses, to wallpaper over behaviours and feelings.

Helen says that if I'm going to do it, she will too and calls her mother before I can get to the phone. They talk about money matters, where to park the cash from the sale of her apartment (the auction is next Wednesday). Just general stuff. Then her mother casually asks, 'Anything else new?'

'Well, yes actually. I have a big announcement. I'm pregnant.'

'You're kidding!'

'No, I'm not.'

'Helen! Oh my God!'

I can hear her voice on the phone from the other side of the room. The reaction is shock and joy. As Janina tries to deal with it, Helen explains the tests and the results we have been waiting for. Her mother asks if everything is fine and Helen says yes, but then launches into her tales of illness, detailing how 'unbelievably sick' she has felt the whole time.

Every time Helen stops to draw breath, the response is, 'Like your mother!' It turns out that when she was pregnant with Helen, Janina was constantly nauseous but unable to throw up, highly sensitive, unable to bear even the mildest of smells. Peanut, you now know what to expect. Biology is destiny and all that.

'Oh, my God,' Janina says. 'You're exactly like me. I didn't have it anywhere near as much with Michelle, but with you, I couldn't even stand my own body odour.'

She asks what sex you are. Helen says you're a girl.

'Congratulations. I love a girl. Oh, isn't it beautiful! Oh isn't it beautiful!'

She tells Helen to be careful with the trip, but we explain that the timing is right, that we are going to places where she won't have to exert herself.

'So when is the second surprise?' her mother asks.

'What surprise?'

'Well, you're going to get married, aren't you?'

Long pause.

'I'm doing it the hard way,' Helen says. 'I'm doing the hard one first, the easy one later.'

Her mother lets it go.

'Beautiful, beautiful,' she says. 'I expected everything in life but not this.'

Helen asks what she means. Her mother says she thought Helen really didn't want kids. Her stepfather, Dolek, chips in to say he's not surprised at all. He expected it.

Michelle is out on the deck at the back of her house when Helen rings, enjoying a sunny afternoon. Nicola wants to get on the phone and talk about going to ballet classes. Then Helen drops her bombshell. I'm on the other extension. Michelle sounds as if she's about to faint.

'Congratulations! Do I fall off my couch and get back up? Is it planned? How long was it planned for? What's going on?' She squeals with excitement as only a pregnant sister could.

Helen fills her in, tells her the gender, that we were waiting to see what happened with the tests, blah blah blah, the whole thing.

'I'm just beside myself,' Michelle says. I hang up as they head into sickness gossip, that kind of macho 'when I'm pregnant I feel so sick I could gnaw my own legs off' ... 'well, I feel so sick I could gnaw my legs and yours off!' stuff. Then it's all baby talk and pregnancy notes and tips and advice and excitement about the fact that Michelle is coming to visit in a fortnight.

'This is such a surprise, I'm telling you,' she says.

My parents both pick up the phone, so I call Helen to the other extension and it's a four-way conversation. I say that I have a small announcement to make: one of us is pregnant.

'You are serious?' my mother asks. 'You're not pulling my leg? You're 100 per cent serious?'

'Yep.'

There's a long pause before they both start offering astounded congratulations.

'This is not something you're supposed to say on the phone,' says my mother. 'You're supposed to see each other so you can hug and weep copiously.'

'Do you realise what you've done?' Dad says. 'You've proved Paul's theory. He said you'd be the first.'

Mum wonders if there will be a domino effect now, if my brothers, both older, will follow. And then it's into the same questions. Is Helen well? How's the pregnancy going? Any problems? When are you due?

'You have six months to fight over names now,' Dad says. 'You know,' he continues, 'I've always thought a woman pregnant is at the most beautiful stage of her life physically. It's not just in terms of how she looks, but in the whole thing, the ethereal nature of it.'

'I'm too old,' Helen says. 'I think if I'd been going to get to ethereal, I would have done it by now.'

March 23

In the end, we don't tell Paul. We are so exhausted from telling the others that we postpone it. I resolve to call my brothers when Helen stops hogging the phone. She talks with her sister for ages today about the practicalities of pregnancy, mulling over crucial questions such as where to find elastic-waisted pants.

Janina rings while her daughter is out shopping. She wants to tell Helen to ask the doctor if she should get a shot for German measles. She also says we have to make sure that we look for a house near schools and hospitals instead of near restaurants. And we have to make sure our wills are in order so that if, God forbid, anything happens to us, we have provided for you. She jokingly says that we can expect a call every 24 hours.

'I couldn't sleep all last night, I was doing so much thinking,' she says. 'I had to take a Valium.'

MARCH 25
Tuesday, 15 weeks

I buy an old rocking chair at an auction. (Who has visions of dadness?) At home, I ring my brothers. Tim and Aleks first. Aleks squeals. This fails to surprise me—the squeal is becoming familiar. Tim takes longer to react, as does Paul. Ah, the male of the species—we're always at something of a loss when it comes time for the emotional response. Both eventually do locate the excitement and the words.

We face all the usual questions. Aleks decides they don't want to know the sex. Paul, for whatever reason, doesn't ask. He does ask if we've had an ultrasound yet. He says people bring ultrasound photos into the office to show him, but he can never quite make out what he's meant to be looking at.

So now, all those who have to know have been told. Telling was great, but there is a small sense of loss too— something that belonged to us is in the process of becoming public property. You are no longer our wonderful secret. You are our wonderful something else.

MARCH 26

Helen gets a terrific price for her apartment, which gives us a little more cash to play with than expected. When we come home from the auction, there's a message on the answering machine from my mother. My parents are thinking of visiting before we go overseas next month. She wants to talk to Helen about kiddie clothes and what sort of colours we like. Hmmm, we think strong colours, not pastels. As Helen says, we can't wear them, so why not make you?

Helen rings her own mother to discuss the auction. I get the feeling our phone bill for the next six months will be catastrophic.

Meanwhile, my mother tells a story about a pregnant woman she knew who would vomit the second her husband came home from work every day.

'Hi, honey, I'm ...'

Bluurrrrgggghhh!

She didn't actually put two and two together and connect her vomiting with the arrival of her husband. The doctors worked it out when she was finally hospitalised for feeling so nauseous. When hubby wasn't around, the symptoms went away. Mercifully, our situation is not this bad. Yet.

March 27

Morning coffee meeting with Sophie, my publisher. We chat about the manuscript I'm working on. I tell her about you and this diary. She says it's like Michael Keaton making the video in *My Life* for his unborn child. I point out that Keaton died in that film.

She tells me of her experiences in birth classes with two types of men, those who look bewildered and embarrassed and those who are obsessively, compulsively involved, with mobile phones and schedules and notes and an over-keenness that is almost painful. As she speaks I am aware of myself sliding pathetically towards the second category.

April

Tuesday, 16 weeks

Is it just me or does April Fool's Day seem like the perfect date to start baby classes? Half a dozen couples gather at KGV's Parent Education Centre, all looking slightly sheepish, as if we've been kept after school and would rather be somewhere else. Name tags are obligatory. Gee, I think to myself, it's enough to have the child, do we have to bond with these strangers as well?

We take our place in a circle of blue plastic chairs. There are pink and grey beanbags too, for those already in the uncomfortable stages of gravidity. They're also useful because they cover the kind of lurid carpet design that could make someone go into spontaneous labour if they stared at it for too long.

Our host for the evening, midwife Cheryl, lectures at a million miles an hour, skipping from idea to idea. She says we'll be learning some anatomy and physiology as well as our options in antenatal care. There seem to be about a billion choices: birth centre, private obstetrician/ward, antenatal clinic, home birth (independent midwifery), midwives' clinics, GP shared care, or Continuity of Care program.

She explains that during labour in the hospital, the mother will be entitled to a partner and a support person. Anyone else will have to remain in the waiting room. There is a first stage room at the labour ward, with reclining chairs and a TV, so if labour takes a long time, we should prepare to settle in, bringing provisions, even books and videos.

Cheryl talks us through some of the physical and emotional changes of pregnancy. She says babies are delivered as early as 24 and 25 weeks and survive. She tells us about the mucous plug in the cervix to stop bacteria getting in, and how its appearance, late in pregnancy (the show) is an omen of labour.

She says that at about twenty weeks, the mother should be starting to feel a little flutter inside her, known as the quickening. At 36 weeks, the uterus gets to its highest point and then drops. This is called 'the lightening'. The baby's head enters the pelvis at about 34 to 36 weeks. At 40 weeks, or when the uterus is ready, the cervix shortens and widens and labour begins.

Cheryl also discusses changes to the breasts (which she charmingly refers to as 'accessory organs') and skin (stretch marks, and the brown line from the belly button to the pubic bone that appears late in pregnancy).

For nausea, she suggests soda water, cordial and dry biscuits. She explains that the stomach is also slower to clear during pregnancy, taking up to six hours longer to do its work. One woman says that ginger beer has helped her fight it. Helen has been having some success with peaches. Another asks about bladder irritability, saying she is getting up during the night—Cheryl says it tends to settle down until late in the pregnancy, when it returns.

She says swollen feet are a sign of fluid retention. She explains that in the first few days after birth, mothers pass a lot of urine. They also bleed as their fluid levels return to normal. She recommends walking as a form of exercise appropriate to labour. As a bonus, it also helps ward off osteoporosis. The fathers-to-be, meanwhile, look everywhere except at each other.

On the way out of the class, Helen asks, through gritted teeth, if I saw the woman who shook her head when Cheryl asked if everyone had been feeling nauseous during their pregnancies.

'I may feel sick every minute of the day, but at least I don't have to go through all this with a haircut like hers,' she mutters with unalloyed loathing.

April 5

Michelle and Nicola are visiting. The three women (four, counting you) are out doing the shopping while I crunch slowly towards deadline on the book. S'funny. Michelle is very excited about Helen having a baby. More excited than Helen is—she's still too busy thinking about sleep. The vagueness is disappearing, but slowly. Michelle is on her third pregnancy. For the first two, they had nothing to talk about. Now there is common, sisterly ground. Now it's advice on everything. I sense in Helen a mixture of gratefulness and shock at the dam-busting torrent of it.

April 8
Tuesday, 17 weeks

Class Two, this one with Eleanor, a physiotherapist. She asks us to calculate our 'timepie'. We are all meant to work out how much we devote to exercise, work and rest. Everyone seems to be sleeping about ten hours and working eight or nine. One woman says she stretches in front of 'Oprah'. Most are already exercising every day like good little girl scouts. For a moment, I see the self-righteous, competitive side of pregnancy, but I beat down my cynicism and keep listening.

Eleanor says that while mothers-to-be are at work, if they're sitting or standing for long periods, they should find activities that break it up. After getting everyone to list their pains, she begins to discuss the common musculo-skeletal problems, the ligament pain, the inflammation of joints. She talks about the need to sit forward, the importance of considering posture during pregnancy, the way the shifting uterus can cause abdominal pain if the mother is not shifting with it.

She says many women experience tingling and numbness, swelling of the hands, feet and ankles. The congestion of the blood vessels is due to pressure from the baby on the lower abdominal vessels. She recommends lifting the legs and support stockings. She explains that, in the other direction, the baby pushing upwards onto the diaphragm leads to shortness of breath.

Groin pain, night cramps, varicose veins, haemorrhoids ... my head spins. Inevitably, the discussion comes (as we all knew it would) to pelvic floor exercises. Eleanor says pelvic floor function takes about six weeks to return after birth, if mum's in reasonable shape. She says those pelvic squeezes should be done from day one, 30 to 50 times a day. She shows us a number of exercises. I'm sitting on the floor trying to do the one where I imagine my groin is an elevator and I'm tensing the muscles in an upward fashion. First floor, haberdashery, manchester. I feel like an idiot. Eleanor recommends plenty of sex for the pelvic floor workout—it's a grip thing. At least that makes sense.

When it's over, what stays with me is the guy who puts his hand up and asks if, when the midwife said the mother would be consulted about any Caesarean options or drugs to be administered, she was implying that the father would be too. 'Do I have any rights?' is the constant question of the soon-to-be father. Where do boundaries begin and end? It's our child too, but we're constantly aware that we are not the ones carrying it. More than once Helen has said that she may be having an awful time, but at least she's in the middle of it. In some ways, I'm perpetually on the outside, nose pressed against the window, knocking and asking if I can come in.

April 11

Last appointment with Dr Andrew before we go overseas. He has the full results of the tests with him. 'It's a normal healthy baby,' he says before reminding us that they can't test for everything. Helen says she's having trouble sleeping again and wants to know if taking something for it would be okay. Dr Andrew says yes, and recommends a little Scotch.

Helen weighs in at 52.5 kilos and the examination begins. Her blood pressure is fine. Dr Andrew puts his hands on her stomach. 'That's pretty good,' he says. 'It's perfect in size for that period of gestation. It's exactly where it should be.'

He's glad to hear we've done the tour of the hospital. He tells Helen she will have an ultrasound and a swab at 28 weeks. We run through a handful of minor questions. Dr Andrew is reassuring. Helen has been sniffing a lot and asks if that is normal. ('Is this normal?' must be the question obstetricians hear all day, every day.) Dr Andrew says the vessels are stretched to the limit.

'Pregnancy affects your nose?' Helen asks incredulously.

'Pregnancy affects everything,' he replies.

APRIL 13

The flight to Los Angeles (yesterday) is not great. I sleep less than an hour. Helen manages only a few. We are up the back of the cattle class, near the toilets. I have the aisle seat, which means everyone elbows me in the head as they stumble to the loo in the dark. Clearing Customs takes forever. Helen has to sit down while I keep our place in the endless queue.

We're staying with Shelli-Anne, a friend who covers Hollywood for an Australian magazine. She sees that Helen is pregnant the minute we walk through the door. I don't know who is the happier. The rest of the day is spent wandering around like zombies. Late at night, still in some mid-Pacific time zone, I insist on visiting a 24-hour supermarket. I have this thing for American supermarkets— they have so many stupid foods. The cereal aisle is my favourite.

This morning I wake up, take a shower and emerge from the steam to find Helen finishing a bowl of strawberries. A full-page ad in the *LA Times* warns about the dangers of eating contaminated strawberries. Apparently there's a Hepatitis A epidemic. I have a quiet anxiety attack and try not to upset her.

By the time we're moving, the day is half over. We go trinket-foraging at the Pasadena flea markets and check out apartments with Shelli-Anne. Helen is running on a weird clock, fading in and out.

APRIL 15
Tuesday, 18 weeks

Shelli-Anne asks when we're going to get married. She's the second one. Helen says her mother brought it up again on the phone last week. It would be better for us if we did, her mother said. It would make things easier. I wonder how much pressure is to come.

Most of our time is taken up with shopping and seeing friends. My vision is of Helen walking out of change room after change room, holding up pairs of trousers and saying, 'What do you think? This is too big now, but in a few months?' As if I would have any idea.

We splurge on clothes for you. It's the first stuff I'm aware of us buying, five months out from your due date. I don't feel so superstitious about it here; it's easier to do it away from home.

Shelli-Anne wants to get into naming discussions but we shy away from them. You're a strange public/private thing to us. Sometimes it's okay to talk about you and sometimes it makes us uncomfortable. Helen, meanwhile, looks shockingly healthy after a couple of days away, though she zonks out around 4 pm. Then again, so do I.

We are in a bookshop. Helen has been perusing the back cover of a sad book. After putting it back on the shelf, she says that previously, she might have enjoyed it, but now she couldn't. Pregnancy has made everything more real. Her nerves are exposed.

April 17

I have an idea today for the world's lamest comic strip superhero, Pregnancy Woman. I can't draw, so I'll just have to tell you what it looks like. I see a three-panel series.

First panel: a whole lot of humans running in all directions and looking terrified.

Caption: 'Panic grips the city as a giant meteor, on a deadly collision course with the Earth, enters the upper atmosphere.'

Second panel: shot of superhero in command, looking upwards.

Caption: 'In the nick of time, our hero, Pregnancy Woman ...'

Third panel: Earth explodes.

Caption: '... remembers she had something important to do today, but can't quite put her finger on it.'

All good comic strips are based on telling the same gag over and over. This one would be no different. Just change the nature of the cosmic threat every time, and add an alternative third panel caption: 'In the nick of time, our hero, Pregnancy Woman ...

'... vagues out and goes to sleep in the corner.'

'... develops a craving for cornflakes.'

'... worries about how dry her hair is getting.'

'... finds a nice chair to sit down on.'

'... succumbs to a sudden urge to recycle her breakfast.'

'... decides that finding a bra that fits is more important.'

APRIL 19

'Is there anything in any of the pregnancy books about going more girly,' Helen asks, 'because I have definitely gone more girly.' She's holding up a spangly hair clip. 'I would have bought this clip before on the argument that I could give it to Michelle or Nicola, but now I want it.'

New York. Visiting friends Ken and Judith. Judith says she could see the pregnancy in Helen's face. Not that she'd need to look there. Helen has been growing like crazy in this last week. The little voice from the bathroom tells me that her breasts are bigger again and she'll have to buy another bra.

'I think all this girly stuff happened early on,' she says. 'I think I started to feel a lot more female as soon as I knew, more feminine. That's okay by you, isn't it? You like girly stuff anyway—you grew up with boys.'

Food is still a problem. Helen's on four meals a day and can't eat too late or too much, it gives her indigestion. She says she can feel her uterus pushing upwards. The hardness of it is past her belly button now.

Lying on the bed in our hotel room, I think to myself that it took me 26 years to get overseas. You've done it before you're even born.

APRIL 20

I ask Judith what it was she saw in Helen's face, what gives the pregnancy away. She says it's something about Helen's skin, a softness, a clarity. Helen says her hair is getting thicker and healthier too. I start to make a list of the things I am learning about travelling with a pregnant woman.

1. They're a great excuse for not walking anywhere.
2. They're a great excuse for sleeping in.
3. They're easy to manipulate. To get your own way, just say, 'You're looking tired, perhaps you'd better rest.' This is particularly useful when bored with shoe shopping.

APRIL 22
Tuesday, 19 weeks

I take Helen into Tiffany's on Fifth Avenue and buy a second little silver ring, the same as the other one, except it has a tiny emerald instead of a ruby. She decides that the first could be a little larger and we leave them both for refitting. At dinner tonight, the new girlfriend of a friend tells Helen that during delivery, she should make sure I'm next to her head, instead of at the other end. Apparently, I should avoid, as much as possible, looking at the actual birth, or I'll never see Helen in quite the same way again. It's not the first time someone has said this to us and probably won't be the last. I find it a little alarmist.

APRIL 23

Helen says the breathlessness has started. She says it's very light, as if she had walked up a gentle hill, but it's there. She is lying on the bed, reading *What To Expect When You're Expecting* and ticking off the symptoms. 'Forgetfulness ... check. Breathlessness ... check. Don't fit into clothing ... check.'

We pick up the rings. Helen now has one from New York and one from Sydney. I have kept my end of the bargain. I have bought her jewellery. So she has to go through with her end and actually have you.

APRIL 24

Splashed across the front pages of today's papers is the story of a 63-year-old mother who lied about her age (she said she was 50) so she could be implanted with a fertile egg. Sixty-three. That's a quarter of a century on from Helen's age. I can't imagine what it would be like to have an 80-year-old mother during high school. I can't imagine what it would be like to be 70 and trying to handle a hyperactive seven year old.

It's only a few weeks since this whole thing was a secret. Now, as has become obvious from the reactions of friends, we couldn't keep it a secret if we wanted to. Helen has the beginnings of the classically recognisable profile, the silhouette. Her travel adrenalin, meanwhile, has dried up. She is tiring in the afternoons, so we're trying to relax more. We were never going to have a particularly difficult holiday, but we've even wound down from our low expectations.

APRIL 26

A two-day work trip to Las Vegas leaves me exhausted. Helen says she was mostly fine without me, though she did feel very breathless walking through Central Park. She says she had to stop a few times. She doesn't think it's right that she should be breathless at this stage of the pregnancy. According to the books, these feelings are not due for a couple of months. She looks bigger than when I last saw her. Or is it just me?

April 27

Flight to London. We put together a care package for the trip, with the sound expectation that Helen will not find the airplane food attractive. It includes a banana, a couple of hard-boiled eggs, some licorice and figs. 'Who's going to be a fat little piggy?' Helen says, surveying her spread at the airport. Most of it is gone before we're even on the plane.

April 28

We're staying with our old friend Chris and his partner Sharon. It helps to be with someone comfortable, but we perhaps should have thought twice about it. Chris and Sharon are smokers and that's pretty rough on Helen's overtuned senses, as is the noise that filters through the floor from the upstairs flat, making sleep past 6 am impossible. The situation is not improved by the fact that Helen feels increasingly enervated. On the third leg of the four-part holiday, she seems close to collapse. She wants to hibernate. I'm not much better—the Vegas thing took it out of me. We force ourselves to do and see things, but the byword is 'slowly'.

May

MAY 1

Thursday, 20 weeks and two days

A couple more tips on travelling with a pregnant woman:

4. Carry an emergency apple, or other suitable blood sugar enhancement
5. Know where the toilets are
6. Black may be slimming for all shapes and sizes, but if you must wear it, try to avoid staying with people who have cats.

Actually, there are warnings in the books about keeping pregnant women away from the rear ends of cats. Exposure apparently brings with it the danger of toxoplasmosis. I'm not sure what that is, but it's quite clearly not to be trifled with. I helpfully suggest to Helen that she not handle the faeces of any other animal or human, just to be safe.

Let the record show that as of today, Helen's stomach has pushed ahead of her breasts. I'm impressed. She lies on her back and I hum the theme from *2001*.

'It's disgusting,' she says.

She doesn't mean it, Peanut.

MAY 3

'I think I had tummy fluttering today,' Helen says. 'It was sort of like my stomach doing flipflops, but it wasn't my stomach.'

The rest of the day is dominated by a barbecue get-together for three old uni friends and their partners who are now living in London. Helen has to drift off for a nap—she is semi-comatose during the ritual viewing of

the Eurovision Song Contest, which is halfway to the best
state in which to watch it. She's having real sleep problems,
and the more we see friends, the more she feels a function
of her pregnancy rather than a human being. I sense she's
not interested in talking about it any more. She feels as if
she has disappeared.

MAY 5

Paris. More fluttering. Helen keeps dismissing it, unsure
of the veracity of her own senses. Her latest rationalisation:
'It was just a muscle twitch after the long walk.'

She continues to slow. Perhaps this holiday is too much
work. Perhaps it's the jet lag, the constant moving, the
obligation to see people. We're both determined to take
these last few days at a snail's pace. Imagine. Flying to
Paris, then hanging around the hotel watching ice hockey
and 'Conan the Barbarian' dubbed in French (oddly enough,
it makes no less sense). We venture out, but not far. We
walk as much as we can, and sit down whenever the
opportunity arises ('Ah, another café ...'). We sleep. We
eat. We let the primitive state rule.

MAY 6
Tuesday, 21 weeks

I love Helen's profile. Front on, not much has changed.
Side on, she's a relief map of the Himalayas. And she has
finally noticed. 'Oh my God! I'm pregnant!' The voice
comes from the bathroom. Disrobing is a shock.

More fluttering during dinner. Helen says it's like the
pages of a book flipping over. She is eating vegetables with

couscous at the time, so it's doubtful that it's the meal doing it. In a food capital like Paris, we've been searching out simple, bland fare. It's all that will go in safely.

Helen's latest suggestions for names arrive while we're on the Métro. Eden or Zoe. Eden I can do without, but the latter goes onto the possibility list. Your middle name looks at this stage to be Rachel. A good Jewish name. In biblical terms, Rachel was the wife of Jacob and did a lot of begatting (this is fine by me—I wish you a healthy sex life).

M AY 9

Singapore. A 24-hour stopover. Some last minute shopping. Peanut shucking (no reference to you) upstairs in the bar at Raffles. Gin and tonic. Helen drinks too. We work on the principle of moderation. We undertake the minimum of duty-free shopping and spend the rest of the night in the hotel, making use of the large bath and even larger bed.

M AY 1 1

It passes over me like an eclipse. I am sitting on the plane and the light suddenly changes. I can feel the fear near to me. I close my eyes and see myself in a warm, white, weightless room. The fear, in vaguely human form, is banging on the window, shouting to get in. If I float towards the window, I can see it, but I can't hear it.

What fear? The fear of entrapment that the books say hits many men during pregnancy. I look across at Helen, quietly under the spell of a John Updike novel, her Miss Peabody reading glasses perched on the bridge of her nose, one strand of hair drifting across her forehead. And I think, well this is it. I've made my decision. The rest of my life is mapped out. It is no longer a blank page, an unwritten, undrawn, endless list of possibilities. It's this woman, this baby, this family. And I am not scared by the thought at all. I am comforted by it.

Back home now, padding around in winter, the weather squalling outside, we wonder what time zone we're passing through. We went away abstract, mouthing the words of pregnancy, telling people, listening to the way things sounded, gauging our own feelings by the reactions on the faces of others. 'Oh, that's right, we're happy about this.' 'Yes, it's great.'

We have returned with the concrete reality. Pregnant. The difference is huge, and in more than waistline terms. For the last few months, your existence has been, if not a joke, then something to be played with, to be enjoyed, to be made fun of. It hasn't felt real. Now, it has come into sharp focus. Now, we get serious.

MAY 13
Tuesday, 22 weeks
Five Lines to Kill Your Sex Life During Pregnancy

1. Have I told you that spherical objects turn me on?
2. If you don't let me take my chance now, I may never feel breasts this huge again.
3. I'm aware that you haven't seen your genitals for three months, but I can assure you they're still there.
4. Ooh, I fancy a threesome, don't you?
5. Honey, it's never too early to try for another.

MAY 15

Back at work, another round of telling begins. People split into consistent types of reactees. The first response of some is to ask what we're going to name you, as a prelude to a long and convoluted discussion of options (usually involving, at some point, their own name). Another group, probably the most spooky, are the people who seem more excited than we are. A third reaction, usually from singles, is blankness, the people who offer congratulations but have an expression that reveals they have no idea what they should be saying, how they should be feeling. I was one of those until recently.

Our friends Hannah and Andrew tell us they will have a baby at the end of the year too. Hannah is much less circumspect than we have been. She's telling people only eight weeks in. It's great news. Now Helen will have someone to talk to, a friend to share it with. And when you're up and moving, you might have a playmate.

MAY 16

Appointment with Dr Andrew. According to our calculations, the pregnancy is 22 and a half weeks in. Helen says she is having trouble eating, feeling constantly full, no matter how little she puts away. The indigestion is still very much present and we wonder if perhaps the jet lag hasn't played some part in making her feel so fatigued since our return.

Dr Andrew says it's not common for an expectant mother to feel sick this far into the venture, but it's not unheard of. It's nothing to worry about yet. Just bad luck.

Helen says there has been regular fluttering for the last two weeks, which tallies with textbook expectations. Dr Andrew says you will have been moving about for around seven weeks. Helen weighs in at 55 kilos. Her blood pressure is fine. Dr Andrew checks her abdomen and decides that the shape is 'not too big, not too small'.

May 18

To me, it seems big. The growth rate is amazing. For the first time, I can put my hands under you and lift. When I do, I feel Helen's whole abdomen move. She has small hips and a small torso—she's a small person. Peanut, you have nowhere to go but out.

We were speaking to another couple today, due to have their baby a week after us. The mother-to-be was hardly showing at all. Listening to the two women talk, sharing their nausea and foul smell stories, trading scars like battle veterans, I began to feel, more strongly than ever before, that this whole parenthood thing is another one of those clubs that you don't know about until you join, like the Masons.

May 19

'I've had enough now,' Helen announces, looking down at her swelling tum. 'I'm going to have a monster and I don't want to do it. It's not fun any more.'

I haven't been making much of it, but these last weeks have continued the trend that seemed to start on the holiday. Helen's discomfort is worsening as she inflates. Her sleeping patterns have deteriorated. As much as I hoped being at home would help, any advantage has been outweighed by the increasing size and volume. And being back at work adds to the demands on her. As I sit at the table, she rises from the couch, carries her stomach over in two hands and rests it against me.

'Look, it's too heavy. I don't see why I should have to do this any more.'

I don't think she should have to do it either. My stomach muscles hurt just thinking about it. I have guilt attacks when I see her, when I hear the wince as she moves, the effort it takes to get up. This is meant to be the easy second trimester. Ha.

MAY 22
Thursday, 23 weeks and two days

Hey, Peanut, you're not doing much. I'm talkin'. Are you listening? I'm singing, but I don't hear a harmony yet. There's a bit of Helen's stomach that feels harder than the rest. Is that your head? Should we wake you up? Helen says the fluttering is growing louder, intensifying into what will soon become kicks, but only she can feel it as yet. From the outside, you're just a giant flesh-coloured beach ball. You're a girl in a float tank. Which disturbs me. I don't want some kind of New Age kid.

MAY 24

Life with the Hunchfront of Notre Dame moves on. We make light of it as much as we can. We joke about the size. We try to keep our spirits up, but we're both wondering why she's having it so hard when other women we know have sailed through. This past week, Helen has gone from having a pot belly to an undeniably pregnant shape. The muscles at the top became obvious first. As she pulls off a T-shirt, I can see the curve of them below her ribcage.

Worries aside, there is something undeniably lovely about being able to feel the shape and size of the bulge, its strength, its solidity, its aggressive thrust. But there's also no denying that with its arrival, Helen has entered that weird state of 'the other'. She has gone from being a human being to a 1950s B-movie alien-colonised incubator.

The last vestiges of my disbelief are falling away. In another week or two, I'll be able to feel you elbowing your way around in there. The sense of looking at two people when I see Helen is taking some getting used to. Who would have thought there were so many stages of acceptance and realisation to go through?

May 25

Sitting at the breakfast table, Helen tells me that this morning she tried rolling over onto her stomach to sleep ('I really miss it') and the fluttering became very intense, as if there was someone in the flat below banging on the ceiling with a broom. 'Hey, Mum, back on your side.' She says that until recently, it had felt as if it were *her* body that was changing; now it actually feels as if there is an entity, a presence. You.

I remember a dream I had a couple of nights ago. Your mother and I are in a train station and all our belongings are wrapped in a towel—we don't have a suitcase. The towel comes loose and everything falls to the ground. As

I frantically pick up the bits and pieces, struggling to keep them from rolling away, I lose sight of Helen in the crowd. I finally make it onto the train, but I can't see her. Then, just as the train begins to move, I glimpse her through the window, seated on a train going in the other direction.

This, to me, is about my growing need to protect, and my perfectly natural fear that I won't be able to do it. My dreams used to be crappy, idiotic tableaux based on images I had picked up during the day and had no use for (I'm out bowling with Michael Jackson and he explains his love for marzipan). Now they actually mean something.

May 28

Wednesday, 24 weeks and one day

Dinner with my brother Paul, who says there have been ripples in the family since the announcement. For him, it has brought the issue of children to the fore. He suspects similar debates have been happening with Tim and Aleks. He says Helen being pregnant has made things easier for my parents though. They're happy about you, Peanut, but it's more than that. Given that Helen and I are not married, they find the thought of us having a child to be a comforting sign of commitment, something that actually makes Helen a part of the family.

May 29

We're watching television, catching up on something we taped, when Helen takes my hand and puts it on the left side of her stomach. About two seconds later, thump! A little limb bangs against the wall. I jump, but not as much as a second later, when there is a real, solid, full-extension kick. I am later informed that I squealed. So there we are, Peanut. At about nine o'clock on a Thursday night in the late autumn, I first feel you kick, first have some kind of direct physical knowledge of you. I let my hand stay for ages, resting against the warm, taut shape of the belly, feeling these bumps and thumps, these squirmy stretches. I could stay here forever, but Helen gently extricates herself and heads off to bed.

June

JUNE 1

The last week has been like wading through concrete. Helen is overtired, irrational, inconsolable. She has no reserves, no strength and seems to be swelling like a hot air balloon. Even the simple things—decisions about dinner, getting the washing done—seem like unclimbable mountains. The physical changes are huge and constant, and nothing I do seems to lift her spirits. There are still moments when this is fun, and knowing you're there brings us a lot of joy, but life could be better. Meanwhile, we still haven't found a house.

JUNE 4
Wednesday, 25 weeks and one day

Helen has her glucose tolerance tests, which take two hours and leave her with bruising on the inside of her elbow that looks like the result of junkie self-abuse. Her breathlessness has taken a turn for the worse. She says she now has to sit down every five minutes when she goes for a walk. The books say the second trimester is the happy-happy time, a rich and beautiful period which abuts the difficult last couple of months. This is rubbish. If things don't look up soon, I'm going to send this pregnancy back and ask for a refund.

JUNE 5

Helen declares that after a few months of living without coffee, it is now good for her nerves. To be more specific, it helps thin the fog, the caffeine jolt lifting the spell of bovinity. One espresso nails her eyelids open. After dinner we sit on the couch, taking turns to hold her belly up and take the pressure off. You kick away, your elbows and heels pressing against our fingers. Helen thinks you can hear now, that you can detect her tone of voice. I'm not sure why, but I feel a swell of what seems like pride. 'My daughter's so smart she knew what I was talking about before she was born.' How dumb is that? Pregnancy means getting to laugh at yourself a lot. I'm in bed as I write this, with Helen snuggling against my back for warmth. And you kneeing me in the kidneys.

June 6

I overhear Helen on the phone telling someone that since the kicking has started, she has actually enjoyed this gestation a lot more, no matter how hard it is. The reality factor is comforting, reminding her why she's going through so much. She hasn't said it to me though. I guess she just assumes I will have noticed.

June 8

It's late, sometime after eleven. And it's dark here in the bedroom. Dark and quiet. The window is open, but there are no sounds making their way inside, other than the occasional swish of a car heading up the street. Helen has been asleep for an hour or so, lying on her side, bump turned inwards, breathing gently. I'm whispering to you. This is our time together. I know you're awake because I can feel you move. And when I run out of things to say, I take out the tiny portable radio, put one of its earpieces in my right ear, and hold the other up to Helen's stomach, so you can listen too. And the two of us lie here under this roof, in this pinprick spot on the globe, listening to the Ashes broadcast from England. Oh yes, my sweet baby, you *will* be a cricket fan.

JUNE 10
Tuesday, 26 weeks

The books mention something I've been waiting for in vain. It's called 'couvade'. The word comes from the French 'to hatch'. It's sympathetic pregnancy. Studies estimate that 30 to 80 per cent of men go through it. Apparently, a lot of blokes have weight gain, nausea, mood swings and food cravings while their partners are doing the same things. I've been watching myself and my behaviour, hoping for phantom symptoms, but so far, nothing. What a gyp. If anything, I've lost weight. I've been drinking more, but I can't even seem to work up a beer pregnancy. I did have nausea, but that was traceable to a bad curry. My moods are no better and no worse (give or take the anxiety produced by the difficulty of the situation). And my interest in food has lessened, subsumed by Helen's requirements. It's much, much easier just to want whatever she wants.

JUNE 11

We bid on a house, the only one we have followed all the way to auction. When the price makes it to $50,000 beyond our comfort zone, we drop out. Back at home, I find Helen's nose buried in the pile of baby books. She has been reading them more lately, looking for answers, for explanations of why everything seems to be getting harder.

She tells me that she's looking for comfort. Every time she feels cruddy, she goes to the books to remind herself what other problems she could have. 'Ha,' she beams, 'at least I'm not constipated.'

June 13

Appointment with Dr Andrew. Helen weighs in at 58 kilos. The glucose tolerance test has come back normal, which is the good news. We explain that the weeks since the trip have been seriously difficult. Helen has been alternately panicked and exhausted. If she walks 5 metres, she becomes breathless. Her emotions are swooping out of control and she is suffering. Dr Andrew says some pregnant women have huge emotional shifts.

After examining her, he confirms our suspicion that she is too big. He doesn't appear particularly nervous about her state, but reminds us that if anything goes wrong, the easiest place to go is to the labour ward. The resident or registrar will check Helen out and call him immediately.

'It could be a sudden accumulation of fluid around the baby, which is not normal, so we should check it out. It might be abnormal. It might just be part of this pregnancy. The only way to know is via the ultrasound.'

He mentions something called hydramnios, but says he doesn't want to frighten us (as if we're not just that little bit scared already) by talking about possible causes too much. At this stage, he suggests that we forget about them and just make the ultrasound appointment.

'The most common outcome of this,' he says, 'is that we don't know what's going on.'

JUNE 16

Helen arrives home from a short trip to Melbourne to see Michelle's new baby. She says you kicked a lot on Saturday night, which she felt was reassuring—like having a travelling companion. She spent an hour on Sunday with the new baby asleep on her chest and thought it was a lovely feeling. She describes the tiny hand gripping her collar. So far, there is no name, but Belinda and Maxine are the front runners.

I've been proofreading the book, which I feel strangely detached from. There's too much going on elsewhere in my life to care about work. I'm nursing an undercurrent of nervousness about the next ultrasound. We have felt something was wrong for weeks. Now others agree and that's an invitation to get uptight. I keep trying to tell myself that there is nothing to worry about until we have something official to worry about. It works, but only sometimes.

JUNE 18

Wednesday, 27 weeks and one day

Ultrasound day. Part of me is excited because I've been waiting to see you for ages. The last time we looked, you were a peanut. What will you be now? We know you have limbs—we can feel them. Of course, resolution on the other front would be a comfort too. Either way. If something is wrong, I want to know. I want a name and an address.

12.30 pm. Into the small dark room. Fiona, the operator, asks why we're here, and Helen explains that at 23 weeks she started to grow very quickly, and is breathless and tired.

12.46 pm. I see your hands for the first time. Your head. Your spine. Your fingers. The level of amniotic fluid is judged by averaging the distance from baby to abdominal wall in four quadrants of the womb (the normal Amniotic Fluid Index range is 10 to 25 millimetres). The operator says she thinks, just from the look of the pictures, that there is too much fluid.

Back to looking for body parts. She checks through the list of biological landmarks. Here's a bladder. There's a thigh bone. Lower legs. Feet. Fiona measures the circumference of your head and that of your waist. And then, good God, your face, your lips, your nostrils, the scanner rolling over your features as we stare at images of you. I am surprised—I didn't think the ultrasound would be so clear.

Your heart is beating. We see its chambers. The machine says it's doing 136 beats a minute, which is a great speed for babies and dancing. So much is appearing on the screen that I'm beginning to lose track. It's like a 1960s psychedelic light show, shapes moving, colliding and merging.

What she has not found is a stomach with any fluid in it. Dr Jock arrives and asks if there has been a sighting: 'If there is an obstruction [in the passage from mouth to stomach] fluid builds, so we're looking for a stomach to make sure there is no obstruction, that baby is swallowing.'

He finds what he thinks is a stomach, but there's not much in it. He says he can't tell if Helen is carrying an abnormally large amount of fluid or just more than average.

He says you're 'nice and active' and that the stomach he spotted appears to be emptying. Nothing definite. We'll need more time, more tests.

JUNE 24
Tuesday, 28 weeks

Ours has been a household of few words this week. What is there to say? We have retreated inside ourselves. Anyone standing outside our door would think no-one was home. We're both afraid, but neither of us really wants to talk about fear, to admit it. Neither of us wants to put into words the possibility that something is wrong. Neither us of wants to even think of the words 'might die'. We need to keep our blackest thoughts private. So we don't talk. We are silent, waiting until there is more information.

Helen feels no better. Indeed, the confirmation that something may be wrong, like the confirmation of the pregnancy itself, has allowed her to feel as awful as she truly does. Her bulk is now a psychological upset as well as a physical difficulty. And it's hard to forget when it's attached to the front of you. Finding distraction isn't easy.

JUNE 27

Appointment with Dr Andrew. Helen weighs in at 59.5 kilograms. The doctor says he doesn't think there's as much fluid as there has been, but we should talk about what it all could mean. He explains that amniotic fluid is produced by the lining of the uterus. The baby swallows it, uses it and pees it out. Excess fluid could be produced at any point in the cycle. More could be coming from the lining. More could be building up because you're not swallowing properly. More could be building up because you're peeing excessively, which would mean that your heart is not functioning properly.

You're around 28 weeks, but Helen's actual size suggests 34 weeks. He can tell the number just by looking (he'd probably be really good at the jelly beans in the jar thing). He says her size means we must continue to check for potential problems and recommends we have another ultrasound next week.

'Very likely there is not a problem,' he says. 'They may not find anything. Not everything can be found. But in medicine, there is always a worry when things are not exactly as they should be. Too much fluid is not diabetes, and it's not chromosomal, so we test for other things.'

He says that what they're looking for in you is mostly an inability to swallow, a narrowing of the gullet, abnormalities in the alimentary canal. He says there could be an area of the placenta which produces excess fluid.

'They'll look at everything,' he says, 'but the problem, of course, is that they're looking at shadows.'

He assures us that Helen looks better, that her stomach is not as taut as it was. He says he's an optimist, but that we're not in a position to ignore what has been going on. Better to test for everything now than wait until you're born and find we've missed something.

On the way home in the car, Helen says, 'I can't tell if he's worried or if he's just trying to reassure me.' Neither can I. There's a lot of silence during the evening as we disappear into books and magazines. Not knowing hurts.

JUNE 28

Helen's crying wakes me, muffled sobs in my neck. A bad night. She's tense and upset, having trouble breathing while lying down. More than once, she has to sit up to restore the air flow, pulling the covers around her to stay warm. She says she has been thinking about who will be her support person at your birth. But I know there's more to her anxiety than that.

July

July 1
Tuesday, 29 weeks

In bed. Late. Snuggled up as tight as the huge stomach *bermp* will allow. We are quiet. I am concerned for you. For the first six months of the pregnancy, I was worried about Helen. You were an extension of her. You were like another organ, an extra liver. Now you're you. You're someone who *does things*. You make decisions. You kick, therefore you are. Tomorrow, the ultrasound.

July 2

In the morning, I pick up a box we sent from New York. It's full of books and gifts and baby clothes, lots of baby clothes. Helen drags them out one by one and holds them up. We realise we should have bought more with booties sewn in. Everything stops at the ankles. What would we know?

On the way to the ultrasound clinic, Helen is busy fighting indigestion. At least she's more comfortable than usual—wearing the new maternity underwear that arrived in the box. Sitting in the waiting room, listening to the soundtrack of quiet burping beside me, I begin to wish I hadn't eaten either. Dr Tom (Dr Jock is not available today) is running late. My feet tap. I look at the other women coming and going, all with slightly pained expressions. Maybe they have problems too. Maybe it's just the full bladder you have to hang onto for the ultrasound.

Eleven o'clock. Fiona asks about Helen's breathlessness. Yes, it's been pretty bad again. She is starting to scan as Dr Tom arrives. He backtracks through the full story of the pregnancy, the number of scans we've had, the age question, the chorio. We ask for his thoughts on possible reasons for excess fluid. He says the most common cause is idiopathic, a medical word which, he says, translates roughly as 'we don't know'.

'It's pretty much a closed circuit in there,' he says, pointing to Helen's swelling stomach. 'They just drink and wee, drink and wee. Sometimes they just wee too much. The regulatory elements of it are not fully understood. There are some foetal abnormalities that can show up on the scan and explain what is going on, but many don't.'

Dr Tom talks (another well modulated, calming voice) as Fiona skates across the surface with the scanner. They're not entirely certain what they're looking for, he admits. We spot the lengthy femur again. Helen says she was a long, skinny baby. Dr Tom says, 'Well, you're going to have one too.'

The bowel is not dilated, he says. By this, he basically means that the stomach is empty and hard to spot. This could be evidence of a possible obstruction. Dr Tom says he'd be happier if the stomach were bigger, if it were full. But on the other hand, he reassures us that he wouldn't want a *really* big one. They keep looking, coming back to the stomach often to see if it's filling up. It isn't.

Through all this I am sitting in the corner with my teeth clenched, willing him to say, 'Everything is fine, everything is fine.' In another part of my head, I'm singing a little song to comfort myself.

He raises the question of what we do about excess fluid. Sometimes, there is so much that the doctors will decide to drain it, for fear that it will precipitate labour. But he thinks that would be premature in this case. He suggests bed rest, saying it has helped in similar cases before. Today, he says, they're just gathering information. Decisions will come later. Helen is at the upper end of the normal liquid spectrum. There's too much fluid, but not way too much. It's more about monitoring than acting at the moment.

'There's a question of how much we can scale down your activity,' Dr Tom says. 'The discomfort is nature's way of telling us things are not going as well as they might.'

They're still watching the stomach, moving the scanner back and forth. No change. It's quiet and Helen closes her eyes. I listen to the air-conditioner hum and the occasional sounds from the other side of the door, chairs scraping, a child's voice. Dr Tom tells us to go have lunch and come back in an hour so they can have another look.

1 pm. Helen finds it hard to breathe and has to sit up. The pillows are re-arranged to make her more comfortable. Her eyes shut again. Seeing the screen means swivelling uncomfortably, so she doesn't bother looking, letting herself relax.

You're moving, kicking around. Your stomach is not filled. We look at something else for a moment, your hands and feet. You have five fingers, five toes on each foot. I am mildly relieved that you're not some three-fingered cartoon creation. Fiona finds your face. Your lips are moving. You could be swallowing, she says, or you could just be sucking your tongue. Scanning down to the stomach ... it's the latter. Dr Tom says we'll have to have an ultrasound on a fortnightly basis.

'I don't know if the absence today of a stomach is significant or not,' he says. 'It [that's you, Peanut] might not be drinking when we want it to drink.'

JULY 7

I start telling people that we have a size problem. I email Paul and Tim. I'm not sure if it's just offloading my worry, but I find it comforting to get it out in the open. This thing has been upsetting us for a month now. I hear myself repeating what doctors have said: 'it could be normal', 'nothing to worry about just yet', and it almost sounds convincing.

Baby class. The expectant fathers sit around talking about ultrasounds. Judy, the physiotherapist in charge, asks the gravid mums to line up in order of their gestation stage, the lowest week at one end and the highest at the other. The range of the half dozen women covers 28 to 33 weeks. Stomach size means nothing, though I see in Helen's eyes that it's obvious to her how much bigger than the others she is.

Judy stresses the importance of perineal massage. Sounds like fun to me. The massage reduces the likelihood of tearing (and the episiotomy that goes with it). She asks each woman about the changes they have noticed in their pregnancy. They talk about breathlessness, the Braxton Hicks contractions.

Then it's time to ask the men the same question. On the way around the room, one guy says he doesn't think his wife has changed at all. 'But she's not a whinger,' he proudly says, as other faces darken. What, you can see the women thinking, by implication we are? I hear the word 'Prick' muttered from my right.

Judy drags out a model pelvis to show us where the ligaments attach, how the muscles work, where pressure builds up and what sort of posture exercises can help. The rest of the class is based on exercising, mostly of the pelvic floor. Then it's a discussion of the value of calmness. Calm, she says, can be your biggest ally.

July 8
Tuesday, 30 weeks

House auction. On the way, Helen tells me about a dream she had last night, a dream in which you, Peanut, were born and could talk. You were giving her advice, calmly chatting in a totally comprehensible way. And Helen says she remembers feeling very reassured by whatever it was you were saying.

We are the third lot on the auction list. Helen freezes in the auction room, so I do the bidding. Just before it's our turn, she puts my hand on the upper right side of her bulge. 'Push here. You can feel something. It's a hand, I think. It's Peanut putting her hand up. She wants to bid.'

We get the house, but pay more than we would have liked. (Isn't that always the way?) We celebrate at the restaurant of Matt, a chef friend. Helen goes into minor meltdown, worried that we've done the wrong thing. We can afford it. We'll just have to scrape a little, be careful with the cash while she is off work.

July 11

In the ultrasound chamber again. Fiona swishes back and forth with the scanner, trying to find a stomach. Dr Jock asks Helen how she is feeling. Not bad, better than a few days ago. Fiona says she hasn't seen a stomach. I find, as I watch the tumble of shapes on the screen, that I'm getting used to recognising organs, your kidneys, your bladder, your internal geography.

Fiona finds your face. You look to be sucking your right thumb, though you may just be resting it against your mouth. You are head down. It's your bum that's pushing into Helen's ribs. Fiona finds something fluid-filled in your abdomen 'where I would expect to see a stomach'. Dr Jock has a look. He agrees that it is a stomach, 'but there's not much in it, is there?'

'The heart's on the left where it should be,' he says, moving the scanner. 'The lungs look fine. Now we should see the stomach just under the heart ... but we really don't ... That's the gall bladder there ... That's the aorta ... I can't honestly say that I can see stomach ... Well, it's going to have a stomach. When I say that I can't see it, I mean it hasn't got any fluid in it ... So why is there so much fluid? To me, it seems like more than last time ... The baby's skull seems all right ... right orbit fine ... left orbit fine ... five digits on that hand ... five digits on this one.'

He totals the AFI level. It's 36.3 millimetres this time, and was 24 millimetres last time he saw it.

'The baby looks a pretty good size. But I cannot say that I've seen stomach today. I don't know that it's functioning. If the baby's stomach hasn't filled, it might mean she's not swallowing. And if the baby is not swallowing it might mean she can't swallow. If her oesophagus is blocked, that would mean she can't swallow and that would need to be surgically corrected.

'Basically, I'm becoming a bit suspicious. We can't see everything, though. You just can't see the whole lot. It's good that we're aware of this. And you're definitely going to have the baby in the right place, the hospital.'

He says we should have another scan soon. From the look of Helen, he says he'd guess she was 38 weeks. We're both quiet in the lift on the way down. The anxiety and upset that came after the last visit is not here. Instead, there's a chest-squeezing numbness, an acceptance that possibility has crossed over into probability. In the carpark, I remember that I haven't answered an email from Paul, asking what I want for my birthday, which is in two weeks. Usually I have no idea what I'd like. This year I know exactly what I want, but I also know, with increasing certainty, that I can't have it.

5 pm. We arrive for our regular appointment with Dr Andrew. Helen excuses herself to provide a urine sample. Two minutes later she's rushing back towards the desk. 'I'm bleeding,' she says frantically, a look of terror on her face.

Dr Andrew is seeing a patient. We are hustled into the consulting room next door, where Helen lies on the bed, her hands between her legs, holding a gauze pad in place, willing the haemorrhage to stop. In seconds there is blood everywhere, pushing through her clothes and spreading across the mattress. The bottom is falling out of my chest. I do what I can to calm her down, stroking her, talking to her, telling her not to worry. A single tear rolls down her cheek. I've never seen her look so scared and small.

Dr Andrew tells us to go straight to hospital.

'It's very likely that you will come into labour,' he says. 'It is also possible that it might settle, but you'll have to stay in hospital.'

He sees the size of the stain spreading, the amount of blood coming out.

'This is not good. But the chances of a baby surviving in a big institution are 95 per cent. The biggest problem is still the possible abnormality.'

All we can do is get to hospital and see what happens. If Helen comes into labour, he says, he will let her, because of the bleeding. If not, we'll have to reassess the situation tomorrow. We make our way to the car as quickly as possible. Helen is on my arm, both of us in silent panic, the kind that makes you feel wrapped in a force field. At the car, I tear my T-shirt off and put it on the seat to soak up the flow. Helen carefully straps herself in. We drive. It's peak hour, but the journey flies.

6.15 pm. Helen is shuttled straight into the labour ward, stripped of her clothes and wired up to monitors which measure her heart rate and the contractions of her uterus. A registrar explains that there will be a blood test and more ultrasounds. A drip will also be put in. She says the kind of problems you'll have at this stage, if you are born, will be with feeding, growing, keeping warm. She's very reassuring. She has to be—we must look as anxious and afraid as we are.

I move my car from the emergency parking area. By the time I get back to the ward, the bleeding has slowed. You're still agitated according to the monitors, but not as much as you were. Helen is calmer, lying back, breathing carefully, safe now. If something is going to happen, this is the place for it. Your heart rate is 140; anything between 120 and 160 is okay. We wait.

The blood test is done and the cannula is put in after much foraging for veins. What's worrying the staff is the possibility that you may have bled. You don't have a lot of blood to spare. Helen is given a shot of steroids to help your lungs mature, just in case she does go into labour. We sit, holding hands, touching, saying nothing. From somewhere down the hall, we hear the first cry of a baby entering the world.

At 7.45, the portable ultrasound is wheeled in. The operator notes the fluid level immediately, finds a beating heart and then sees what she thinks is a stomach. Empty. She calculates the AFI at close to 40 millimetres. You appear to have gone to sleep. The image is fixed on your face. Come on, we're all urging, open your mouth.

The registrar returns to say that the first blood test suggests everything is normal. The foetal blood test will not be back until Monday. The bleeding has all but stopped. The monitors are quiet.

Left on our own, we realise how hungry we are. It's almost nine. I sneak out to secure takeaway food from a local pizza joint, a favourite haunt when we're in the area. Around ten, Helen is moved upstairs to another ward. I settle her in, then leave. On the trip home, the events of the day close in on me. I am so shaken that I find it hard to get out of the car when I stop. It's midnight. I sit there, music at full volume, and cry it all out.

July 12

I was too tired to have a sleepless night, too worn out. Inside, I found four messages on the answering machine from Helen's sister Michelle, the first upset and each subsequent addition more frantic. Though the last said to call any time, I wasn't up to it.

Today dawns bright and beautiful. No bleeding. No pain. No major contractions. I walk around the house with the cordless phone as Helen directs me to clothes, toiletries, books, food, specifics. She made a list in her head at 3 am.

Paul rings. I fill him in. My parents are at their beach house. They have a mobile phone, but they never seem to turn it on except when they want to use it. We have no real way of contacting them, short of Paul driving two hours to the coast. Since things have settled, we decide to wait.

Michelle was ringing because Dolek, Helen's stepfather, has had a stroke and is in hospital. What a piece of timing. It's difficult for Helen to cope with the news—she is already disoriented. She says she feels like a big jug, like these crazy emotions are being poured in and she somehow has to hold onto them all. She feels light-headed, and finds it impossible to even comprehend the idea of Dolek being in hospital. It's hard enough trying to get past her fear that you might have been hurt or suffered. Your heart rate is fine and you're moving around like normal, so the signs are good.

We sit out on the balcony in the warmth of the late morning sun. Dr Andrew arrives and says he's relieved everything has settled, but Helen isn't going anywhere.

No-one is certain what caused the bleeding—perhaps, he says, it was a broken blood vessel. Helen's cervix has partly dilated, so we now have an unstable pregnancy. It's like volcano watching. There's a lot of rumbling going on and sooner or later she's going to blow. The doctor thinks it could happen any time. I ask what the outside possibility is. He says it's highly unlikely we'll make it to 36 weeks. We're at 30 and a half now. Helen has to stay in hospital for as long as it takes, and every additional day is a good one. Every day is a chance for you to grow stronger, faster, smarter.

In the afternoon, I round up some of her friends, leaving messages on answering machines suggesting they call or drop by. Helen, meanwhile, is discovering hospital food, strange Anglo-Saxon cooking that she, like any self-respecting migrant child, does not recognise—exotic dishes such as baked sultana rice pudding. I thought she might be horrified, but she finds it funny. And she's very hungry, perhaps because of the blood loss, perhaps because of the steroids.

In the evening, we scrunch up on her bed and I watch TV as she reads, our bodies pressed tight. I talk to you, hold you both, feel you next to me, try to be as soothing as possible. To be honest, I'm surprised at how well Helen is handling the thought of being trapped in a two-bed ward, with all the noise and lack of privacy.

JULY 13

I ring in and Helen is shaky. Just before she went to sleep last night, a nurse arrived to give her another steroid jab ('And this time, it was a jab!'). The pain and the shock, she says, made her have a good cry. It had been coming.

She says she's feeling strengthened by putting the tears behind her. 'But I think the novelty has worn off—even the meals don't look so exotic.'

JULY 14

Helen started bleeding overnight, contracting as well. I believe it had a lot to do with the emotional pressure of her situation, compounded by the news that Dolek is unlikely to live more than a day or two. She was strapped into the foetal monitor, then taken in a wheelchair for an ultrasound. Dr Andrew asked the scanners to find out how much you weigh (1.4 kilos) and whether Helen's cervix is dilated (no, it looks long and closed).

Back in the ward, the contractions and bleeding continued. Helen says you were moving around, making her tender and sore. She felt as if her muscles were about to split. After an hour or so, the contractions started to slow down. It was a scary reminder of the delicate balance of our situation. Neither of us feels there is much time before your arrival. Stay in there as long as you can, little one.

Helen is extremely uncomfortable, with pain in her rear and at the top of her legs, cramps which seem to be moving up and down. When I get there after work, she says, 'I've had enough.' She holds me as closely as she can. She wants it all to go away.

JULY 15
Tuesday, 31 weeks

Chef Matt sends a care package to the hospital, an extravagant and delicious picnic, just what Helen needs to lift her spirits. An odd image has snagged in her mind, the kind of small detail that can seem more upsetting than the big picture. This morning, while sitting out on the balcony, she saw a neonatal delivery van come into the carpark. It's the type of van that will transport you, when you're born, to the Sydney Children's Hospital, where you can be operated on. It seemed to symbolise everything that has gone wrong for her.

After hearing from Dr Andrew, the situation becomes clearer. They suspect there may be a blockage in your oesophagus and a hole between it and your trachea. The likelihood of surgery is now very high. So you will be delivered by Caesarean section. I reassure Helen that it means she gets to keep her pelvic floor. She looks at me oddly.

J ULY 16

Dolek died this morning. I can see the pain on Helen's face, the helplessness, the loss. She has been crying all afternoon. Thankfully, it hasn't affected her physical condition. I spend the evening crammed into the hospital bed, pressed up against the bits of her I can get to around your bulge. She has now achieved a snail look, clearly carrying a house on her body. You are tumbling and turning and running about the whole time. They say that the extra fluid means your joints will not ache from being so tightly held in place. There's a little mercy for you.

I've finally located my parents. After the call, I look at the baby books on the coffee table and think, well, their advice no longer applies. We've moved off the page.

JULY 18

The funeral in Melbourne. Janina opens the door to her apartment, takes one look at me and bursts into tears. She wants to know about Helen. Her own grief is put aside for the moment, consumed by maternal fear. I explain everything, and though she remains worried, I can see her fear beginning to dim as I talk.

We speak of families and children and how lucky Dolek had been to have a family around him when he died, how important it was to Helen to know that he had seen her pregnant, and how important that had been to him. Helen's brother-in-law, Brendan, wants to have more children. Michelle isn't so sure. I tell Janina that given the current situation, I would be ecstatic just to have one. Maybe two children would not be out of the question (Helen has been broaching the subject lately), but no more than that.

I entrust Janina with a secret. In the last week, I have decided what your name will be—one of Helen's early suggestions. I'm not going to tell you and I'm not going to tell Helen just yet. I think it should be a secret. Hope you like it . . .

JULY 20

A quiet weekend. On Saturday my father is in town for the day, and I pick him up and take him by the hospital. He and my mother will be back during the week—this is his reconnaissance mission.

JULY 21

Helen isn't sleeping well. There's been another growth spurt, another accumulation of fluid pushing her shape in all directions. She's very sore. The doctors have measured and there seems to be an agreement that yes, the bulge is growing, but it's not in the danger zone just yet. When I arrive after work, Helen is pushing you, her hands pressing on the top of her stomach, trying to force what we suspect is your bony butt down and out from her ribcage.

'I have to push her down now,' she says, 'because it hurts so much. This one's going to be a spoiled child, you know. She has so much freedom to move in there [patting her stomach]. Other foetuses get all cramped.' She drops her chin. 'Life isn't always going to be like this, Peanut . . . Ouch! I'm going to push and I don't care if it's a problem and if she hates me for the rest of her life . . . Do you think she will?'

Helen has talked bank representatives into dropping by the hospital, two tonight and another couple in the morning. In the middle of all this, we're trying to get the finances together for the house. It's funny to see the corporate suits sitting by the bed. It makes their spiel even less believable.

Later, on the couch at home, I wonder if I feel the right things, if my own emotions can be trusted. Should I be more worried, more nervous, more uptight? I feel remarkably calm now. After months of worrying when there wasn't much to worry about, now that there is, I seem to have switched tack. I'm as focused as the situation allows and demands. Maybe it's numbness.

Some days it seems almost impossible to keep up with this diary. I make notes on scraps of paper, which I leave around, hoping I won't lose them. But it seems more important to me than ever. I can't control the future. I can't guarantee that the world will treat you well. I can't guarantee it will recognise you, bring you good tidings, comfort and care for you. But whatever happens, I want you to know that you were born into love, that you had parents who wanted you, who had nothing but the purest hopes. Nothing else in your life, in our relationship, will be that simple, that non-negotiable.

JULY 22
Tuesday, 32 weeks

Still there.

JULY 24

Still cooking.

JULY 25

My father arrives during the afternoon and finds his way to the hospital. My mother has been ill and is not well enough to travel. It's my birthday, but I've tried to play it down, not because I'm unhappy, but because a birthday seems like a useless thing for me right now. For you, Peanut, it would be even less of a thing to celebrate (though there was a little part of me wishing for us to share a date). I'm 33. The age of Christ. I'll keep an eye out for men with nails.

Dad has a present for Helen, a jewellery box he made. Inside is a felt pouch containing an opal brooch, a warm, white stone filled with fire. Dad explains that it is one of three. They belonged to my great aunt Peggy, wife of Boy (whose real name was Keith), brother of my grandfather

Tim (whose real name was Theodore). Peggy's dad ran a boarding house in White Cliffs at the turn of the century. He would put up miners, punting on them getting rich and paying him back with gems. The three opals were set around 1902, and were given to my father by Boy, who never had children of his own and wanted one to go to each of the wives of my brothers and me.

Helen has surprisingly managed to buy me a present, a book I wanted, with the help of Ruth. And three separate hampers have arrived for Helen, who sits in bed reading imported magazines and nibbling on fine foods. My father and I trek off to secure another pizza banquet. And all in all, I reckon I've had a pretty good birthday.

July 27

Helen calls in the morning, feeling positively whalish, sleep-deprived and unhappy. I ask my father to hang around the house while I visit on my own. Helen is convinced she has had another growth spurt. Breathing is a harder and harder proposition. I hate to see her so uncomfortable, so wrecked by what's happening inside her. My father sees it too, when we return in the afternoon. Though she is larger, her spirit has shrunken. Something must break soon. I can't see her making it through the week like this.

July 28

Another difficult night. Helen insists she has grown in the last twelve hours. She's due for an ultrasound and promises to call if there's any news. When I get to work, after dropping my father off at the train station, there's a message waiting. The ultrasound has shown that you haven't grown much. But Helen's fluid level has jumped again. Drs Andrew and Greg, the head of the neonatal department at KGV, have decided that it's time to attempt a drain. If we don't, the pressure created by the extra fluid will bring on labour. If we do, there's a chance that the sudden change will bring on labour anyway.

Helen is waiting at the neonatal ward when I arrive. In the theatre, she is laid out flat on her back. The doctor, midwife and nurse fuss about her. They take four pieces of green cloth ('If it's green, it must be sterile') and make a square around her protruding belly. It looks bizarre, even weirder when they paint her skin with iodine, which has the colour and consistency of soy sauce, and stains it a burned copper.

Dr Greg explains that the fluid level on the morning ultrasound was 52 millimetres. (Remember, normal is 10–25.) A week ago, Helen was 40 millimetres. He says he'll drain off as much as can be comfortably taken. He says you will undoubtedly stab yourself on the needle a number of times during the procedure, and that we shouldn't worry about it. As it happens, the second the needle pierces Helen's skin, you lie down and go quiet. Later, Helen wonders if it's not some primitive instinct, a reaction to danger or intrusion. The needle goes in through the abdominal wall, right next to what used to be Helen's belly button, before it flattened out and disappeared. She winces. They give her more local anaesthetic. When the needle is secure, a tube is added, which is run through a machine that slowly pumps liquid out.

The amniotic fluid itself is yellow (mostly urine) and viscous. I'm not sure what I'd been expecting, but it wasn't this. The liquid snakes along the tube and into a large container. As it fills, the assistant and Dr Greg keep an eye on what's going on inside. 'It's a very photogenic baby,' says the assistant after finding your profile.

Helen's abdomen is visibly shrinking, the skin loosening. Though Dr Greg had said he was only planning to take a litre, maybe two at the most, the container fills up and another is brought in. Two litres. Two and a quarter. Two and a half. Helen starts to get pains around her cervix. The drain continues. Three litres. At 3.3, the doctor stops it. Three point three litres. It seems hard to believe that much could have been in there. Dr Greg says it was less than half of what's actually there.

I have just seen a woman lose half a stone in less than an hour. Many would pay a fortune for that. Helen looks pale. She is given drugs to ease the pain and to relax the muscles of her uterus, which have begun to contract. It's a wheelchair trip back to the ward, where she fights the soreness as the drugs take effect. I feed her jelly beans bought from the chemist across the road.

Her belly is softer, flatter. Her navel is back. We greet it like an old friend. Well, I do. Helen is too busy going into what we think is a mild shock. She begins to shake, offering a passable, if involuntary, Katharine Hepburn impersonation. Later, Dr Greg wanders past and says, 'Oh, that's just the ventolin in one of the drugs. It gives you palpitations.'

When I come back after a few hours at work, you're grooving around. I put my hand on Helen's stomach. It feels different. Your movements are closer to the surface. You don't have to stretch out now to make your presence felt. We wonder how you'll feel about being made to live in a smaller house. You're still doing all right—as the assistant says, you've come down from a castle to a mansion. The drain has brought Helen's AFI level to 32 millimetres.

If labour is going to be brought on, it will probably happen in the next 48 hours, Dr Greg says. If not, then maybe the drain will buy us a fortnight. By the end of the evening, Helen is already feeling better, lighter, more manoeuvrable in the bed. Fingers crossed.

JULY 29
Tuesday, 33 weeks

The next morning slides in and she's fine, though sleep has been awkward. Various medical staff have been by, asked the odd question, smiled and mumbled positives. Dr Greg seems to think Helen might be able to go home, that we might have earned release. Helen is definitely feeling much better. And looking smaller.

'I could paint my toenails this morning without gasping for air,' she says proudly.

JULY 30

No sign of Dr Andrew yet. Helen's theory is that he's avoiding her. He doesn't want to be the one to tell her she can't go home. Not that he would ever say a thing like that. No. He'd just furrow a brow, look off into the distance and say, 'Well, of course you could, but *I* wouldn't do it,' with an air of impermeable finality.

Janina arrives at lunchtime. I pick her up from the airport and deposit her at the hospital on the way to work. Helen is glad to have someone around for company. It's good for both of them.

July 31

Helen rings from the hospital in the afternoon. Dr Andrew has finally been by and told her she's free. She can hardly contain her excitement. Three days after the drain there have been no complications. We have enough fluid insurance to let her come home for a while, perhaps a week, perhaps even more. Janina decides to stay an extra day.

I load the possessions into the car. How can one woman accumulate so much in such a short time? The back seat looks like a flower shop. The books are wrenchingly heavy. Bags of fruit spill out everywhere. As I pack, I realise how much I have come to enjoy King George V, how comforting I find its smooth, cool hallways. While on first sight, I was surprised by its age, now I find it full of character. On the way home, Helen looks out the window and sighs loudly. 'It's such a big world,' she says.

There is celebration in the household. We dine on the finest takeaway offerings of the local Chinese establishment. We sit on the couch, drink tea and feel as normal as we can. The best moment, one that fills me with life, comes in bed, when I feel my thighs tuck in behind Helen's, her rear against my stomach, my chest against her back, the smell of her hair in my nostrils, my hand stealing under her arm and across the bulge, my fingertips gently pushing into its newfound softness.

August

August 1

Now that a little optimism is creeping into view, the question of whether we can have a sex life returns. Helen is convinced it's possible. I am holding out, scared about the fragility of the situation, about what that sort of activity could precipitate. I want to hear it from a doctor first. It's a pleasure to feel the awakenings though, the toe-curling fleshiness of desire. For weeks, that side of ourselves has been shut down, sidelined by worry. Helen says her mother saw her nude and told her how beautiful she looked. It's true.

August 2

Janina went home today. Though it has been both lovely and helpful to have her around (she was a cooking and cleaning demon the other day), there's a part of me that is not sad to see her go. It's not her fault at all. I just don't seem to have the emotional space for it. After sharing Helen with a hospital for three weeks, what I really want is to have her to myself, to let the stiff upper lip pretence melt away, to rest my head in her lap, my cheek against you, and disappear.

August 5
Tuesday, 34 weeks

The fluid is coming back, with all the inevitability of a movie monster. ('Ohmigod! It can't be killed!') Helen is sleeping well, but the growth spurt brings discomfort. She's swelling out on the sides. Misery loving company as it does, we spend the afternoon wrestling with housing loans.

We're also trying to organise removalists, so there's paperwork all over the place.

It's surprisingly hard for Helen to be at home. In hospital, she had to sit still, shut up and accept the situation she was in. At home, all the alternatives are in reach. She can see everything she'd like to do spread out tantalisingly in front of her. She could be cooking or walking or organising things. But she has to rest, she has to do nothing. Home is a constant, cruel reminder of what is not allowed.

AUGUST 6

The weekly ultrasound. Swimming Girl (when I put my ear to Helen's stomach, I can hear the ocean), you're now in the breech position, head up, feet down. This explains why Helen has been complaining about you stomping on her bladder and colon. Her cervix is still closed.

'Great hair!' says the operator and shows us the shadow of a good thatch. We spot your face and you're definitely taking fluid into your mouth. Measurements are taken and it's decided that you're around 2 kilos, up from 1.6 ten days ago. Most of the gain, apparently, is in the head and bones. You're still a long, skinny baby. The AFI readings are taken. Helen's at 35.5; up, but not alarmingly.

'And in all that time,' the operator says, with a certain predictability, 'I didn't see a stomach.'

In the afternoon, I ring Dr Andrew and ask if we can, you know ... He says, 'Sure', with a tone that suggests I was worrying about nothing. He calls back after talking to the ultrasound clinic. I think I hear worry in his voice, but he has nothing to tell us that we're not aware of.

There's still no stomach on the scan. The fluid is rising.

It's getting to the point where the idea of what is wrong with you upsets others more than it gets to me. I'm working hard on acceptance, so that I can move on. I think it's very sad that you won't come into the world smoothly and easily, but things could be much worse. And once the problems are isolated (or as close as we can get) then we will know what our obstacle race looks like. Knowing what has to happen is calming. We can do nothing more than wait, try to keep you in, and prepare ourselves for those events.

AUGUST 8

I speak to Paul on the phone. When I hear myself describing what is going on, I catch a hint of what I'm really like. I don't know if Paul can pick it up, but there's a rattle of fear in my voice. I hear how worried I am. I may think I'm calm and confident, working on acceptance, but my skin is giving way. I have a red blotchy scalp—something I've never seen before. And my bottom lip, which always cracks in times of stress, is riverbed dry. Some days I think this whole thing is under control. Others I think I'm just holding it together.

Later, an appointment with Dr Andrew. 'Well, what's happening? You look very relaxed. I think it has been a sobering experience for you.'

Helen comes in at 60.5 kilos.

'I think you've regained a lot of the fluid,' he says. 'Two kilograms for the baby is very good though. The chances of it surviving are very, very high at that weight.' I hear

the words: 'the ... chances ... of ... it ... surviving ...'.
Surely there isn't another option.

'Let's assume that everything is normal,' Dr Andrew
says to Helen, 'that you won't suddenly come into labour.
If that is so, we should plan for an elective delivery. Either
we induce it and allow the birth to happen naturally or
we opt for an elective Caesarean.'

The advantage of the elective delivery, he suggests, is
the timing. It can be arranged for a day of the week, and
a time of the day, that will allow us to have the right
people around and awake enough to deal with whatever
will happen after the birth, with the probable surgery. It
wouldn't be the end of the world if you chose 5 am on a
Sunday to arrive, but it would make things a lot more
difficult. Dr Andrew suggests the 38 week mark. That's
August 26. He consults his schedule and recommends the
28th. I remember, with a surge of joy, him saying how
unlikely it was we'd make 36 weeks.

Given the probable surgical complications, he recommends the Caesarean option. Helen will be admitted to
hospital the day before for an amniocentesis, to confirm
that your lungs are mature enough. At 38 weeks, that's
pretty likely. She will be given an epidural, which will
continue after the delivery to help with pain relief. If
uncomplicated, the procedure will take 30 minutes. If it
gets a little tricky, maybe ten minutes more.

I ask what will happen at the moment of birth. Dr
Andrew says you will be given to us to hold. If everything
is okay, and that is still a possibility (a long shot, but a
possibility), you will be handed over to us for a while, as

usual, for a first cuddle. If not, you'll still spend a few minutes with us before being whisked away.

He says there is the other option: to induce and allow normal delivery. This has the timing risks. I can see Helen wavering. There's a part of her that would like to go in that direction, but I think she knows that she can't. But will she make it to August 28? Another drain is more than likely in the interim, but will be determined by just how uncomfortable Helen is and what the ultrasounds show.

Helen asks if they have an idea why 'the problem' (no-one is giving it a name yet—the hydramnios Dr Andrew mentioned refers simply to the excess fluid) could have happened. Is it genetic?

'It's not genetic,' Dr Andrew says. 'It's a statistical misfortune.'

Helen says she is fighting depression.

'It *is* depressing,' Dr Andrew says. 'This was meant to be a positive time, when you're planning to be new parents. It's quite appropriate that you should be depressed. But you should be optimistic too. You're dealing with a serious, but minor abnormality.'

I turn around and Helen is crying. She says she is sick of waiting.

'Yes, I know,' Dr Andrew says patiently, 'but it's not ready.'

We book for another ultrasound next week. Dr Andrew says he is also concerned about your size. You're small, he says, which could just mean you're a small baby (Helen and I both were), but could also mean you're not getting enough food.

At home we talk about grieving for what we can't have, for the normal version of parenthood we can't get to. One of the books suggests that women who have Caesareans often feel as if they have failed at a simple task of womanhood that so many millions of others pass with flying colours. Equally, we feel a bit idiotic being sad. There are so many people with problems much worse.

AUGUST 10

A quiet weekend. Helen has a big day out on Saturday, getting her hair cut, then sitting for a couple of hours in a café. More than once she has said that this whole thing has given her a new perspective on small pleasures. She sits in the café watching the people go by, smelling the smells coming from the kitchen, being part of a world she hasn't been near for weeks. She pays for it today. Tired, breathless, worn out. Constantly eating and drinking.

I'm starting to plan for the move. And you? You're practising tumble turns, standing, stretching, pumping out rhythmic beats. It's the ripples that feel strange, when you push against the wall and slide along it. Helen is left feeling faintly queasy.

AUGUST 12
Tuesday, 35 weeks

It's odd actually finally having a date: the 28th. It's comforting and frightening at the same time (particularly because I have to move house on the 25th and 26th). Most babies have a due date, but it's more like a use-by date with you. There is a definite end, a definite number. And unless something happens in the next few days, you're a Virgo. Or are you? I'm thinking of writing to an astrologer to find out if you can actually claim a star sign if you're surgically removed rather than born. Maybe, left to your own devices, you would have chosen to stick around inside Helen long enough to be a Libran. Should a doctor's whim change that?

AUGUST 13

Okay, hands up everyone who's sick of the ultrasound room? Your head is down again. Your heart is beating fine—we see all four chambers. Dr Jock reminds us that it could still all be nothing, though that is increasingly unlikely. He has a bit of a poke at Helen's abdomen and announces cheerily that 'there's nothing the matter with that, it's nice and soft'.

'If we're gonna see stomach, we should see it ... about ... there ... I don't see anything today either.'

Fiona takes over. Your kidneys are fine. There's your bladder, your femur, your face. You suck in some liquid— we watch your lips move. Around you, the amniotic fluid, black, looks like the Milky Way, the tiny little particles shining like stars. The AFI comes in at 32.8, less than last week, though there's a fair margin for error. Dr Jock says everything is biophysically fine. You're sucking, moving, exercising the respiratory muscles, doing 'everything we like to see'.

AUGUST 15

Dr Andrew's office. He's trying to get in touch with a Children's Hospital surgeon, Dr Ian. 'I don't know if he does this operation, but he will certainly know who does.'

We realise we have mixed the dates up. The elective delivery date is shifted to 4 September, where the real 38 week mark is. That would mean Helen is now 35 and a half weeks. Her weight is 61.5 kilograms. Her blood pressure is normal. During the examination, Dr Andrew says he suspects the growth this week might be more baby than fluid.

'I'm very happy with the way things are going. With any luck, whatever this is will be a minimal defect.'

Helen asks for a reprieve from the weekly ultrasounds. They don't seem to be telling us anything we don't know. Dr Andrew agrees.

August 16

Late afternoon. The white and watery sun grows yellower as the shadows of leaves and branches move across the room. It's a gorgeous, skin-tingling day, the end of a week of perfect winter weather. As I type, Helen is sitting in the sunroom talking to a friend, Miriam. Their voices mingle with the clacking of keys in here, the hum of the television in the background, and the distant roar of a football commentary on someone's radio.

Something has lifted. Whatever burden we have been carrying has become lighter. We are both happier. Maybe it is just the weather. Maybe it's that we can see how far we've come in five weeks, that we have made it further than we thought possible. Maybe it's the slow shift from uncertainty—even though our new knowledge is not pleasant, it does, at least, arm us to deal with the situation. It does put us in some kind of control.

Actually, I think it's all of these things and more. I think the fluid growth has slowed down. When Dr Andrew said he thought the recent growth spurt might be more baby than fluid, it made perfect sense. Helen seems to be bigger, but in better health, stronger, more spirited. The last time she was this size, a month ago, she was weaker. She looks well and relaxed. Maybe the fluid problem will not be as bad again. Whatever, today I think we look like a normal couple, instead of two bleary people with plastered grins covering fear.

AUGUST 18

I've got to put this down in writing. Helen surprises me by saying she is still wavering on the delivery decision. My gut feeling is that she'll go the Caesar route. She's turning the idea of normal delivery over and over in her head. I point out that if she opts for it, she has no right to spend the rest of her life looking at you and saying, 'I went through 26 hours of white-knuckle pain for you.' If she chooses that route, she will choose the pain. You will have the right to say, 'Hey, Mum, it was your call. I would have had the Caesar.'

AUGUST 20

Wednesday, 36 weeks and one day

The mortgage preparations are insane. The move won't be any trouble (I hope) but the paperwork has been arduous. The constant screw-ups of the bank have pushed our stress levels towards the ceiling. Just what we need. Settlement day passes, but we don't settle. My biggest nightmare is that Helen will go into labour during the next few days, driven over the edge by the trauma of the move. I'm insisting that she stays with her friend Jenny when the packing and moving is actually happening.

Michelle and Maxine are visiting. By the end of the day of talking and cooking, Helen has a fresh source of exhaustion, but at least this is a good one. I'm grateful for anything that distracts her.

AUGUST 21

Sigh. The bank situation just gets more stupid, venal and bungled every day. I can't believe how much idiocy has been drawn into this circle. Anyway, we asked for it, didn't we? Could there be a dumber thing than trying to move at about the time you're due? No, I didn't think so. We deserve everything we get.

AUGUST 22

Appointment with Dr Andrew. He says he's been having a lot of difficulties finding the surgeon, whose ears must be burning—he calls while we're talking about him. Dr Andrew promises to ring back. Helen is sore top and bottom and hasn't been sleeping, but we believe that is more stress-related than anything else—the result of the loan debacle. She says she is still not sure about the mode of delivery. She admits that, talking to other women, she keeps being told to take the Caesar option. Dr Andrew says he is not trying to railroad us, but reminds us of its logistical advantages. Helen replies that her concern is recovery time. He assures her she will be surprised at how quickly she recovers.

There's not much else to report, besides a lot of activity. (Have I mentioned that you're a hiccuper?) Helen's weight is 62.5 kilograms and her blood pressure is normal. Dr Andrew says the pregnancy has moved down, but her abdomen doesn't seem too tense. A good sign.

I ask what Helen's chances are of not making the planned September 4 delivery date. He says they're high. 'There is so much distention there that the cervix could be opening.' You would no longer be considered premature though, because we have passed the 36 week mark.

There's a message from Dr Andrew on the machine when we get home. He says he has spoken to Dr Ian, who can do the operation. Dr Andrew sounds delighted. At our request, he has made an appointment with the surgeon next week so we can find out more.

I call my parents. We're moving into organisational mode, trying to make sure everyone who wants to be around for your birth can be. My mother's health is improving. She might be able to make the trip by about the time the baby thing happens.

AUGUST 23

Helen calls her mother to arrange her travel details too. Janina asks, 'How's my little grand-daughter.' It's the first time anyone has said anything like that. I think everyone around us is starting to grow calmer as well. This makes me wonder just how out of control we sounded a few weeks ago, because everyone else seemed to go weird then too, and I presume they were following our lead (what an appalling presumption). The answer to Janina's question is 'Busy'. You're still doing aerobics, putting your head and behind where they're not really wanted. It's a constant battle between you and your mother for the comfortable position. When she's comfortable, you're not. And vice versa. I hope this is not going to set a tone for your future relationship.

AUGUST 24

More settlement hassles. The whole medical side of our lives has been so smooth and well organised, while the bit that should be easy, getting some paperwork done for the mortgage, has been a nightmare. We inspect in the afternoon. The vendors have left the kitchen in a mess. Helen is deflated by the visit. This makes me unhappy because she should be excited by moving into a new home, especially one she's going to spend a lot of time in over the next few months and years.

In the baby book I've been reading (I'm not sure why, but I haven't lost the curiosity factor about normal pregnancies), it says, loud and clear, that I should expect my beloved to behave in a completely insane fashion in the last month. Certainly, Helen's moods have hopped onto the swing. Today, she is in the 'why don't I just kill myself—it would be a lot kinder to all of us' stage. Tomorrow, who knows?

AUGUST 26
Tuesday, 37 weeks

Packing. I spend the whole morning watching guys putting things in boxes, thanking God that I made Helen go to

Jenny's place for the duration. She would have hated to watch the corners cut by the packers. Juggling glassware is a great trick, but I think Helen would prefer it wasn't her own.

AUGUST 27

The guys move as if they're on drugs (I don't ask). They do it at a trot and by 3 pm, the new house is full of our possessions. Everything is on shelves. The wrong shelves, sure, but at least there are only a couple of boxes left to be unpacked. I spend the rest of the afternoon making the living areas presentable, adding bunches of flowers to warm up the rooms. Helen has been visiting a friend, Nora, and has cheered up by the time I retrieve her. As soon as she comes through the front door (no, I don't carry her over the threshold—I am not mad), she decides she loves it after all.

For me, there is an enormous sense of relief. Even though there is a lot left to be done before we will have properly moved in, I realise how scared I was about the possibility of Helen going into labour. I'm still hoping you'll stay where you are until our elective date, but if you don't, well, it doesn't matter much now, Peanut.

Or whatever your name is. We did think we'd worked it out, but we were wrong. Or maybe we weren't. Anyway, we're back in debate. The name we picked has been shelved at the moment. I'm pulling for the safe, lazy, blokey option—'We'll make up a name for her when we get a bloody good look at her. No point calling her Doreen if you look at her and realise she's a Fifi.'

August 28

I wake at 3 am to the sound of Helen crying. Not quiet, sniffly sobs, but loud wailing, little bits of her heart breaking off. She can't sleep. The pain in her back and sides is sharp. It's a terrible thing to hear crying in the night, to know there's nothing I can do about it. I reach out, but she pushes my hand away.

Tonight we sit in our new house, eat pasta, drink tea and imagine that the orange cake is not so stale. Helen tells me we should think about what questions we're going to ask Dr Ian at our appointment in the morning. How long will the operation take? How long will it take you to recover? Exactly what is involved? Will you be able to play the cello again?

The new house has a deep bath. Helen says she can fill it to the point where her legs float, where the pressure lifts and the water renders her weightless. Right now, she is lying on the couch, her dressing gown falling open, belly pushing through, tight as a drum and contracting slightly. Every time she moves, there's a sharp intake of breath.

With the event closing in, people keep telling me I must be excited. But I'm not. I'm hoping things will go okay, talking to myself a little under my breath, reminding myself of what is to come and how we're going to get through it. We haven't had the nesting instinct yet, and I don't lie awake dreaming of the person you're going to be, of the things I'm going to teach you, of the A-1 brilliant father I'm going to make (and I *am* going to make one, out of mud and twigs). It's not like that.

August 29

Dr Ian's consulting rooms are in a small white bungalow, a block away from the hospital. 'So,' he says, seated behind a desk in his dark, businesslike office, the only bright spot a Chagall print on the wall—he obviously doesn't spend much time here. 'These are exciting times, are they not?'

Before getting to the details of the operation, he reminds us that ultrasound diagnosis is not 100 per cent accurate. It might not be what everyone is saying it is, something called TOF. There's an 80 to 90 per cent chance that it is, but it might not be. There are, he says, other, far rarer conditions that have similar outward symptoms.

Dr Ian explains that Oesophageal Atresia (OA—atresia means a complete blockage) is an event that takes place very early in gestation. Normally, in the course of the embryo growing, the lungs and trachea derive from the oesophagus. They separate, sharing the nerve and blood supply. What has most likely happened here is that yours have failed to separate properly. With this atresia, there is a complete gap in the throat—instead of a tube, there's an upper pouch from the mouth, and a lower pouch heading up from the stomach. In 90 per cent of cases there is also a connection between the lower pouch and the trachea, the Tracheo-Oesophageal Fistula (TOF). The normal separation has not occurred because of a lack of blood supply to the area. The emergency in the situation is that acid can come up from the stomach into the lungs and damage them.

So, he says, it's important to diagnose and operate quickly. At birth, a tube will be passed down your throat to confirm the suspected blockage. Air will be squirted down a tube to fill out the pouch that is the top end of your oesophagus and see how far south it goes, then an X-ray will be taken. Dr Ian says that in about 50 per cent of these cases, there are also other problems, with heart, kidneys or bones. Our ultrasound results are not suggesting that they are likely here. Still, we shouldn't rule out the possibility.

After the diagnosis, you will be prepared for transport to the Children's Hospital where he will operate. He has already booked a bed for you in the intensive care unit. He will do the operation in one hit, going in through the chest on your right side, through your rib cage. Inevitably, he will fracture a few but that, he says, is not really a problem. Once inside, he will tie off the fistula and stitch the two parts of the oesophagus together. The crucial element is the distance between them. Wounds heal better without tension, so the shorter the distance, the better the chance of a speedy recovery.

The best oesophagus for you, he says, is your own, but there could be a problem if there's a big gap. If there is tension then the junction, called the anastomosis, might leak. A tube will be inserted through the side of your chest to help drain anything from such a leak. Leaks are not uncommon, he says, and should heal normally.

He tells us there will also be a tube in your nose which will thread down to your stomach. This tube, a naso-gastric tube, will be used to feed you when you're ready. Until then, you will be fed intravenously.

All up, the operation will take about an hour and a half, with time on either side for the anaesthetic to take hold and wear off. When you return from theatre you will have a drip, and probably also be on a ventilator, which means a large tube going into your nose. If everything goes well, he says, you could be home in as little as a week. Babies, he reminds us more than once, are fantastic healers.

But it won't all end there. In the long term, he foresees two major problems for you. The first is reflux. It is almost inevitable, he says, that you will be a vomiting baby. The valve between the stomach and the oesophagus will be weak. This could be a temporary situation and is normally treated by drugs. But one in three babies end up needing an operation if the drugs don't work.

The other problem is the anastomosis, the join in the oesophagus. It will form scar tissue and tighten up, causing a stricture, a narrowed, tightened part of your throat. With reflux, the food goes all the way down and then comes back up. With a stricture it doesn't even get down. The nature of the stricture depends on the size of the gap. Mild ones are treated very easily. With severe ones, the solution is a further operation.

Another possibility is that the trachea cartilage will soften. TOF babies typically have a barking cough, which they usually grow out of.

He asks if we have any questions. We're reeling from the information, but I manage to stammer something about the timing of the surgery. He says that if he gets the baby two or three hours after birth, he will be delighted.

He tells us that TOF is rare but not unheard of, and says he has done many TOF operations. If you're well, he assures us, the chances of not pulling it off are extraordinarily low.

Helen asks about the scar. Dr Ian says it will be about 10 centimetres, and will come around horizontally from under the breast to the back, more in the back. He asks if we know the sex and we tell him you're a girl. He flinches just a little, then reminds us how well baby scars heal. I find myself thinking that I'll have to make up some stories for you about how you got those scars battling pirates and tigers and saving yourself and the world.

We drive home in silence. We wanted and needed to know all this, but hearing it put so matter-of-factly stuns and numbs us.

Later, we have our last appointment with Dr Andrew. He asks how it went.

'I think the big shock was how long the scar will be,' Helen says.

'You almost never see the scars on adults who've had congenital surgery,' he replies. 'Babies heal very quickly.'

He confirms next week's Caesarean. We will need to be at the hospital at 8 am the day before for the amniocentesis. He has made the booking and he gives us the forms we will need.

'I don't even see the point in examining you,' he says with a laugh, but we insist. Helen weighs in at 65 kilograms. ('It's all fluid,' he says. 'It must be.') Her urine is clear. Her blood pressure is fine. He prods at her stomach. 'It's not as bad as I thought it would be. It's not too tight.'

AUGUST 31

Sunday afternoon. As I type I can hear the grunts and groans, the staccato exhalations of a woman trying to get comfortable on a bed, settling in for a nap. Maybe her straining, crying muscles will allow it, maybe not.

Today feels like the proverbial calm before the storm. It seems a time to draw breath, to take stock. If I look at myself, these are some of the emotions/states that I seem to be in: optimistic, scared, numb, calm, nervous, nauseous, quiet, apprehensive, confident. I'm like a roulette wheel. The ball stops at one emotion for a few moments before spinning onwards.

We've made it through another month with you still inside. Want to take a bet on lasting the next one? You're never too young to lose your pocket money to your old man.

September

The first day of my official break. So, of course, I spend the morning trying to finish work. Then I buy the couch-bound Helen the baby names book she has been asking for—we glaze over when we try to read it.

Every time I look at Helen, she is holding a muscle and trying to find a position, any position, that will provide at least fleeting comfort. In a quieter moment, I drop my head down to her abdomen and explain exactly what will be happening in the next few days, what will be done to you, where you'll go, what we'll be doing and what we'll be thinking. I ask you to be brave.

I send the following email out to the Net-connected friends I have.

All things going to plan, an enormously large (and yet, somehow still radiant) Helen will be transported by forklift to King George V Hospital tomorrow morning. There, she will have an amniocentesis to determine the lung maturity of the baby. This should be a formality, given that tomorrow will also mark her entry into the 38th week of gestation, a place we were told we had no chance of visiting. Also, she had two shots of lung-boosting steroids six weeks ago when the fear and hospital stuff was at its peak.

On Wednesday morning, at the unquestionably ugly hour of 7.30, the rescue workers will go in and cut the baby free. The C-section is elective, a decision made to make the rest of the day go as smoothly as possible. The pre-birth diagnosis (which, for the record, is oesophageal atresia and tracheo-oesophageal fistula) will be confirmed.

The baby will be with us for a few minutes before being transported from KGV to the Children's Hospital. There, around lunchtime or early afternoon, the operation will be performed. If all goes well, it will take about an hour and a half. Helen will be stuck at King George for at least 24 hours, possibly longer. I will stay with the baby. All available grandparents will be on deck. The best case scenario is that the baby will be at home in a week. There are a number of long-term follow-on problems, but nothing too scary.

Don't I sound confident?

September 2
Tuesday, 38 weeks

Up at 6.30 to get to the hospital by eight. Every bone in my body begs me to go back to bed. A headache materialises the second I achieve verticality. I've been up and down all night with intestinal problems. Now is not the time to worry about my own health.

In the ultrasound room, Dr Greg asks, 'How many weeks now? Thirty-eight? That's great, tremendous.' The amount of fluid around you makes it difficult for him to get a decent picture. Your face is nearly 12 centimetres from the outside wall of Helen's abdomen. She asks for a pillow to go under her back to ease the pain.

Dr Greg tells us that you're a smaller baby than he would have expected, and than one would normally see for a TOF baby. 'It's a surprising finding. I'm not sure if it means anything at all, it's just a little surprising.' He says some research has speculated that there is a growth-promoting chemical in the amniotic fluid. If that's true, you wouldn't be swallowing enough of it. But you also have a genetic predisposition here (Helen and I were both less than 6 pounds).

We ask what effect the excess fluid will have on the Caesar. He says, and it's hard to gauge the extent of the facetiousness, that Dr Andrew always operates with the mother's pelvis tilted slightly away from him. 'That's what you pay an assistant for, to get wet.'

There's no anaesthetic for the amnio, because the needle is tiny, three times smaller than the one used for the drain. He covers Helen's stomach in iodine, and the needle spikes in and out.

'So what do you think the baby will look like when it's born?' he asks.

'Well, I think, from some of the ultrasounds we've seen, that it has my family's forehead,' Helen replies, but that isn't what he is talking about. He just wants to make sure we don't expect you will be a fat buddha with rosy cheeks.

We're finished before 9 am. There isn't an available bed, so we have to go home for the day. I still feel like something the cat dragged in, ate, threw up and then ate again, so it seems a good plan to me. This way, I'll be able to lie face down on the couch for a few hours.

Back at 4 pm. An hour later, Dr Greg turns up. 'Do you want to hear the bad news?' he asks. According to the amnio results, your lungs are not mature enough. The finding might be wrong, but they don't want to take the risk of having to operate on a baby who has breathing problems, who needs to be on a ventilator.

Dr Greg tells us to go home and give it another week. Helen replies that there's no way she could make it through another week, and asks if it's possible to drain her again. After conferring with Dr Andrew, he says she can stay in overnight and he'll drain tomorrow. Assuming it goes smoothly, Helen will only have to stay in hospital for one night this time.

When they take the date away from us, September 3, I realise how much I had psyched myself up for it, how much I had worked myself into emotional shape. Helen and I are disoriented and destabilised by the thought of another week. Then there's the problem of having all three grandparents here, at significant expense, waiting for this show to go on.

I call around and tell the family. Paul says you're bound to arrive on September 7, because it's Father's Day: 'You can't mess with that kind of narrative force.'

SEPTEMBER 3

The day that was to be your birthday dawns cool and mild and blue, a beautiful spring morning for a glamour queen to come into the world. I ring Helen, who is grumpy and bleary, having been kept up half the night by a nervous registrar having problems measuring your heartbeat. She says while the fuss was going on, the nurses were remarking how amazing it was that she has no stretch marks, something which she is quietly very happy about. 'They can still come,' was her mother's cheerful assurance (Janina arrived yesterday).

I pick up my own parents and head to the hospital. When Dr Andrew arrives, he has more bad news. He'll be in Singapore next week, giving examinations. So he won't be able to do the rescheduled Caesar. He suggests an alternative obstetrician, Dr Geoff.

The second drain begins at midday. The AFI comes in at 47. Dr Greg says he'll drain for as long as he can, but won't push it if things get painful. 'We're only trying to buy you a week this time.' He explains to the operator, Danielle, that the needle should be pushed into the abdomen at an angle so that if any contractions happen (very likely) the needle will straighten up, rather than pull over or out. A sound piece of advice should you ever have to do it yourself.

'You are going to give me a local, aren't you?' comes the voice from beside me.

'Only if I like you,' says Dr Greg.

Helen squeaks as the needle goes in, but says she's not sure how much it has to do with needle pain and how much with the fact that she tensed up in anticipation and her tender back muscles cried out.

'The amnio is a lot murkier than last time,' Helen says.

'Yes, that's supposed to means it's mature.'

We can see the needle quite clearly in the middle of the ultrasound screen. 'Don't touch,' Helen warns you. Can you hear her? We're helped by the fact that, as Dr Greg says, 'Babies don't float, they sink to the bottom.' This means that we can draw fluid from the top area without much likelihood of you getting in the way.

When it's over, about 40 minutes later, 3.1 litres have been taken. Helen is visibly smaller again. The contractions start immediately. For 20 minutes, Helen wails as they pick up speed, pushing the pain down through her pelvis. Then the drugs kick in and everything calms down, though the familiar side effects (breathiness, palpitations, shakes) are there. This time around, Helen finds them comforting evidence of normality.

Because we're not married and because we all live in different cities, today is the first time the grandparents have met. Not the easiest of circumstances, but it gives them something to talk about, I guess. They head off to lunch together while the drain is happening and return an hour later, when the difficult stage is over. The day takes a toll on them. Their feelings of helplessness are compounded by the fact that, while the natural process of pregnancy remains essentially the same, the hospital process has changed remarkably since our own births. Most of the machinery and techniques are unfamiliar to them. When we talk about ultrasounds, their eyes widen. When Helen's mother hears your heartbeat, it worries her because it is going so fast. She never heard the heartbeats of her own children. She never saw them on the screen.

The AFI is at 29. Now there's a number we haven't seen for ages. (I am thinking of entering Lotto using our favourite AFI numbers.)

September 4

Helen tells me on the phone that she feels better. The reduction has had a similar effect to the last one. Her stomach is still very tender. She's also spotting, but doesn't think that will stop her from coming home.

By lunchtime, Dr Andrew hasn't shown, so we get the ward staff to page him. He says he's been talking to Dr Greg and they agree that there will be no amnio next week. Dr Greg says that even if the result came back too low again, he wouldn't trust it, because the amniotic fluid is always a mixture of fluid the baby has urinated and regurgitated—if you're not doing either thing because of the TOF, then of course the result would be wrong.

So they're going to go in regardless on Wednesday morning, September 10. Your new birthday. Unless, of course, you have other ideas.

I bring Helen home. She's still contracting, with quite a bit of pain. The best thing that could happen to us now, as I see it, is that we get an extra few days of breathing space. Our biggest problem is keeping the grandparents occupied. I don't want this downtime to turn into some kind of Amish working bee, with everybody raising the barn in the backyard and trying to get lots of chores done before you arrive.

SEPTEMBER 5

Minor contractions continue through the night. After a couple of weeks of waking up around 6 am, we manage to struggle through until after eight, which cheers us both. I visit my parents at the beachside apartment they've taken for the week. It's reassuring—they're somewhere pleasant enough to make the waiting more tolerable. Janina is staying with us, but will move to a hotel near King George V to be with Helen when you're born. With Helen's blessing (indeed, at her urging) I have a drink and a few games of pool with two friends, Tony and Andrew, at a nearby pub. It's a moment of normality, a chance to act for a few hours as if the last couple of months have not been happening.

When I get back, I find the contractions have picked up pace and strength. 'I've started to leak,' Helen whispers. The contractions, which had been squeezing out clotted old blood, are now also bringing a clear fluid. They seem to diminish, but in the evening return just as strongly. We ring Dr Andrew. He asks how regular and how long. They're every ten to fifteen minutes and last for anything from 30 seconds to a minute and a half. He says if it gets regular and worse, to ring the labour ward or just take her straight in. In the meantime, lying down seems to help. So does Panadeine.

SEPTEMBER 6

A fairly peaceful night, by which I mean that planes do not crash into the house and waters do not actually break. The contractions continue. Helen's sleep is broken. But things seem to calm down a little in the morning. Lying in bed, Helen looks at me pitifully and then snuggles up.

'So?' she says, raising an eyebrow.

'I don't think so,' I reply.

'I just want it on the record that I offered you sex this late in the pregnancy,' she gloats, knowing I won't call her bluff.

The grandmothers dig in the garden. My father and I go out looking for sprockets and nuts and thingies we need to hang pictures, and change washers in the shower. Helen continues her occupation of the three-seater, glued to the old movie channel on cable TV.

5.30 pm. Helen calls me downstairs to the bath. 'Can I gross you out?' she asks, before showing me a brown, squishy, clotty kind of thing. It looks like the sort of substance that scientists find leaking from a broken jar on a crashed spaceship, the sort of thing that two days from now, will have eaten half the world.

Maybe this, we think, is the show. Maybe not. Who can tell? She has been contracting since breakfast, pretty much every eight minutes, for around about a full minute at a time. This afternoon, while I watch a football match on television, she goes to sleep on the couch beside me, with her socked feet tucked underneath my thigh. For a while, I stop looking at my watch, but I know the contractions are coming from the way her toes curl into me.

We look up one of the books to see if this could be real labour, but it says that unless the pain is in her back (it's mainly in her abdomen) and unless the discharge is fresh (the blood is old), real labour is fairly unlikely.

'What do they call this then? Fun?' moans Helen.

9.15 pm. The pain is worsening. The timing in the last hour has looked like this: nine minutes, seven, seven, five, five, eight, eight, nine, eight, eight, eight ...

I call the labour ward to ask for advice. The woman who answers suggests that Helen have a shower. Apparently, it will often stop this sort of contraction and bring on the real thing. We're not sure we really want to do that late on a Saturday night. With not a little trepidation, we decide to take a crack at sleeping, and hope that we'll still be here in the morning to reassess the situation.

SEPTEMBER 7
Sunday

4.05 am. We drift in and out of consciousness for hours, waking up with the rise of Helen's moans and zonking straight out again as they subside. Then I hear a voice, calm, collected, matter-of-fact.

'Okay, my waters have broken.'

We get up. Well, I get up. Helen leaks and squelches and gushes her way to the bathroom, where the flood continues. We both shower. Surprisingly, neither of us is inclined to panic. The hardest part is that Helen can't stop the fluid. Every time she puts a pad in place, it soaks through in seconds. She wants to get to the hospital with some kind of dignity, but goes through three sets of underpants before reaching the front door. 'Just give up,' I tell her. 'You won't be the first mother to get there trying to hold your insides in place.'

The contractions speed up. On the way to the hospital, I am driving, watching Helen wriggle on the towel and trying to keep an eye on the dashboard clock, timing the distance between contractions ... five minutes ... four minutes ... five minutes ...

5.20 am. The hospital. Checking in involves all the usual paperwork, with the desk staff manfully tearing themselves away from the US Open tennis telecast to attend to the forms. Helen stands there in bare feet—her shoes, discarded beside her, have filled with the renegade fluid.

In Prep Room 801, monitors are attached and a cervical inspection done. Huge, tea towel-sized pads, called blueys, are placed under Helen's rear, but don't seem to last long.

Each movement brings with it a new gush. The midwife, Sylvia, says Helen's cervix is 2 to 3 centimetres dilated, and very thin—a thick cervix doesn't open quickly (yes, I wondered about the distinction too). The contractions are now coming every two or three minutes, and getting harder, curvier, more powerful. The midwife is called away and we sit. All I can hear is the ticking of the clock on the wall and the solid thumping of your heart on the trace . . . 121 . . . 132 . . . 137. A bird calls in the background. Dawn can't be too far away.

Helen contracts again, this time jack-knifing as the pain slices through her. But even as it's all happening, she is somehow detached, floating above her body and watching. 'What gets me is how violent the whole process is,' she says. 'For so long, you are driven by the need to hold this thing in, then all of a sudden, you have the need to expel it.'

6.20 am. Labour ward, Room 8. I suspect the hospital has been designed with theme rooms. We are in the Chalet. It's all wood panelling and cork-tiled floors. Very Scandinavian. Put some hot rocks in the corner it'd be a sauna. Sylvia asks Helen if she's okay. Helen throws her a quizzical look. 'Yeah . . . I think . . . I don't know . . . I have nothing to compare this to.'

Dr Andrew is caught before heading to the airport. He says to let things go ahead spontaneously, just to see how far we'll get. And to get an epidural as soon as possible. A nurse puts the cannula into Helen's hand. It goes in without much hassle and the saline drip begins pumping cold liquid into her arm. Fluid in, fluid out—the pads on the bed need changing every few minutes.

Extracting blood is less successful. Helen can't see the doctor having trouble finding and milking the vein, but I can. One attempt. Two attempts. Three. The sight of it makes me go light-headed. I have to stand up, walk around, strip off my sweater and take a drink of water before I recover. If I feel this ill now, I wonder how I'll cope with whatever happens in the next few hours.

Helen notices she is shaking between contractions, unable to stop her legs from quivering. When the contractions hit, the blood rushes to her face and her toes clench. Once, I see her bite her own hand.

6.45 am. An anaesthetist puts the epidural in. It seems to start working immediately—the next contraction comes and goes without shouting. Helen is more concerned about her arm—the saline has been making it so cold that it's beginning to hurt. It feels as if it's been kept in a freezer, dead for a month. It's because of the speed of the drip— a pair of one-litre bags empty down the tube in less than 40 minutes. We ask a nurse if the third litre can be slowed to give her arm a chance to warm up.

Things are beginning to quieten down. The leftover adrenalin pushes my brain into overdrive. Headlines run through my mind, announcing possible scenarios. I see myself on the phone telling grandparents they have a healthy grand-daughter. Then the same scene, but with the opposite message. Both ideas make me teary. The last few months crash through my brain.

The contractions are still happening, according to the quietly whirring trace machine beside the bed. To look at Helen, you wouldn't know it.

7.30 am. The waiting stage. Helen is allowed to suck on ice mixed with lemon cordial, but I can flaunt my soothing cup of tea at her. I make it in the first stage delivery room, where mums-to-be go through their early contractions. A couple in the room have brought with them a bag of video tapes. They're watching *Loch Ness*. I reckon the sight of Ted Danson at this time of the day would hurry my labour along too.

8 am. I call Janina at home. She's downstairs in the laundry, dealing with towels and sheets and underwear and everything else we left wet. I think about calling my own parents, but decide to let them sleep in. Helen is dozing, just drifting along, occasionally noting a contraction, but mostly on the edge of dreams. I curl up in a recliner chair and go out like a light for half an hour.

9 am. Another cervical examination. Helen is now fully dilated. Midwife Kelly takes the straps off Helen's belly. These have been holding the heart rate and contraction monitors in place. Her stomach now looks like a camel, with a large hump at the top and a smaller one below. The smaller one turns out to be her bladder. It is decided to insert a catheter to relieve it. While I'm on the phone to my mother, Kelly confirms that it will definitely not be a Caesarean—Helen's too far gone. My mother reminds me that it's Father's Day, something I had completely forgotten. My family has never believed in Father's Day. I do now.

9.20 am. The epidural dose is lowered. It's important for Helen to regain some feeling downstairs, enough to actually help with the pushing. When the feeling comes back, labour will really start.

9.40 am. Dr Geoff arrives. He says he's very happy that it won't be a Caesar, that nature will get to take its odd, idiosyncratic course. Helen agrees. She says the randomness of the event, the unpredictability of the timing, the pain, all the things that medical science can take away, are also part of the appeal of giving birth. That seems way too deep a thought to me.

10 am. I call Paul and ask him to call Aleks and Tim, then grab a bite to eat in the cafeteria with about six other people, all looking the worse for wear. I think I'm going to cry, but I don't.

10.20 am. The epidural has slowed down, but the contractions have stopped. The room has gone quiet again. Helen is talking to me, but she's a little delirious—it sounds more like she's saying the words to herself. 'There's going to be a baby here soon ... Not just something in my tummy ... A pooing, pissing, vomiting, crying little thing ... How does that feel? ... How does that feel? ... And you have to ask it things every five minutes ... You want sleep? ... You want a clean nappy? ... You want food? ... You want attention? ...'

On a trip to the ice machine, I spot my parents in the corridor and for some reason, I'm surprised to see them. On the phone, I'd said they were welcome to come but that there wasn't much they'd be able to see. It's a mark of how preoccupied I am that I thought they would stay where they were. Helen's mother arrives soon after and the three of them sit in the waiting area together. I shepherd them into the ward for a quick visit, then go back to waiting for the contractions to return.

11.15 am. Oh, oh, here they are. Helen is on her left side, trying to learn how to push. I'm thinking maybe we should have read those chapters after all. Nurse Troy is guiding her, recommending that she consider it all like a gigantic bowel movement. There's a sudden shaft of pain in Helen's lower back during the middle of each contraction, so we change her position, sitting her up and propping a beanbag behind her.

11.20 am. Dr Geoff examines her. 'It's perfect,' he says. 'What's happening is perfect. The baby's head is almost in view. And it's facing the right way.'

11.40 am. Each contraction arrives, after a few minutes of peace, with a warning from Helen: 'It's starting again.' She takes deep breaths and pushes three times before it's over. I'm stroking her forehead, whispering encouragement as Nurse Mary and Dr Geoff stand with their heads bent down between her legs, the doctor's gloved fingers helping where possible. Mary keeps assuring Helen that her efforts are 'Fantastic! That's great! One more push! Fan-tas-tic!'

11.55 am. In the middle of another contraction, I notice that I'm breathing just like Helen, mirroring her. The sweat is accumulating at her hairline. Her face is flushed. But there's no swearing at me, no name calling, no discovery or denouncement of God. She seems on track, if distant and internalised, wrapped up in her own process. I can see a lot of strain, but not a lot of pain. In between contractions, I feed her ice chips. She stays quiet, her eyes closed, her breathing rhythmic, working up strength for the next round. I look at her coping so well and feel a sudden burst of confidence, as if this is exactly the right thing to be doing, exactly how I should be spending this day.

12.10 pm. Four pushes to each contraction. Dr Geoff invites me to have a look. I can see you starting to crown, the top of your head just visible at the height of each push. Black hair, purplish with the mucus covering it. Dr Geoff asks Helen if she'd like a mirror, so she can see what's going on. 'No,' she says, looking aghast. I can tell it's not fear or squeamishness. She has to stay focused.

12.25 pm. At Kelly's suggestion, Helen switches to her hands and knees. I sneak another peek at what's going on down south, then resume my position at her northern end. She's growing tired, muttering that she's not sure how much longer she can push like this, how much more effort she can give. I mop her and kiss her and tell her I'm so proud of the way she's handling it.

12.39 pm. Another push, Helen. One more. One more big one. And then it happens. I'm standing at her right shoulder, a hand in the middle of her back, steadying her, looking down across her rear. The top of your head bulges out, then suddenly your forehead, your eyes, your nose, your mouth, your whole head is free. And covered in fluid, in mucus. The paediatrician, Anne-Marie, does a quick suction, catching as much as she can. 'Go on!' says Dr Geoff excitedly to Helen. 'Oh go on!'

12.41 pm. Everything happens so quickly. With one push, you're out. It's over in an instant, like one of those David Attenborough films of the deer giving birth in the wild, a shiny, slimy, slippery fawn tumbling onto the grass.

I half expect you to try to stand up and totter about on confused and unstable legs.

You're pink and healthy looking. And you're crying. I'm surprised but I'm not sure why. I guess I thought the problems in your throat might affect your voice. Dr Geoff asks if I want to cut the cord. Before I get to think about it, everyone is chanting, 'Do it! Do it!' as if this is a university keg party. I take the scissors and cut into the cord, feeling the fibres snap as I do. It's a tough little thing and the scissors feel blunt—it takes about four attempts to crunch through it. I am faintly nauseated.

You're carried over to the paediatrician's table for a quick examination. Helen is still on her hands and knees— she has to stay there until the placenta is passed. Remembering some good advice, I shoot three quick photos of you, new to the world, held under the light by the nurse and paediatrician, bubbling at the mouth and squealing.

While the examination is taking place, I rush out to the waiting room to tell the grandparents. It's only 20 metres along a corridor, but by the time I get there, I am crying so hard that I can only blurt, 'She's out and she's gorgeous, but you can't come in yet,' before turning and running back.

You have been placed between Helen's elbows, directly under her face. 'Hello, darling. Hello, darling,' she is repeating over and over, tears rolling as she does. 'Oh,' she says when she sees I'm back, with a hint of surprise in her voice. 'Oh, it's a baby.' I hug her tight and tell her again how proud I am of her. She says she thought she was a failure—she was sure nothing was happening when they were telling her to push.

12.48 pm. You're taken away to the nursery for a more thorough examination. You also need to be stabilised and put in a humidicrib for the journey to the other hospital.

1 pm. The placenta is gently coerced into appearing by Dr Geoff. It arrives in what looks like a shiny blue wrapper. One by one, the staff are leaving.

1.10 pm. Half an hour after you joined us, Helen and I are alone again, left to get our breath back, to relax and come to terms with what has just happened. Dr Geoff reappears to tell us we've 'got a great little girl', and that the diagnosis of the oesophageal blockage has been confirmed. Helen barely registers. I feel nothing much either way—it's what we expected. You've weighed in at 2.1 kilograms. All signs are that your other organs, heart and lungs, are okay.

1.20 pm. It's time to bring the grandparents in. Helen asks for a mirror. I tell her she looks beautiful, but she doesn't believe me. I dig one out of her overnight bag and she is surprised by how unravaged she looks.

I'm a little more composed as I make it to the waiting room. Helen's mother is first in the queue to get by, almost stampeding me. My mother is next. My father gives me the biggest hug of my life. Back in the room, Helen is propped up regally in bed, allowing her court to fuss around her. The event is relived until we are told we can visit you.

1.50 pm. Helen is wheeled in front of us as we all troop off to the nursery. There are half a dozen babies locked in their humidicribs, which look like perspex submarines (SS *You*). Visitors are strictly two at a time, so Helen and

I take it in turns to look after individual grandparents keen for their first viewing. It takes Helen and her mother a grand total of four seconds before they're divvying up your attributes. Your nose, they claim, is theirs. I reckon it's yours. Your huge feet, they sniff, are obviously from my side. The porthole is opened to let Helen and I touch you, your tiny ears, your downy hair. I try to get the grip reflex going on your purplish hand.

When everyone has seen you once, we start over again. Then we go back to the labour ward so you can be prepped for travel. The parents disappear to find some lunch. Helen is hungry too. All that's around at this stage of the day is tea and dry biscuits, which may never have tasted so good.

3 pm. The team from NETS (Newborn Emergency Transport Service) arrives. The transport process is explained —a doctor, a nurse and I will travel with you—and we sign the consent forms.

Left to our own devices for a while, I bring up the subject of your name. Now that we've seen you, I know for sure. So we decide, right there in the Swedish sauna, that you are Naomi Lee. For the record, the Naomi is biblical, the Hebrew name all Jewish people need. The Lee just sounds good, though Lee Remick and Lee Miller add a little weight to the choice. We say it over and over and it sounds like music. Naomi Lee. Welcome to you.

Helen talks about how much she likes the hair on your arms, the little soft tufts on your ears. She says that while she was watching you in the humidicrib, she could see you making the exact same movements she has been able to feel these last few months.

4.05 pm. You're wheeled by, wrapped in the 120 kilograms of machinery required to transfer you safely. You look like a kamikaze pilot strapped into your plane. The nurse points out that you have a wayward eyebrow— we parents know which of us that came from. You also have beautiful long eyelashes. We'll both claim those. You're asleep as Helen says goodbye to you.

4.20 pm. I leave the hospital with you. It's late in the afternoon and the shadows are moving across the city streets. You wake up halfway, with the sun in your eyes for the first time, wail and then immediately disappear into sleep again.

4.40 pm. The colour scheme at the Children's Hospital— purple, blue, aqua and green—is a little hard to take after such a long day. I doubt if it's better at other times. I'm parked in a waiting room at the intensive care unit while they get you cribbed up and ready to go. It's a small, windowless room with a few old magazines and newspapers from weeks ago. I'm in no mood to read.

5.30 pm. My parents arrive. Helen's mother has stayed with her. There's nothing to do but wait.

6.25 pm. We're allowed in. You're in the Atom Infant Warmer V-3600, an open cot with its own heating system. It's a lot less threatening than the humidicrib. But you're not happy. My stomach tightens when I see you. There's a tube in your mouth suctioning the mucus, a splint holding the drip that's attached to your arm, another monitor taped to your right palm, and two more to your chest. Then there's the heat sensor, a gold disc attached to your torso.

And what I am thinking is that it's not fun for you. I

know it's not fun. I can see it's not fun. I am standing in front of you wishing the floor would swallow me. I am so sorry, so sorry that you have to start your life this way. I feel as if it's all my fault.

Dr Harry, the anaesthetic registrar, explains what will happen to you in theatre, but I'm not really listening. I see his lips move, and I take in every third word or so. I hear enough to know that you'll end up with a tube in your nose, attached to a ventilator, which will keep you breathing for a day or two. There will also be morphine. Lots of morphine.

7.15 pm. Dr Ian is here. I reassure you that I'll be around when you come out of theatre. You're asleep. I ask you to be brave, kiss you twice on the forehead (once for Helen) and try to smell you, but there's nothing but the antiseptic hospital scent. Because they have to unplug the heater to move you, it's decided that you should wear booties and a hat for the trip to theatre. One booty is pink and one is orange. The hat is striped pink and yellow. I hate to say it, but your first fashion statement is not a good one.

Dr Ian shows me the X-rays. He thinks there may also be a blockage below your stomach, at the duodenum, but we won't be able to check for that yet. When you've gone, I call Helen to tell her you're okay, hear her voice wavering and decide not to tell her about this other possibility. It will be at least an hour and a half before you're brought back. My parents and I walk up the road to get some Chinese food. I have no idea what is said over dinner. Not much probably. By nine o'clock, we're back at the ICU. Waiting.

10 pm. Dr Ian says the news is not all good. The gap in your oesophagus is very big, at the upper end of the scale. Three centimetres. He says it is almost certain to spring a leak. What is there has been stretched and joined. If it doesn't respond, the operation may have to be redone. The sooner the leak appears, the more predisposed to infection you will be. Dr Ian says 48 hours is about the average length of time it takes for a leak to turn up.

He says it is also pretty certain that you will have a longer term problem with the stricture, with the tightness of your throat. The worst scenario is that you will have to have another operation. He can't say when that would be, maybe soon, maybe years from now.

I call Helen to tell her what has happened. Shortly after that, you are wheeled by us in a hurry, a blur of machine and tubing.

11 pm. You're covered in red marks where things have been taped to your skin. There are yellow iodine blotches all over you. There is masking tape on your forehead, nose and cheeks, holding in the ventilator tube. Details of the tube's width are scrawled on the tape. You're a very, very saddening sight. We have been so well prepared by everybody for all the things that have happened, but nothing could prepare me for this. I feel myself losing balance, growing shaky. I want to double over. I want to scream. I want to curl up and go into shock.

My parents, when I bring them in, are white. I hold your gripping hand—you're still under the anaesthetic. 'I wish I could show you what she'll look like in ten years' time,' my mother says encouragingly, but her voice is small and upset.

'It's not the best way to start, is it?' says my father, talking out loud and not hearing himself. Then words fail us and we just stare.

Sister Mary-Rose, the nurse looking after you, explains what will happen overnight. Mostly, they just want you to sleep. This has been quite enough for a first day, she says, her Irish lilt a comfort. I want to stay, but there is nothing I can do here. I kiss you, say goodnight and put my parents in a cab. Then I hail another and head back to Helen.

11.45 pm. I walk Helen's mother back to her hotel, then snuggle up to Helen, who's suffering badly. It's been a very hard evening for her, stuck here, unable to be where her heart wants to be. There's a powerful sadness in her. Even so, she's so beautiful. Every time I look at her, I see flashes of the birth and I fall in love with her and you all over again.

1 am. I crawl into bed. And as I'm falling into sleep, I am thinking of you, there in the cot, hooked to the nightmare of circuitry and plumbing. My poor girl. My poor, lovely girl.

SEPTEMBER 8

I wake after six clean, smooth hours of dreamless sleep and call Helen, who managed to put away a similar amount. She's already heard from Mary-Rose, who has given her a full and reassuring briefing about your condition.

Armed with a list of names and numbers, I begin the ring-around to announce the news, calling the friends and helpers, the people who have been so good to us in the last few months. The pride I'd expected is there, but it's tempered by a sense of what has only just begun. I put on my bravest face for the email version of the birth announcement:

MONDAY MORNING ...

Best laid plans being worth the paper they're written on, Helen went into flood at 4 am on Sunday. A little less than nine hours later, at 12.41 pm, Naomi Lee pushed her way into the light of the delivery room. She arrived without the Caesarean section we'd been promised, preferring to make her own way, thank you very much. This attitude, it strikes me, seems to hint that she's taking after at least one of her parents. If such a thing can be said of so violent a spectacle, the birth was elegant, silken and beautiful, a tribute to the calmness of the mother and the value of having a small bub.

Naomi arrived pink and healthy and a little under five pounds. She's the proud owner of a stylish head of brown hair and a pair of deep blue eyes. The pre-birth diagnosis was confirmed and she was moved and operated on last night to fix problems in her oesophagus. Medically speaking, so far, so good. This morning she's breathing well enough. The signs are positive. Now we just wait and see. Mother Helen is well and happy and glamorous and hoping to move today to a hospital closer to the baby.

By the time I see you, it's mid-morning. You've been out for a little less than a day, and through so much already. They've tied a white ribbon in a bow at the top of your forehead, where the tape that holds the oxygen tube in place begins. It's comical, but sweet. Anne-Marie is looking after you, another Irish nurse, this time from County Laois. (Mary-Rose is from Tipperary.)

I am flooded with joy and wonder when I see you, even though you're still part baby, part machine. It's a new day, I tell myself. You're still here. And already looking so much better, so much happier. Fighting. Or do I just imagine that? There's not much of you available to touch. I stroke your forehead, hold your hand, feel your fingers grip mine, feel your heel push against my palm as I tuck your knee up into your stomach, in the position it would have been inside Helen. You seem to find it comforting.

I drive to KGV to pick Helen up. She has been learning how to express colostrum, on the way to milk. She looks surprisingly well, with the cutest post-pregnancy mound in front of her. After a few hours up and around, she feels as if she needs a sling to hold her stomach up, to stop it from sliding down. We switch hospitals and rush (as much as Helen's state allows) in to see you, through the airport terminal decor and that colour scheme. We're not allowed into the ICU. You're apparently busy, and don't have time for your parents already.

My family arrives, Mum and Dad and Paul—he's just driven into town. We cram ourselves into one of the small waiting rooms. When it's all right to go in, I take Helen first. She pales when she sees you, though to me you look so much better already—the big ventilator tube has gone. After a few minutes of sitting, talking to you, touching you, holding each other, I start bringing through the others, one at a time, leaving Helen at your side.

When everyone leaves, we go back to Helen's room. She's so upset that she can't express and has to have a shower to try to calm down. An hour later, we go back and sit with you, cooing and talking and gently pushing the hair away from your forehead. And I see Helen smile and get over the shock. The warmth starts to flow as the ice-cold fear melts into love. You're sleeping and peaceful. Occasionally you even make a mewling kitten noise.

SEPTEMBER 9

A little Panadol to ease your pain. A little respite from distress. A sign that things are mending. Any sign. A confused look (I know you can't see us yet, but you can hear us and point your eyes in the right direction). A touch on the shoulder from one of the nurses. A grip on my finger, baby digits wrapped around me. Small mercies.

It's one hour at a time. One action. One reaction. For all the worry and panic, ICU is a calm place. Helen tells me that expressing the colostrum makes her feel as if she is doing her part. Of course, so does sitting quietly beside you, touching you, willing your recovery onward, promising you an easier path later on. (I'd hate you to know some of the promises we have already made about what will happen when you get through this.)

Today is a little quieter than the last couple. I run errands and then go to the hospital, where Ruth, the first of our friends to meet you, is waiting with Helen for a visit. In the afternoon, it's family time again, with all three grandparents and Paul on a tag team visit.

You aren't breathing well. An X-ray shows what appears

to be an air pocket in the right side of your chest cavity. The lung has collapsed there. It's where the leak is from your oesophagus. Yes, the leak, pretty much bang on the 48 hours predicted by Dr Ian. There's a tube stitched in through your side which drains matter away from the internal wound. This tube, which looks as big as a hose pipe to me, is moved a little to try to suck out some of the air and other junk in the cavity. It actually slips out, at which point it is discovered that it is blocked. Another tube is inserted, and the material, mostly mucus, drains away. It isn't a comfortable process for anyone. There is one moment where you are particularly upset and your mother is crying into my chest. It passes (we have to keep telling ourselves it will pass) and I take your hand and talk you towards sleep.

Helen, like you, grows stronger with each passing hour, more able to deal with the situation. She can reach into the cot far enough to kiss you on your hand, on your knees, but not yet far enough (her stomach muscles have a way to go) to kiss your sweet face. That time will come, and it can't come soon enough. Neither can the day when we are able to pick you up and hold you, to do that simple thing most parents get to do immediately.

I wouldn't want you to think we're having a terrible time as parents. Hospitals teach us just how lucky we are. Whatever the problems, things could always be much worse. There's a couple with a newborn son two cots away from yours, hunched over with concern, going through all the worries we have and more. I watch them come and go, see the mixture of fear and determination, of hope and panic. It's ICU policy to keep patient details confidential, but it doesn't take much brain to know that whatever their son has is more serious than the situation confronting you. I almost feel a fraud when I look at the other parents around me. And even outside this large, quiet unit, every corridor we walk down takes us past another specialist wing, each representing another set of problems we don't have to deal with. Here are the kids with head injuries. Here are the kids with cancer ...

That said, it's still overwhelming. We are so focused on you that we lose track of time, place and people, of what is going on around us. I come home at night and find I can't remember what people I spoke to looked like. As I type this, I find details evaporating. There is you and only you.

Night-time is quiet time. Like last night, tonight the two of us just sit there with you, each holding a hand. Helen pushes her finger in underneath yours, attached to the splint on your right hand. I see a mostly serene face (you're a pretty jaundice-yellow colour), a pair of deep dark eyes casting about for something to focus on. I have a warm spreading feeling, like honey leaking from a jar, that everything will be all right.

SEPTEMBER 10

Helen had a dream last night that she was you, lying in your crib, looking up at the world. She dreamed your little kicking movements, felt the tubes coming out of you. I tried to call her this morning, but she was already with you. You had a peaceful night after all the activity of yesterday, and when I arrive about nine o'clock, you are still asleep, serenely dreaming of whatever it is you dream of—small, dark, wet places, no doubt.

We ferry the grandparents through in longer turns. They sit with you for an hour, Helen with her mother in the morning and me with my parents in the afternoon while Helen is trying to express, sleep and worry about why her bra doesn't fit her engorged breasts.

Tonight we change your nappy, clean your eyelashes and wrestle with the dried, caked saliva on your lips. I try to get a swab in to clean your mouth, but you aren't letting me. The strange thing is, I feel less worried about you than perhaps I should. This is because, and I'd be lying if I said I expected this, I find I have an extraordinary belief in you, in your strength, in your will.

As I write, it's 10.30 pm. You've been off the oxygen for seven hours. If you don't need it turned back on during the night, it's possible that another tube can be taken away in the morning. Which will leave the naso-gastric tube, the drain in your side, the drip in your hand (through which you're being fed a protein mix called TPN—Total Parenteral Nutrition), and the various monitors. They put you on lipids last night too, after deciding you were advancing well enough to begin to metabolise fats. So your svelte, slim, chic physique might be on the way out. The last thing I'd want is for you to have a modelling career, so I'm okay with that ... all right, maybe not the *last* thing, but you know what I mean.

There is talk of you switching to a ward tomorrow if your mending path continues. No-one seems bothered by the leak at all—it almost seems to reassure people, along the lines of 'that is exactly the sort of problem we're used to at this point—the whole thing is going as planned'.

Meanwhile, your mother, who matches you wince for wince, is beginning to calm down. She is very tired today, which I take as a good sign. It means that her fear has slowed to the point where she is no longer producing the adrenalin needed to keep going. She thinks you're doing okay and can breathe out.

September 11

We're travelling with you, Naomi. You're steering. If you have a bad day, we have a bad day. If you have a good one, we have a good one. Today was a bad day. It began with Helen sitting bolt upright in bed at 5.30 am, convinced something was wrong. She talked herself back to sleep, but soon found out that something *had* happened. At that time, it was decided to move you from intensive care to a ward. And though that's a good sign, it is hard to see it that way.

You have moved from a place where you had one-on-one care, to a six-bed ward with nurses handling multiple patients. In ICU, you were the healthiest baby. In the ward, you're the sickest. ICU was soothing. This place is noisy, full of tears and cries. It might have been easier if you made the transition successfully, but today is the one step back that was due after our two steps forward.

Today is whingey, difficult and pain-filled. I arrive to find Helen in tears at your screwed-up face, at the pitiful cries you are making. Though you settle down into sleep, it is broken with regular scrunches, little howls. The only bright spot of the morning is a bowel movement, which means we might be able to hope that there's no duodenal blockage.

I carry the icky feeling all day that something is going wrong. Which, of course, it is. The drain has clogged again, so you're full of gunk. The material trying to get through is too thick and oozy. This time, it is decided to flush it. They try to give you a pain-killer, a syringe-full into your rectum, but you promptly poo it out. So it's back to morphine through the drip, albeit at a smaller dosage than you were having a few days ago. Even that doesn't seem to calm you down. You have a look on your face of, This is all too much and I just want to be left alone.

I spend most of the day shuffling paperwork, dealing with Helen's maternity leave forms, adding you to our health fund and registering your birth (you officially exist now). Oh, and I visit a familiar store (Tiffany's), but more of that later.

SEPTEMBER 12

Today is a blur. If I shut my eyes and think about it, I get a whirl of distress and upset. I see you cry for the first time, a tear escaping from the corner of your gorgeous blue eye.

This wasn't meant to get harder. You were meant to be born, have an operation or two, then get progressively better. For the last couple of days you've been getting worse. When I arrive this morning, you are wriggling and writhing, recovering from a tough night. Helen is with you already, trying to calm you down. Dr Ian shows up and says he thinks you should be moved back to ICU (unfortunately, it's not his decision to make). Your breathing is ragged, your heart rate up and your blood oxygen levels down. You are visibly and audibly stressed, finding life a hard road.

Dr Ian says he's considering the option of a gastrostomy, an operation which involves putting a tube into your stomach to drain it of the natural acidic juices (the tube could also be used to feed you). This would help with the reflux problem. The acids and secretions coming up from your stomach are stressing the oesophagus even further, leaking out and clotting the pipe. Your lung has collapsed again. The acid content is also attacking the wound, retarding the healing process. The gastrostomy would drain it away before it had the chance to head up your throat. But it would mean another operation.

After quietening you down a little, and only a little, we move Helen back home and go shopping for cots and baby baths with the grandparents. The next thing I remember is standing in a department store crying my eyes out. I have just spoken to one of the surgeons on the phone. They've decided to go ahead with the gastrostomy. Tomorrow. While you're under anaesthetic, they're also going to put in a central line, a tube that will go into one of the main veins in your neck to feed you and supply your drugs. That tube has been going into the veins in your umbilical cord (it was in your hand for a while), but these veins are outliving their usefulness. The thought of another operation seems suddenly too much for me and I stand and sob while shoppers walk past me. I stop caring what I look like, and what anyone might think if they see me.

When we get back to the hospital, mid-afternoon, your pain is worsening rather than improving. The nurses try everything, moving you, sucking the drool (can you drool!) from your mouth, adding a little heating, stroking you, Panadol, extra morphine . . . nothing works. You grow more tired, irascible and noisy, your tiny face contorting. By 7 pm, your pain is almost unbearable, then some morphine kicks in. We sneak out to eat something. An hour later, the pain is back and just as jagged, ripping up and down your torso. I sit stroking your forehead, hoping that I'll never have to see anything like this again. There is a moment I recall with crystal clarity, with Helen sitting beside the bed, tears rolling down her face, and tears rolling down yours. And I have to look away, because I don't want to be the third.

At 9 pm, your heart rate breaks the 200 beats per minute mark. They have been giving you a drug to help your breathing. A side effect is that it has been making your heart race. You snap out of a sleep, scared, bewildered, and begin to flail your arms and legs as if you are having a seizure. I have to hold you down, one hand pinning each of your arms, and my chest leaning in to stop your feet jerking. It is an awful 20 minutes, with Helen trying vainly to express beside the bed, her pain as vivid as yours.

Your oxygen levels drop. God knows what your breathing rate is, because you are either running yourself ragged or holding your breath to ward off the waves of pain cycling through you. Before now, pain has been like a train passing through a station, a rumbling build-up with a few seconds of flashing, jagged distress. Now it's as if you're tied to the tracks.

I drag Helen away at 10.30, after you've achieved some sort of stability (heart in the 150s, the pain only coming every couple of minutes). There's a rash and swelling on your chest, on the right, above the lung that has still not re-inflated. We don't know what it means, if it has any meaning, yet. Maybe tomorrow will bring an answer. I don't really care what tomorrow brings, as long as it isn't more of this.

SEPTEMBER 13

At 6.46 am, I snap out of a dream of dead babies. Of lifeless pink–white remains handed to me in a blue bag by someone unknown. I look inside and see a tangle of limbs and torso and your plastic hospital ID bracelet still attached. It's a vision I try to shunt away, but if I close my eyes, it returns, so I give up on the sleeping idea and get up. The insides of my cheeks are tender, chewed up from a night of teeth grinding. The fear that you could die has not hit me often, but occasionally it sneaks through. I don't think we'd be normal if it didn't creep in somewhere.

Nurse Jackie says you've had a peaceful night. Helen doesn't believe it, but she shows us the records of your evening. You were a little agitated around 3 am but from then on, you slept. You look better, with clearer skin, smoother breathing and less pain. When the hurt comes now, it is like it was before: as a fleeting visitor, a few knotted seconds. Helen places a sprig of fragrant jasmine on the blanket near your head.

You're wheeled away to the operating theatre at 9.30 am. Helen holds your hand and talks to you. Dr Ian looks at the red, inflamed area of your chest and decides it's probably an infection, but nothing too major as yet—it hasn't driven your temperature up or affected the rest of your body. We leave for an hour to find some breakfast and a breast pump so Helen can express milk at home, instead of having to be in the hospital every few hours.

Later, in ICU again, Dr Ian says everything was 'technically a success'. The central line has gone in under your collarbone. They have tunnelled it across the top of your chest and attached it to a vein in your neck. This trick makes the line stable and likely to last for as long as it is needed. The gastrostomy has gone directly through the wall of your belly and into your stomach.

When we try to push Dr Ian on the timing of anything, your recovery, danger periods, whatever, he just shrugs. Nothing is for certain. We can only sit it out. He explains that he plans to put some dye in through the stomach tube and see what happens to it. He's clearly still concerned about the possibility of duodenal obstruction or constriction. My father asks how long doctors have been able to treat children with these obstructions. Dr Ian says the first reconstruction surgery was in 1943.

My father had an older brother who was born in 1925, but died after two days because of a duodenal obstruction. Maybe your problem comes down to my genes. It would make Helen happy to have an answer. Though she says otherwise, she has been looking for a guilty party, for someone or something to explain why you should have such a difficult hand. Me, I'd rather not know, particularly if it's my fault. I don't know how much more it can hurt.

Shortly after Dr Ian leaves, they wheel you past. Though you're covered with iodine splotches, with a plastic tube jutting straight up from your belly and a coil of smaller tubing taped to the top of your chest, we are mightily relieved. You look peaceful for the first time in 48 hours. We don't care if it's just the drugs talking. For now, you have some kind of rest. Helen and I look at each other and feel ourselves breathe out.

My parents are leaving today, so they've come to wave goodbye. I'm watching them closely as they approach the cot. They saw you after the first operation, at your worst, and I can see the relief cracking the lines on their faces too. Now I know we're not fooling ourselves. My mother cries, saying, 'I don't often do this,' as they leave. She should cry. She has a right. This has been a long week.

Helen's mother reckons you've put on some weight. You seem bigger to me too, less frail. Though there are more tubes in you, we're all feeling more confident. You're a tough critter, and there's so much love around you that it seems impossible that you wouldn't get better.

SEPTEMBER 14
Sunday, one week

Another peaceful day. We check in at 9 am and find that Mike the registrar has drawn a little sheep on the bandage that holds the ventilation tube in place. You don't care because you're still on more drugs than Keith Richards (hmm, given that you'll probably be twenty when you read this, I should tell you that Keith Richards was a guy who was famous from the 1960s through until your toddler

years for warding off death by actually embalming himself).
The sheep adds a light, comical touch to your predicament.

You've made it through the night fairly comfortably.
The occasional drool, a snore or two, a little yelp, nothing
to report. Your oxygen intake is good enough that they
turn down the morphine to see how you'll breathe on your
own. If it works, the ventilator will be removed. It will
take anything up to eight hours for the morphine to clear
your system, so we drive Helen's mother to the airport
and have a quiet afternoon at home, alone again.

At 6 pm, you're still sleeping. They haven't extubated
you. You didn't like it much when they turned the ventilator
down to ten breaths a minute, so it went back up to fifteen.
Now they're leaving it in overnight. While we're there,
your heart rate drops and it's clear you've gone into deep
sleep, which registrar Mike says is the best healing time.

Nurse Fiona asks when you're going to have duodenal
surgery. Mike talks about it too. Everyone else is treating
that as a given now, as an inevitability. We have heard
nothing. They have to try the dye test first, Peanut . . . Helen
says you're no longer a peanut to her. You've become a kitten.

SEPTEMBER 15

Hospitals are extraordinary bureaucracies. Everything has
to be written down, signed and counter-signed. This works
to the benefit of the patient in the end. The first thing I do
every day, though I'm not meant to, is read your case notes
from the night before, to find out exactly what happened.

Physiotherapy. The therapist sits you up (you don't just
exist in the horizontal plane) and pats you on the chest

and back, stimulating your right side, the area where your lung has been weak and collapsing. You are a little thrown at first, but Helen holds your hand and you soon calm down. You almost seem to enjoy it.

Afterwards, you are rolled onto your side. Your new position gives me the first good look at the wound on your back, which was cleaned up after Saturday morning's operation. It's a neat, simple line that goes under your arm and across towards your spine. The gastrostomy and central line are going to leave scars as well. That's a couple more stories I'll have to make up.

The quietness of these days is now becoming odd in itself. Late last week, when things were at their worst, it felt as if we were being thrown about by a raging storm. Now it's as if we're strangely becalmed, out there in open waters, no land in sight, wondering what will happen next.

SEPTEMBER 16

The ventilator tube stays in. The morphine stays off. You are kind enough to present us with a bowel movement of power, texture and surprisingly green colour. You gurgle and sleep. No more tests are done. We spend a few hours sitting by your bed, watching your chest move up and down. Here's half an hour of your life, chosen at random from the 48 that today offered:

5 pm. Your heart is doing 140 beats a minute. You're breathing 30 to 40 times a minute, without the help of the ventilator. There's what looks like rapid eye movement going on. You're either chasing rabbits or in a little pain.

5.01 pm. You stretch the fingers on your right hand. Your eyelids flicker and your face moves, as if you're about to wake up and say something. You don't.

5.03 pm. Bubbles of spit escape from the left side of your mouth.

5.06 pm. Your breathing is a little shuddery. Nurse Sharyn thinks it might be time for you to take another hit of the Liquigesic (a paracetamol–codeine mix).

5.10 pm. I tuck my index finger into the palm of your hand. You curl around me.

5.11 pm. One eye flashes open. You wince a little, then fall instantly back under the surface of sleep.

5.13 pm. Your legs are hoisted ever so slightly skyward and the Liquigesic is pumped in rectally. You don't complain.

5.17 pm. You think, now would be a good time to drool, and do it.

5.19 pm. Your temperature monitor starts beeping. It just needs readjusting.

5.21 pm. Sharyn decides your temperature is a little high and turns the heater down.

5.23 pm. The oxygenation monitor strapped to your foot is checked.

5.28 pm. Your breathing slows down as your sleep gets deeper.

SEPTEMBER 17

A special day. At 6 pm, with the help of Nurse Sharyn, we wrap you in the soft white blanket that lines your crib, pick you up, making sure not to pull on any of the tubes and wires escaping from the folds, and put you in Helen's lap. When I ask her now, a couple of hours later, what was going through her head at the time, she says she wasn't thinking, she was just feeling. For the first time, she was able to hold you, to feel your weight in the crook of her arm, your warmth coming through the blankets. She was able not only to see what you were doing, but to feel each breath, each wriggle, each movement of the secretions inside you.

She has been dying for the sense of physical connection, real connection, with you. The protective, soothing embrace. I could see how much it meant to her, but it didn't stop me elbowing her out of the way after half an hour to get my share. To watch you drifting off to sleep in my lap made me so happy I was light-headed.

Sharyn snapped a couple of Polaroids of the three of us. The only visible tube is the small one taking oxygen to your nostrils (the ventilator was removed this afternoon). It's as Happy Family as we have been able to get so far. The only thing that could make you prettier would be a better haircut. They gave you your first snip this morning, cutting off some fringe because it had stuck to the tape on your forehead. Not even two weeks old and having a bad hair day . . .

I just showed the Polaroids to Helen's nipples to get them to express milk more freely. Apparently, thinking of your baby makes your milk come faster. When she's in the hospital, and near to you, Helen expresses twice as much milk. At home, it's always a bitter struggle.

Dr Ian told us this morning that the best case scenario is another two weeks of hospital. More likely, it will be at least a month. And I have no reaction to that. I don't feel happy or unhappy about it. It just is.

We've been getting to know some of the other parents in ICU, which is to say, we nod hello and exchange the occasional word in the expressing room or kitchen. None of our kids has the same problems, but as parents we share some of the same feelings. The baby boy next to us has almost none of his lung capacity—they've so far predicted his death twice, but he's still here. A girl on the other side has an infectious viral disease that has broken out in purple splotches. Her limbs have had to be amputated. You, Peanut, will get better. It's a sobering thought.

SEPTEMBER 18

Arriving back at ICU after lunch, the door is opened for us by a priest. He is looking for the father of the boy with lung problems. The curtains around his cot have been closed all morning, with staff coming and going in full surgical gear. The baby is hanging in there, but the thread is weakening. To this man and his wife, the priest is there to help. To me, he looks like the grim reaper.

This family were there on the night we arrived. They've maintained a bedside vigil ever since. Often, I've looked over and seen the father sitting quietly on the chair by the cot, hunched over, smaller than his height, a picture of silent worry. Once or twice I've spotted him with his head in his hands, or gazing into the distance with his eyes red. This is a very raw place.

On a day like this, I feel guilty about things going right. You had a good night and you're more alert now. The morphine has gone, the Liquigesic comes and goes. You grizzle a little when you're moved around, when the chest drain pulls, but you settle quickly. The physiotherapist says she thinks your right lung, partially collapsed, is mending well.

While I am out, you wake and want to play. Helen introduces you to your feet and your knees. She plays stretching games with your arms. I haven't seen her so happy since, oh, last night when she got to hold you.

At 2 pm, you are wheeled, along with all your drips and attached machinery, up to the X-ray department in the old part of the hospital. The X-ray room is like something out of a 1950s sci-fi movie, with a large Frankenstein table in the centre. You look so tiny as they lay you on the bunny rug in the middle of it. It's time to test the duodenum. Dye is injected into your stomach through the gastrostomy tube and then, wow, Naomi is on TV.

Standing behind the protective screen, we are able to see continuous X-rays on the monitor as the fluid moves and spreads. Unfortunately one of the first things we see is reflux, the dye moving up your oesophagus and ... yes ... disappearing through the leak into your chest cavity. Well, that answers that question, and we weren't even asking it.

Slowly, the dye begins to move down from your stomach, across what looks like a centimetre or so, collecting at the duodenum. And then ... nothing. The radiologist explains to Helen that a duodenal atresia is easier to fix than an oesophageal one. A follow-up X-ray half an hour later confirms it. Dr Ian will operate next week.

At least you're looking better with every passing hour, so it's pretty certain you'll be back in the ward for a few days, probably from tomorrow. We will be less worried this time around. You've had six days to recover—last time you had three. Tonight we sit and hold you again. You are wide awake, but as soon as you are placed in my lap, you start to drift off. We change your nappies. We clean your eyelashes and keep tabs on the spittle you're pushing out, wiping it away or using a suction tube. I am getting so good at this that I suspect I may have been a dental hygienist in a past life.

SEPTEMBER 19

Shhh. Helen is throwing the breast pump around the house. It won't work properly and her breasts are crying, swollen and painful. It's taking ages for the milk to come down. We've been experimenting with different machines and suction arms, with very limited success. Tonight, it is all too much for her. She asks if I'm going to put her tantrum in the diary. I say I think not. She says I should. If difficulty is the truth, then it's the truth.

The freezer is starting to fill up with tubs of breast milk. Five or six times a day, every day, Helen fights the machine. I can see how hard it is for her, but I know there is much more to it than the physical pain. She is expressing milk that we may not ever be able to use. Who knows how long it will be before you're able to drink? Who knows if you'll ever get it straight from her?

You have a rough patch this morning when they flush out your chest drain, drawing mucus and air and other nameless gunk that has been giving you grief. It's not a great experience to watch you go beet red and start your strangled yowling, but our consolation is the speed at which you return to calm after being upset. You're mostly okay, except for occasional moments when you cough and splutter and look as if you're choking, then present us with the saliva equivalent of a hairball. They seem to surprise you too.

Back in the ward in the afternoon, it appears to us that your eyes are beginning to focus. We can see you actually looking at us now, focusing on our faces, on our hands, on Russell, the teddy bear we brought in to watch over you.

SEPTEMBER 20

More hairballs. I know we had that conversation about you not becoming a model a while ago, but you do seem to be accumulating all the attributes. You're long, skinny and gorgeous. You don't eat much and you seem to like bringing stuff up.

Helen has been worried that because of the way you're treated in hospital, you will come to associate being touched with discomfort, with having things done to you, drains flushed, wounds tampered with, tape stuck on and removed. I think you can already discern the difference between activities. Also when you're awake now, you seem to recognise us. For about half an hour, you are clearly looking at Helen, committing her to your mostly empty memory files.

We think you're getting hungry. You'll chew on a knuckle, suck the mouthwash off a cotton bud. But you can't eat yet. We have a freezer full of frozen breast milk, if that's any consolation. Actually, it really is getting to Helen. She has been more upset about problems with the pump today than about anything during the entire pregnancy. It's a combination of exhaustion and frustration and those fabulous Zen hormones wearing off. As I type, she's in the lounge room, hooked up to the machine again (like mother, like daughter). Her mood has at least improved tonight. After holding you for an hour, she expressed more milk this evening at home than she ever has at the hospital. I don't know who the contact reassures more.

S EPTEMBER 2 I
Sunday, two weeks

We visit three times today and manage to miss you being awake at every turn. It is only tonight that you wake long enough for us to see your pretty eyes. I show you your own hand, playing with each little finger. You're still at the stage where you find the relationship between the sight of your hand and the feeling of having a finger waggled kind of strange. But not half as strange as your newly discovered habit of sneezing.

All these hours with you, they just go by. What do I think of when I'm looking at you? I don't know. I'm just lost, dissolved. Helen says when I'm with you, I glow. I know she does. Someone else comes out, someone unfamiliar, yet curiously recognisable. Looking back over all this note-taking, it strikes me that I've omitted to mention just how much in love with you we are. I hope you take it for granted. I hope you always will.

SEPTEMBER 22

When we arrive at 9 am, you're squealing and complaining.
The machines are beeping like mad. Your heart rate is off
the chart. I see it blinking 209 ... 209 ... 208 ... 209 and
shut my eyes. I've never seen it so high. Your chest drain
has blocked and the area around your gastrostomy is red,
puffy and giving off a discharge that is leaking down to
your nappy. The surgical registrar says the gastrostomy is
all right, recommends an X-ray so we can look at your
chest, and thinks we should pump a little morphine back
into you to get you through.

While all that's happening, you are dosed with more
Liquigesic, which seems to work—or maybe it's just having
Helen and me around. I sit next to your bed, telling you
stories. I sing to you too, when no-one else is listening.
You like Beatles medleys.

The ward is noisy today, full of chatting mothers,
bouncing kids, new admissions, trainee nurses, visiting
families, student groups, televisions ... it's a wonder you're
not stuck to the ceiling like that Warner Bros cartoon cat
in all this hubbub. But gradually we talk you down as far
as sleep, or as close as we can get to it, a sort of semi-
conscious drift.

Lunchtime meeting with Dr Ian in his office. He pulls
a pencil out and begins drawing a diagram of the stomach
on an A4 pad. The duodenum, he explains, is C-shaped
and 'embraces' the pancreas. He says the X-ray showed a
complete block. Instead of cutting out the block, it's easier
to simply bypass it. It's a standard procedure and will take,
at most, an hour. There are two reasons why you're having

the operation this week. The first is that this atresia encourages acid reflux, which is slowing your oesophagus from healing. The second is that feeding proteins and lipids via the central line for long periods of time is not a particularly good thing to do. It's much better to do it the way nature intended.

Dr Ian says that while you're under anaesthetic, he will put a second small tube (a jejunal tube) in beside the gastrostomy and thread it down through the bypassed area and into a clear part of the intestine. Two or three days after the operation, if all goes well, they will start feeding you through it, mixing some of Helen's expressed milk with the acid and juices taken from your stomach, to approximate what would normally be in your intestine. The food will begin slowly, 1 millilitre per hour, and gradually increase.

Helen asks about the scar. It will be a lateral scar, beside the gastrostomy's small round one. She's upset about it. She thinks you're going to end up looking like a road map. I'm just happy to hope you'll end up in one piece.

Dr Ian says we won't bother testing your oesophagus again until 'the moment is right'. The leak will not be healed yet. It all seems like problem upon problem to us. I ask him how well you're doing overall.

'She's good,' he leaps to assure us. 'She's fighting and getting better. In bad cases, they tend to have a setback and just get worse. She's got good stock. I'm confident about the long term.'

They're reassuring words, but they seem to mean a little less when we return to the ward to find you still miserable, in the middle of having your chest drain flushed. It's not an enjoyable way to spend the afternoon, compared with, well, compared with most things.

You settle down very slowly, the pain large and looming, only away from the surface for short periods. You're lying on your left side, the side that doesn't have the drain stuck in it. You begin to arch your back, a behaviour we've never seen before. Your head tilts back, which worries us, because your chin is meant to be down to avoid any unnecessary pulling on your oesophagus. It looks awful, like you're on the rack. We reposition you on your back, but you push your way onto your side again.

The morphine is upped but you're still suffering. I caress you and sing to you and when it seems too much, sit there quietly whispering encouragement. Helen arrives. I take a walk to clear my head, leaving her to pat you and help you (she's brilliant at it, much better than I am, I hate to say).

SEPTEMBER 23

At breakfast your breathing shoots up towards 100 breaths per minute. You're distressed. You don't want to be touched. The drain is not working again. Another X-ray. Another probable aspiration. Another angry, tearful day in South Ward. I am glad I made Helen stay in bed. You're red-faced from squealing and worn out by a day that has only just begun. You open your eyes and look almost frightened by what is happening.

I ask for you to be taken back to the ICU. You're stretched out, craning your neck backwards, bracing yourself against the pain washing through you. With this added dimension of breathing problems, I'm convinced you're just not well enough to stay on the ward. You can't be ventilated here and you clearly need some kind of help. So I ask the nurse, who asks the registrar, who asks the surgeon—the request is handed about like a game of pass the parcel.

The ward is the noisiest I have ever heard it. Two of the mothers have toddlers in visiting baby siblings. There is so much shouting and crashing of toys that your sleep becomes even more fitful. Every time I think you've made it under, something snaps you back. I swear that one of the kids has the ability to make a noise as loud as a freeway pile-up with his bare hands. I'm stroking you, trying to placate your jangled nerves, with a constant background of a four year old shouting, 'Fucking car! Fucking fucking!'

Your condition eases in the afternoon. Helen goes to have her hair cut. It's important that she does things other than express milk (five times a day, an hour at a time) and sit by your bedside. The constancy of this stress is no good for either of us. We're tired and getting snappy at each other. We have to try to stay sane. As someone once put it succinctly, 'Fit your own air mask first.'

Before leaving, Helen gives blood so they can cross match with yours if they need to during the next operation. The woman who takes her sample tells Helen that she worked on the first TOF operation in Sydney, in the early 1970s. One generation ago, Naomi, you wouldn't have made it. If you were my age, you wouldn't be.

Evening. Helen and I sit for a couple of hours, watching you hurting, still breathing fast, improved on this morning, but still, still, still in a bad place. I can hear Helen bleed beside me. When we get home, she breaks down in the kitchen, standing against the pantry door sobbing and moaning, 'I can't do this any more, I can't do this any more.' I hear fear, panic, heartache and fifteen flavours of personal hell rolled into each word. There is nothing useful I can say, so I just hold her.

SEPTEMBER 24

The phone rings as I'm trying to find a pair of socks in the drawer. Dressing seems to be getting harder. It either comes automatically or it takes forever. It's the ward. I have to sign a consent form so Dr Ian can operate today. You're not 100 per cent, but he wants to take the opportunity to move the drain, which has, he thinks, been the cause of your recent deterioration.

I leave Helen in bed, trying to rest (she was up before six doing that milk thing). There's a whirlwind of fuss as they prepare you for theatre. There are so many tubes and devices that have to be plugged, unplugged, reconfigured and replaced that they need an hour of warning to move you. While they're at it, they figure they might as well administer the antibiotics (your gastrostomy area is red, puffy and a little weepy) and maybe, if there's time, sneak in a little morphine to make the trip smoother. You're not exactly happy about any of it, though you're not, as Helen and I keep saying to each other, a whinger. It's something that continues to amaze us, your ability to pull through, to buckle down and cope with the pain, then quickly return to normal on the other side.

Though the duodenal operation will take only an hour, there's always at least half an hour on either side of preparation and recovery, and another hour or so of getting you comfortable back at the ICU, so I figure I can go home and bring Helen back in the afternoon.

We pore over the photographs that have been developed, deciding which ones we should send to our parents. There are ten or so that are safe viewing, which is a great relief. I could hear the distress in my father's voice on the phone last night as I told him you'd had a couple of rough days. It's hard for our parents, being so far away and so powerless to do anything to help their own children and grandchild get through this.

Back in ICU in the afternoon, I feel like an old hand, surveying all the new, nervous faces, the parents who are where we were three weeks ago, a place overwhelming and scary, with a baby fighting to stay afloat. The couple who were beside us then are not here. After the ward, it's so quiet that it seems unnerving at first. All I can hear is the constant exhalation of the air-conditioner and the occasional soft beep of an alarm.

You're brought back in, covered in the usual iodine splotches, with a brand new set of stitches right across your stomach, the new tube next to your gastrostomy and the ventilator tube hooked into your nose. You'll be on the ventilator at least until they can bring the morphine down. You've got more of the drug than ever before inside you. It's one of those things that the body develops an immunity to, so the dose has to keep going up. If they took you off the ventilator now, you wouldn't breathe for yourself.

It'll be 24 hours before you're anywhere near the state of consciousness, let alone the city, street and home of consciousness. I'm keen on an early night; I can't stop yawning as I walk around the room. So I take Helen gently by the shoulders and drag her away from your bedside.

Dr Ian rings just before dinner to tell us that the operation went very well. Not only did they clear a lot of gunk from your chest, they also got the air pocket. The chest drain has been replaced with a bigger one, which shouldn't clog up as often—your quality of life should, fingers crossed, begin to improve. He sounds very happy, and says the problem in the duodenum had been exactly as he predicted. The feeding tube has been placed easily, and he plans to start feeding you milk on Friday. Finally, some good news to tell people.

SEPTEMBER 25

A few short weeks have made such a difference to our attitude. Before, the day after a major operation would have been a day consumed by worry and nervousness. Now it's a day of calm. You're sedated, and unlikely to need your hand held, or even know about it. At home, Helen puts photographs of you into frames and spreads them around the house. Tonight we even take ourselves out to dinner. You approach wakefulness but never quite get there. You're content to lie about and secrete.

SEPTEMBER 26

A new day, a new problem. It's hard to stay on top of everything. If I weren't keeping this diary, I'd probably have lost track by now. The latest difficulty is that your gastrostomy tube has come loose and is leaking horrible green stomach acids all over you. We're worried about the possibility of infection at the gastrostomy site and at the wound from the duodenal operation alongside it. Every time the nurses put a new dressing on, the leak stains it bright green in minutes. Your skin is so raw from the acid that the protective zinc cream won't stick to it. A specialist promised to look at it this afternoon, insisted that she was the person to do it, and then didn't show, after we waited for six hours. We're not happy.

Other than this ghastly sight, you're okay, still sedated, still sleeping it off. Occasionally you get around to breathing, if something like a passing pain bout reminds you that you're alive, but mainly the machine is breathing for you. They have started feeding you milk from Helen through the new tube, the little one that goes in beside the gastrostomy. All her hours wrestling with the pump are finally having some meaning. At the moment, it's just a single millilitre an hour to get you used to it, to coat your intestines. It's not even enough to show up in your waste output.

Meanwhile, it's crowded in ICU again. In the bed beside us a girl, who looks about ten, asks for a drink of water. She was hit by a car yesterday and has internal injuries. Her grandmother sits quietly beside her. She's on the mend. But the same cannot be said for everybody. All afternoon there has been a dreadful intermittent wail, an unearthly sound from a five-year-old boy in a bed two down from you. Sitting quietly in the corner, touching your soft thigh, I hear enough of the goings on to understand there are neurological problems, that these spasms are getting worse, that each one is damaging the boy's brain even further. The long-term outlook is not good. His father stands by the bed with tears running down his face.

SEPTEMBER 27

Lucy, the girl who was hit by a car, made it out to the ward today. She's not eating, because she's had damage to her spleen and they don't want to rupture it, but she's improving fast. A friend of Lucy's mother comes over, a woman with a spray of dark curls and a love of Lycra. She sees you and swoons, particularly when she finds you have the same name as her own daughter. 'I'm going right upstairs to pray for your Naomi,' she says. 'I've got a crystal altar up there. I might even bring back the power stick and get her to touch it.' A few months ago, I would have told her where she could park her hippie tendencies. Now I just say thanks, every little bit helps.

In the morning, Nurse Libby changes your gastrostomy dressing. After caucusing with the other nurses and available doctors (it's Saturday morning—not everyone is around), she decides to try duodermal tape, an adhesive bandage that allows your skin to breathe, but stops the leaking acid getting to it. You seem to calm down pretty quickly after we try it. Mind you, that could also be the increased dose of Panadol you had half an hour before. You wake up, your eyes wide open and inquisitive. You look up at my face, watching my lips as they move, as I sing you a song. By the way, I've discovered that Helen also sings to you when no-one is around, little songs she makes up about what a kitten you are. I ask her to give me a demonstration, but she declines.

Your milk intake is doubled! You're now on 2 millilitres an hour of, get this, EBM (Expressed Breast Milk—there has to be an official name for everything). At this rate, you should catch up to Helen's output in about the year 2011. Mind you, that's if her output continues. Her relationship with the pump is an ongoing disaster. Her breasts are in permanent revolt, making sleep increasingly difficult. The night is a chorus of grunts and sighs. She is up and attached to the pump at 1, 4 and 7 am. It would be a lot easier if she were attached to you.

SEPTEMBER 28
Sunday, three weeks

At 3 am, your gastrostomy tube works its way loose and falls out. It has done so a couple more times since. The whole area has broken down. What's there now is an open wound the best part of a couple of centimetres across, swollen, puffy, irritated, with a hole in the middle where the tube was. The colour of the skin not covered by the duoderm is the deepest, angriest red. Across the top of this, green bile and acid oozes.

It's a frightening, blood-draining sight. Helen goes straight into shock when we get to ICU. 'I've never seen anything like that before,' she says twice, as if she hadn't heard herself the first time. It takes me a few seconds longer to react, but if anything, my reaction is worse. I can't look. I have to sit down and start breathing deeply and slowly. I am sweating, my stomach has tightened and I have that gag reflex going in the back of my throat. While I fight off nausea and distress, Helen soldiers on, overcoming her initial fright to talk about the problem with Nurse Carolyn.

It's not that worse things haven't happened—you're not in a lot of pain—but this one is on the outside, visible to us. And it is something we didn't expect. Every time we think we're through the worst of it, something else happens. Every day, as a passing registrar says, is either a new challenge or a new problem.

Your ventilator rate has been increased. It's been decided to concentrate on the gastrostomy problem and not attempt to wean you off the breathing machine today. You're calm, sleeping and getting a little extra hit of morphine every time anything has to be done to you; Carolyn describes pain relief as her 'obsession', which Helen and I are both happy to hear. I ask if this is a fairly common problem with gastrostomies, or if we're just having a run of bad luck. Carolyn says it's a luck thing. On the other hand, she says, you're passing 'little pebbly bits', which means you are digesting the milk, sorry, EBM.

All that can really be done today is careful monitoring and regular washing of the wound. Your skin has to be kept as free of the acidic irritant as possible. I can see Helen wanting to throw a tantrum. We're particularly angry that the specialist who promised to come on Friday did not make it. This situation might have been averted. I tell Helen it's not the fault of the staff currently on, but there is a desperate urge to find someone to blame, someone to take your suffering out on. I dissuade her from losing it in the ICU. As a parent, you have to pick your tantrum moments very carefully. The last thing you need, as a long-term presence, is to be labelled a troublemaker. It pays to stay friendly, to try to be the best damn patient you can be, no matter how sick you are.

At home in the afternoon, Helen rings Dr Ian, who offers what reassurance he can. Then she gets rid of her nervous energy by rearranging the house, moving things from shelf to shelf, banging in picture hooks. This is a behaviour I recognise. There'll be some kind of crash tonight.

When the tears do come, they're a good thing, a release. But they escalate into slamming of doors before the night ends. I tell Helen she's being irrational, but that's not really the problem—her anger about the situation exhausts me. I don't have the strength to deal with it. I need calm to get through this. She needs something else. She feels best when she's fighting a problem—I feel best when I'm thinking it through. She wants to talk about it. I want to shut down. She's expulsive, I'm retentive.

SEPTEMBER 29

This morning Carol, a stoma therapist (a specialist on openings to the body which have tubes, not Friday's no-shower), was brought in to adjudicate on the appropriate course of treatment. I wasn't there when she arrived, but Helen, who was, says she gasped when she saw the size and nature of your wound. The area has now been covered with a special dressing, which drains the fluid into a plastic bag. This is an enormous relief to both Helen and me.

They have moved you into an isolation room, to lower the chance of any further infection. I say further because we find out today that you are, in fact, carrying an infection, a common hospital gremlin called MRSA, detected in your chest drain almost immediately after your first operation. For a couple of weeks we've been presuming all the antibiotics they plug into you are preventative. Apparently not. I wonder whose job it was to tell us.

Dr Ian explains that the gastrostomy tube has blocked. The acid, which is no longer being drained, has eaten away at the weak point around the tube and leaked out. His main concern is not the leak (our worry) but the fact that the tube isn't working. He asks for it to be flushed. When it is, the saline pours straight out into the bag, not through the tube, but around it. So that doesn't work. It seems likely that he'll have to put another tube in.

He also asks for some blue dye to be put into your mouth to see where it ends up. If it makes it to your stomach, we'll know your oesophagus is at least starting to heal. If it floods out the chest drain, no such luck. You show no inclination to swallow, spitting the blue dye out onto yourself and the cotton bedding. Apparently, babies who don't breastfeed immediately have trouble learning how to swallow. They're going to try the dye again later tonight and in the morning. If you don't cooperate, it will be barium and back to X-ray. Meanwhile, the EBM is at 3ml per hour and being raised 1ml every six hours, with the TPN correspondingly lowered.

Helen tells me tonight, for the first time, exactly how upsetting it is not to be able to breastfeed, how the desire to hold you to her nipple, to be part of you, to have you as part of her, is almost overwhelming. Sometimes, in all this chaos and change, I forget that she has whole dimensions of biology working on her that I don't have. I forget how much more pressure is on her.

Everything has eased again between us. Helen asks me when I am planning to stop disappearing into the study every night to write in this diary. I tell her: 'The first day of pure happiness'.

SEPTEMBER 30

Registrar Mike says he's been trying to phone us. You're looking less well. Everyone agrees that something is wrong. Your temperature has been spiking up overnight, above the 38 degree mark. You're feverish (febrile, I am told, is the word). This means that another infection is present somewhere. But where? It could be in any number of places: your chest drain, the central line, the gastrostomy wound ...

Mike wants to discuss the 'invasive' elements of the tests before going ahead. Because the infection could be anywhere, it's worth screening for all possibilities. So, he wants to take blood from the central line, and blood from a vein. He wants to insert a catheter to get a urine sample to check for urinary tract infection. And he wants to do a lumbar puncture (we blanch when he says it), to rule out meningitis, which is not infrequent in small babies. Some of the results we will know today. The blood-related ones will take longer. Even when they find a bug in the blood, they have to grow it, and then test it against various antibiotics, so it will probably be a couple of days before effective treatment is found. They've put you on a wider range of antibiotics in the meantime, which will automatically cover most possibilities.

Dr Ian took the gastrostomy tube out this morning, replacing it with a catheter and inflating the internal balloon that holds it in place. He wants to see if this will drain any of the fluid. It is already failing. An hour after his departure, the dressing has been changed three times because of the leakage, and nothing is coming through the tube.

While Mike does the tests, Helen and I sit in the expressing room. Neither of us knows what to say to the other. Helen slowly, soundlessly, dissolves into tears.

'It just keeps going wrong,' she says with a voice the size of a postage stamp. 'I feel like it's out of control now.' We talk through what has happened and what it means. Then we go silent again. I know it's not your fault, Naomi, but this is not the birthday your mother was looking forward to.

'Every intervention just seems to cause more problems,' Helen says. 'I don't know what the answers are. It's getting to the point where I don't even know what the questions are. I just don't think this should be happening. I don't think it should be one thing on top of another.'

Dr Hodo, the surgical registrar, has been talking with Dr Ian and they've decided to take the catheter out. The wound seems to be draining the fluid on its own, so maybe that will produce the desired result, for a while at least. It's not the prettiest of solutions, but it's a solution. He organises to remove the tube and have Carol, the stoma therapist, put a new bag over the wound. This time it's done in such a way that the area around the wound is well protected, and the risk of infection (or further infection) considerably decreased. She has to work carefully to keep the small jejunal tube in place—now that its bigger partner has gone, there's not much holding it in.

Hodo sits with us for half an hour, drawing diagrams on the back of an envelope, reassuring us that it's not the end of the world. At one point, Helen asks, 'Is she going to be all right?' It's movie dialogue, the kind of clichéd question you hear yourself thinking but don't often say. She knows the answer (yes) but we both need to hear it anyway.

We go back to see you and you're still under the surface of sleep. Dr Ian arrives shortly before 4 pm to check out the gastrostomy work and is fairly pleased. He says he doesn't know why the drains weren't working, and isn't too sure how this idea will go, but reckons we might as well try. The problem will come if the wound decides to heal over while there's still a build-up of acids and secretions. If that's the case, he says, he'll have to operate and put another gastrostomy tube in.

Just when we think the day can't get any weirder, around 7 pm you screw up your face in what Helen describes as terror, then pass the largest bowel movement of your life, a white, curd-like substance which is obviously the remains of the milk you've been getting (6 millilitres per hour and rising). It is so big that it escapes from the nappy and stains the sheet. While we lift you up to try to change it, your chest drain falls out. I'm holding you, thinking, that's funny, my hand feels wet. I look down and the end of the drain is resting against it, coating me with mucus and whatever else you were pushing through there.

The nurse clamps some gauze to the wound and presses it tight. Registrar Mike seals it. Then he contacts Dr Ian, who is apparently not too disturbed. He reacts in much the same way he did to the gastrostomy problem. If it's out, we might as well just let it stay out and see what happens. If there's a build-up of air and mucus in your chest, he'll have to go back in. If not, then we'll have been lucky.

Helen says to me, 'I know this is going to sound hippie or New Agey, but I reckon she's just sick of all of those tubes. She wants them out and she's going to heal herself. If it were up to me, I'd just take everything off her and wheel her out into the sun for a week.'

Over a quick dinner up the road from the hospital, we decide that this wasn't Helen's birthday after all. We'll choose another day somewhere down the line and do it properly.

October

Sadness wells up in the bones. It's cumulative, a kind of emotional exhaustion. You're three weeks old—it feels like three years. Helen's answer is to get out into the world. Mine is always to retreat into my cave and lick a few wounds. She heads off with a friend, Sandy, to visit an exhibition of Aboriginal art. I sit on the floor and alphabetise my compact discs, a slow and tedious task, but somehow so repetitive and numbing that it feels therapeutic.

You don't seem particularly bothered by the events of the past few days. Mind you, with the chemicals in your system, you probably wouldn't be bothered by being run over by a bus. Your gastrostomy is draining. The skin around it is beginning to lose its crimson anger. This morning's X-ray showed no build-up of air or mucus in your chest after the loss of the drain. Your heart and breathing rates are okay. And your haemoglobin count is stable, so although you're looking very pale, there's no talk of infection-driven transfusion just yet. You're sleeping and everyone agrees you look a little better than you did 36 hours ago.

The central line blood came back clean. The lumbar and urine were discounted yesterday. The swabs from the gastrostomy wound showed only MRSA, the bug we already knew. The chest drain samples are not back yet. But whatever the infection is, it doesn't appear to be knocking you around too much—the new antibiotics seem to be doing the job. Your EBM rate has been stopped at 8 millilitres per hour. No-one likes to eat too much when they're feeling sick.

So we wait. And tend to the everyday things like cleaning your mouth and playing with your toes. Registrar Mike asks me how hard it is to cope. He wants to know if it is possible to bond with something small and frail, covered in tubes, obscured by monitors. It isn't hard at all. The hard part is not being able to pick you up. The hard part is Helen not being able to hold you to her breast. The hard part is realising that none of us really knows where the road is going.

OCTOBER 2

In the morning, I send off an email, a Baby Bulletin, to a long list of friends, the best way to keep people up to date, the easiest way to avoid having to tell the same story over and over on the phone. I fill them in on the details so far, going back over the birth, the operations, the leak, the discovery and repair of the duodenal blockage, and the bizarre week we've just had ...

WHAT'S HAPPENING AT THE MOMENT?

Well, three and a half weeks in, we're still in Intensive Care. Naomi has picked up some sort of infection and is a little sick. On top of that, her gastrostomy tube has broken down and been removed, which means there is a hole in the middle of her abdomen which is leaking bright green stomach juices and bile to the world. There's a sterilised bag over the top of that, but it's odd to look at. Two days ago, while we were changing her nappy, the drain that goes into her chest to pick up whatever leaks from the oesophagus kinda just fell out.

It has been decided that in both cases, the gastrostomy and the chest drain, we will not replace them in a hurry. Instead, we will just wait and watch and see what her body does, see how much of a problem either loss creates. Helen's theory is that Naomi has simply had enough of these invasive tubes and wants to heal herself.

IS SHE GOING TO BE ALL RIGHT?
It's not a life or death situation. It's just upsetting and frustrating. But one of the things about spending all this time in Intensive Care is that you get to see what other people go through. You get a lot of perspective.

HOW MUCH LONGER IS THIS GOING TO GO ON?
No-one wants to say, because right now, there are a lot of variables. But we're getting a loud and clear picture that we won't be out of hospital in less than three or four weeks, and that's if everything goes well. Certainly, we're not out of the woods yet, and there may well be further operations.

HOW ARE THE PARENTS HOLDING UP?
We're pretty tired, but mostly okay. Helen's recovery from the birth has been very smooth, but she has a constant wrestle with the electronic breast pump, which demands her attention for up to six hours of the day, every day. I have taken six weeks off work. The hospital is only five minutes away from where we live and that gives us a lot of flexibility. We're there two or three times a day, but if we need to sneak out and do things, we can.

WHAT DO YOU DREAM OF?

Having a baby at home, one that will wake us five times a night to be fed and have its nappy changed. Sounds like heaven.

You wake up while we're beside your cot. For half an hour, you look at the two of us. We take it in turns to sit directly in your line of sight. Helen pokes her little finger into your mouth and you suck on it, which delights both of you. You clock in at 2.6 kilograms, half a kilo above your birth weight. That may not be a huge amount for almost a month, but what a month it's been.

Nurse Juanita tells Helen she thinks you're a fighter. Helen says, 'How can you tell?' Juanita replies that she can see it in your eyes. I say, 'But don't they all look like that, don't all babies have that?' Juanita says, 'No, some you look at and just think, ohhhh . . .'

In the afternoon, we run into Dr Hodo, who says Dr Ian wants to have a patient conference next week, to get all of us together with Dr Barry, the head paediatrician and director of the ICU, to discuss what to do next. Hodo hints at further surgery but doesn't want to elaborate. He keeps saying that Dr Ian will explain the options. Until the conference, you will just be left to get better.

OCTOBER 3

A letter comes for you today. I am all for leaving it until you're old enough to open it, but Helen tears the envelope apart. Not even four weeks old and your mother is already putting her nose into your business. It's a good thing she does—inside is a pathology bill. What makes the pathologists think you're paying your own bills?

Your temperature is heading up again, and your haemoglobin count is down—it's blood transfusion time. You're drooling like a fiend, and have been since the chest drain fell out. This is a good sign—it may mean that it's not all escaping into your chest cavity, putting pressure on the lung.

Tonight, I go to the hospital on my own. It is 6 pm and the nurse has just left for her dinner break. You are wide awake, lying on your side, contemplating the world. Your eyes are as open as ever I've seen them, your tiny face uncreased by pain. As I sit down, I can see you watching me, your gaze moving from my eyes to my mouth to my hair, which is flopping about because I haven't had it cut for ages (something else keeps soaking up my time). For an hour, we are on our own, just you and me, my fingers in yours, my cheek resting on the edge of the cot, our faces close enough that we fill each other's vision. It is like an oasis of time, a clear, beautiful hour in a desert of frustration and upset. And even though I wish Helen was here, I am also glad that it is just us.

I tell you how beautiful you are, how much we love you, exactly what you mean to both of us. I tell you that you're the best thing that has ever happened to me. Then I think, hang on, that sounds a bit glib. So I stop and consider it, stroking the soft hair behind your ear. I make my whole life flash before me. And I realise that some wonderful things have happened to me (not the least of which is your mother), but nothing better than you. So I repeat what I said. You drool in appreciation. Or at least, that's how I choose to interpret it.

Your colour is better. You were given 50 millilitres of blood before I arrived. It's weird, thinking about someone else's blood circulating inside you. It's different from laboratory-synthesised chemicals. I ask Dr Keith, the paediatric registrar on today, if we could have used our own blood. Apparently it takes six days for blood to be screened and okayed, so it was out of the question. I kick myself for not thinking of it a week ago. And I wish they'd told us. I don't even know what blood type I am. (You're O positive, like your mother, but don't mention it to her, because O positive is the blood of the people, and your mother imagines that she has the blood of princesses. Let her keep her fantasy.)

Keith takes some blood from me to have it tested. If it's type O, I'll donate for any future need. I sit beside you as the needle goes into me. You hold my hand. And you know what? It isn't so bad.

October 4

Peanut, the human being is an incredible, adaptable creature. We get used to things, even if we shouldn't. Repeat our exposure to something and we will learn to tolerate it. So we get used to seeing you tangled up in machinery. We get used to you being in pain. We get used to not being able to hold you. We get used to all these things. And I wish we didn't. It may be smarter to be less worried by everything, but I don't like it. Some wisdom tastes bitter.

In between two visits to the hospital, we lunch with

friends Nora and Michael and, as a treat, take ourselves to the movies for the first time in months. Now, though we're not talking about it, I know we're both feeling guilty about enjoying ourselves while you're where you are. My head is telling me we did the right thing, but my heart demurs.

You are awake when we arrive at the hospital this morning, those piercing eyes just waiting for something like a mother's face to clamp onto. Because I had such a good time last night, I station myself by your feet and let Helen get in close. Mary-Rose asks if we'd like a cuddle. I have been working under the assumption that the number of tubes connected to the ventilator means it isn't possible, but she assures me that it most certainly is, with a little extra care. And now you're recovered enough from your infection (they never told us what it was, but the antibiotics are being cut out one at a time), we should get back to some normal human contact.

You are suctioned for good measure, swaddled and placed in Helen's lap. It has been two weeks since we could pick you up, fourteen days of desperate deprivation.

Later, I have a long talk with Mary-Rose while Helen is expressing. She tells me that it's often the parents who are the hardest for the staff to cope with, who take out their anxiety, anger and frustration on whoever is about. I ask if fathers are the criers. She says no, the mothers cry first, but they get over it first. The fathers bottle it up, then go to water at unexpected times. She says fathers tend to have the tougher time of it in life and death situations. The mothers roll up their emotional sleeves and get on with it.

Mary-Rose says a baby in hospital can be a terrible strain on relationships. She recalls a survey done in a hospital where she spent five years working with premature babies. The divorce rate of couples whose children went through her ward was 70 to 80 per cent. I would have thought it was an experience that would bring couples closer together. I certainly feel closer to Helen after all we've been through. But I guess if something was already wrong in the relationship, this place would magnify it.

Mary-Rose says they try to keep parents of kids with similar problems apart. They figure it's best we don't compare notes, because we'll only end up sad, which makes sense. There was another TOF baby admitted to ICU the week after you were. It had a gap of only one centimetre and was out in the ward a few days later. They kept us on opposite sides of the unit, but we crossed paths in the corridor, so we knew. Helen said she found it heartbreaking to see the other one leave, so well, so easily, when you were having such trouble. My brain, mercifully, has not taken me down such paths. You have to believe that the Universe is an ordered place to see that as an injustice.

October 5
Sunday, four weeks

More smooth sailing. Dr Ian tells us he's happy with your secretions, both the juices from the gastrostomy wound and the added saliva and mucus coming through the mouth and the ventilation tube. I see in your notes that he is planning to tell us about something called an oesophagostomy, whatever that is.

Helen wakes up this morning pining for another cuddle, so our first priority is to get you out of the cot. You were up until almost 4 am partying, so you are very sleepy, so tired you can be suctioned out without waking. It is quiet holding you, but lovely nonetheless.

The length of this ordeal is getting to Helen. She looks at me and says, with real pain in her voice, 'She had to have a three centimetre gap, didn't she?' I keep trying to stop her thinking like that. Start in that direction and you end up at guilt and self-pity, which are cancerous, destructive emotions. You've been dealt a tough hand but we're all making the best of it. What matters is not how you were born, but where you are now. What matters is today, tomorrow and next week. The past may be important, somewhere we can learn from, but it's also somewhere we've left. The present, we can do something about.

October 6

Your breast milk intake has been ramping up over the last few days. You're now on more than 300ml a day, while your intake of intravenous protein and lipids is down to less than 50ml. It gives us all heart.

This morning, the nurses try to get you to swallow some methylene blue dye again. Being your usual cooperative self, you spit most of it straight out, all over the bunny rug (you have rather attractive blue saliva for the whole afternoon). But, and this is a big but, you do actually swallow a decent amount, and most of what you swallow appears to come straight out through the gastrostomy hole. Which means that there is a passageway from your mouth to your stomach. Which means that although there may still be a leak in your oesophagus, it has not broken down completely; it is not two dangling halves. Which means that there has been at least partial healing taking place. Which is a pretty good thing, don't you think?

OCTOBER 7

So you have an oesophagus. And it works. This is what I wake up thinking, much more excited than yesterday. It's odd. We're so used to bad news that good news takes a while to make sense. This morning, I can see yesterday for what it hopefully was, a turning point in your hospital experience—the first simple positive we've had.

Dr Ian rings at 10 am and says he's called the afternoon conference off. He found out about the methylene blue and that has changed all his plans. He asks us to drop in for a chat at his surgery instead and looks very pleased to see us when we get there. 'Over the weekend, I was not too happy,' he says, 'but this morning I got this wonderful news. As soon as I threatened to do something, she got better.'

He pulls out the familiar A4 pad and begins to recap the last few weeks, drawing pictures of the various trouble spots of your anatomy. One by one, he recounts events, stopping when he gets to the presence of the jejunal tube. He's surprised it's still there. In most cases, he says, if the bigger gastrostomy tube goes, so does the smaller one.

'I must tell you also that getting that milk in is the crucial factor. The TPN is not the same. I'm a great believer in breast milk.'

Returning to the problem of the oesophagus, he says that before yesterday there had been two possibilities. The first was that there had been at least some healing taking place, some continuity in the path of the pipe. The second, which he suspected was the most likely, was that there had been a complete disruption, leaving you with two separate pouches again, the lower one probably sealed.

Yesterday morning he noticed what he thought was saliva in the gastrostomy run-off bag. Then he asked for the dye to be put down and *voilà*! A working passage! So his decision for the moment is to do nothing, to let you continue the healing process you have started. You will be weaned off the ventilator, if possible, in the next few days, but other than that, it's a case of fattening you up, keeping you rested and letting you do as much as you can yourself.

Next week, the radiologist, Dr John, will do a test to show us the size of the leak, the size of the cavity it's leaking into and the tightness of the stricture. Then there's the question of what to do with the stricture. The doctors can put a balloon into your throat and inflate it to open the passage. If that doesn't work, Dr Ian will, under anaesthetic, put a dilator down there himself, something more rigid. This dilation process, he explains as we grow paler by the second, will have to be repeated as often as required. It may need to be done regularly for some time. If it's too regularly, and we can't yet really say what is 'too regularly', you may need another operation.

While we're dealing with that idea, he says that if things go well, you may have another gastrostomy tube inserted and be allowed to go home. We'd have to learn how to feed you by pump, but at least you'd be with us. Fingers crossed, he says, it would happen in a couple of weeks, if the cavity is tiny and the stricture stretches up well. If the stricture is very tight, perhaps five or six weeks.

Dr Ian asks how we are, and whether we've been able to have a cuddle with you. More and more people have asked us that question in the last week. Maybe it's simple human concern. Maybe they're trying to make sure that this baby is not going to go home with two exhausted, burned-out parents. Maybe we just look really bad. Most likely, it's all of the above. We tell him the truth, that we have good and bad days, that things have been better lately, that living near to the hospital makes it a lot easier on us, that we're watching ourselves pretty carefully to make sure we don't fall apart.

He mentions what a tough little girl you are. He says you're clearly not about to give up. In the car, Helen says, 'It's scary when even the surgeon thinks you've got a tough kid.'

We go back to the hospital to visit you. You've discovered (yesterday was the first time we saw it) that there's a relationship between your hands, that if you hold those two funny-looking things together, one of them can feel the other one.

We're both a little unnerved by the discussion with Dr Ian. For some reason, it had never occurred to either of us that we might bring you home unfinished as it were. Our dreams have been of triumph, of marching home a girl without tubes. Sure, you'd have a few scars, and feeding might be difficult, but what happened at the hospital would be left at the hospital as you started your new life. Now, we know that won't be the case.

OCTOBER 8

Nurse Carolyn takes a great Polaroid of you today. One of your hands is wrapped around the ventilator tube, attempting to yank it out. You're looking up at the camera with an expression that says, I understand that I have been caught in the middle of a criminal act, but I have no remorse whatsoever—this tube is going.

You are right. The tube has to go. You've made it down as far as eight breaths a minute via the machine. You're 'breathing up', as they say, pumping your lungs 60 or 70 times a minute on your own. That's a work rate a little higher than we'd like, but given that the right side of your chest still has the cavity of air and mucus putting pressure on the lung, decreasing its functionality, the figure is not so surprising.

It's easy to believe, after the last couple of days, that everything will be fine. You look better and stronger. The TPN and lipids have both finished. The antibiotics have ended. Your morphine has been cranked down by nearly a third in 48 hours. And still you power forward.

OCTOBER 9

You receive your first proper letter today. Up to now, it's just been medical bills (and my, you're already an expensive woman to keep). The letter comes from Winnie, daughter of friend David. She hasn't met you yet, but is planning to next month.

dear naomi lee,

we hope you get beter soon and you can come home
from hosbitl and be happy and eat lots of ise-crem we
loke forwood to tickling yore tumy in novemba. From
Winnie David and Lynne.

You breathe on your own for most of the day, 70 or 80
breaths a minute. The tube is slated for removal tomorrow
morning, which can't be soon enough for you. Your
morphine is now on the way out and you're going through
withdrawal, which makes you twitchy. You startle yourself
out of sleep, get upset, require suctioning, calm down a
little, drift away, startle yourself, bang a hand against the
tube, get upset with it, give it a good yank and scream
from the pain.

The better you get, the closer you are to coming home,
the more it hurts not to have you with us. I was standing
beside your cot today and a huge wave crashed over me,
a desperation to have you at home, held against me, away
from all this. Thinking about it, I probably should have
had that feeling before, but there has been so much to
worry about, so many other things to stay on top of. Until
now, the thought of you leaving the hospital would have
been too frightening.

Oh, by the way, an oesophagostomy involves taking the
top end of the broken oesophagus and making it exit
through the side of the neck. That way, all the saliva can
be drained away. Now there's a path I'm relieved (touch
wood) that we didn't have to go down. It used to be a
fairly standard part of the treatment for TOF babies.

They'd be fed through gastrostomies for weeks or months
while they grew strong enough to deal with the operation
to join the oesophagus.

OCTOBER 10

A day to cut out and keep. After a rough night at home,
we struggle to the hospital, arriving later than usual, at
11.10 am. I'm glad we are late, because the good folk at
the ICU have just pulled your tube out. We find you lying
in the cot, your hands moving in front of your face,
searching for the part of you that has been taken away.
You've had an involuntary (though really, much appreciated)
nose job, and it must feel weird. It also must feel weird
to be able to bring up the secretions on your own, and you
are wet and raspy, coughing up huge, soggy furballs every
15 minutes or so.

Your breathing is fine. It isn't even necessary to tape an
oxygen tube to your face. Which means that for the first
time in weeks, we see you free of tape and tubing. I feel
all superficial and shallow saying it, but being able to see
your face makes such a difference. Helen and I are close
to giddy with the excitement of it. You look like a baby
again. We have to remind ourselves not to get carried
away, not to play too strongly with you. For more than an
hour, you stay awake, checking out the world, trying to
come to terms with the removal of this enormous thing
after sixteen long days.

At the back of the room, two men and a woman stand
sipping coffee. They look a little like policemen, with their
short-sleeved blue shirts. In front of them stands a man in

a green suit, staring down at his newborn child with that familiar look of fear, pain and helplessness. The nurse is explaining the care regime as I walk past. Something draws me to look back over my shoulder, and as I do, I see the handcuffs hanging limp from one of his wrists. The people in blue are Corrective Services officers, minding their prisoner on a compassionate visit.

After lunch, I drop in to work to explain to my editor-in-chief that I don't want to come back to work next week. He tells me to come back when I can. Whatever it takes. Like most people, I often bitch about my work, but it has really come through for me.

Helen beats me back to the hospital and swipes you from the cot. Now that the ventilator is off, it's easy to swaddle you in a bunny rug (swaddling helps deal with the morphine withdrawal twitchiness too), taking a little care with the feeding tube and the various monitor leads, and pick you up for a cuddle. You make sucking motions, so she gives you a little finger to go on with. Nurse Julie thinks you may be able to smell Helen's breasts, the secretions on her nipples.

OCTOBER 11

The phone rings at 7.30 am. One of the ICU nurses wants us to know that you've been bumped down the hall to the ward. It was inevitable really, given how well you've been performing since being taken off the ventilator. And given that today is the last Saturday of the school holidays, there were always going to be multiple admissions to intensive care, with kids taking their last chance to fall off a horse, crash into a wall or almost drown in a well. The busy periods are sadly predictable for the staff.

Your MRSA infection, which has still not officially cleared (some swabs sent off to be inspected have not returned results yet), worked in your favour in the transfer, guaranteeing you a room of your own. Swanky! With a good sized-window bathing it in natural light.

We arrive to find you more or less awake, morphine-free and breathing well, on another day where everything seems to be good news, where everything seems to float. I watch Helen sit with you, the biggest of grins on her face as you make those little lip-smacking, sucking noises. Her fear is falling away now. When I mention that my mother will be bringing presents for you today, Helen says, 'Good, I'm ready.' We both are.

My parents arrive mid-afternoon, on the hottest October day in a decade. Though they have driven through the sweltering heat, I am not too concerned. Today is the absolute best day they could have come to visit. Your grandmother thinks, as all grandmothers should, that you are a living doll, absolutely adorable. Tomorrow we'll plonk you in their laps and see what happens.

OCTOBER 12
Sunday, five weeks

No ventilator. No morphine. No painkillers. No chest drain. No gastrostomy. No antibiotics. It's coming down to you and whatever power you can summon up to beat this thing.

In the morning, you perch in your grandmother's lap and then mine, placidly staring up at us. After a while, the pass-the-parcel movement seems to aggravate you, to bring the gunk into play. Every time your throat fills up with secretions, you have trouble breathing and your blood oxygen content goes down. We were going to introduce you to your grandfather at close quarters as well, but his turn will have to wait until tomorrow. At home, your grandmother unveils a few of the baby clothes she's bought for you, which include a gorgeous red jumpsuit. We're not sure where we'll cut the gastrostomy hole, but we'll find a way.

When we put you on Helen's lap tonight, you squirm, turn your face towards her breast, look up at her and start smacking your lips. I can hear it 3 metres away. She offers you her little finger and thinks you might suck it off, such is your ferocity. We're getting the message, Peanut, but we don't know how much longer it will be. If it were up to Helen . . .

OCTOBER 13

When we arrive, you've just had chest physiotherapy and been suctioned, so you're a little groggy. Helen grabs you ('I'm determined to start treating her as normal') and as soon as you're in her lap, you sink into a deep contented sleep. The problem is, the deeper into sleep you go, the more shallow your breathing. And for you, shallow breathing is tough—the cavity of air at the top of your right lung makes it more difficult than it should be.

My parents drop in to say goodbye. Your grandmother is quick to take up the offer of another cuddle, but in the end, your grandfather quietly declines. He's still nervous about your fragility. He's a big man, and you're such a small girl. Your grandmother says he was like that with my brothers and me—fine once we could hold his hand and walk, but tentative before that point.

Nothing has been draining through the gastrostomy wound in your stomach. It appears to have healed over. The jejunal feeding tube is miraculously still in place. Carol, the stoma specialist, decides to take the bag off. All you have now is a duoderm dressing on your skin to help it heal and provide security if there is another leak.

At 1 pm, you're wheeled to X-ray in a pram, the first time you've been out of a cot or bed. As usual, you sleep the whole way, enjoying the movement. The radiologist, Dr John, asks if we understand the risks involved with attempting to dilate your oesophagus, then tells us that the worst thing that could happen is a rupture, which would have to be repaired surgically.

Some preliminary X-rays are taken. Helen stands behind one of the protective barriers, watching through a window. I frock up in the lead gown and help to calm you, standing beside your head, holding your hand, trying to keep the oxygen tube pointed at you. A nurse next to me takes care of your other hand and the copious amounts of stuff you bring up as your distress increases.

The radiologist's assistant offers you barium to swallow. It's in a bottle with a teat on the top. You suck ferociously and we see the liquid heading downwards on the live X-ray screen. It moves down your throat and then pretty much stops.

'There's the stricture,' says Dr John. The leak beside it opens into a cavity shaped like a hockey stick. There appears to be a second cavity further up, a pocket of air on the lung. The doctors theorise that the original cavity has halved, and that the top half, now discrete, will simply absorb itself into the body. Certainly, the two areas appear disconnected.

Dr Ian looks at the X-rays as Dr John tells him the stricture is very tight. He shrugs and says, 'That's what we expected all along.' They decide to try the dilation. Dr John puts a soft tube into your mouth, pushing it down your throat. The end gets to the stricture and then buckles. For a few minutes, he fiddles with it, attempting to squeeze it through the narrow gap. His hands are moving, but his eyes are trained on the screen. He's trying to do the equivalent of threading a needle by remote control.

The room is quiet, tense, as he keeps trying. The only noise is the regular sound of you coughing up secretions, and the howling suction it takes to get rid of them. You're remarkably calm otherwise. Suddenly, the tube is through, and pushing towards your stomach. I'm not wrong in thinking I hear a cheer from the gallery. Helen tells me that Dr Ian leaned over to her and said, in awed tones, 'He's bloody good. He's a bloody good technician. In the hands of anyone else . . .'

A guide wire is pushed through the tube, which is then taken away, leaving the wire in place. A second tube is brought in, this one with a small section near its end, marked by two dots, which is inflatable. After some careful manoeuvring, it finds the spot. Dr John pumps some water into it.

What shows on the screen is an hourglass shape where the stricture is. We can all see how tight it is. The balloon is inflated three or four times, held for a few seconds each time and then deflated. With each inflation, the shape of your oesophagus changes. By the end of the procedure, Dr John is convinced he has at least doubled the width of it.

The wire is removed. The tube is brought most of the way out. More barium is injected into your throat. This time, we see it pour straight down into your stomach, with only the tiniest of amounts heading sideways into the leak. Dr John said earlier that the best way to treat a leak is to fix the obstruction beside it, and now I can see what he meant.

Dr Ian looks extremely happy about the whole thing, particularly the last part. He asks if we can repeat the process next Monday. He says he is also happy that the gastrostomy wound is healing. The stomach juices have not been coming up the throat, so it seems that they must be travelling downwards. Helen asks if the stricture will stay the same size or shrink again. Dr Ian says that essentially what Dr John has done is rupture scar tissue, which will tighten, but not as far as the point it started at.

We wheel you back to the ward, where you go straight to sleep, exhausted by the whole ordeal. I'm exhausted too, and try to curl up on the bed beside yours (it's a full-size one). The nurses come in to cap your central line. It will still be there if needed. Helen and I talk about how far we've come. The only thing going into you now is breast milk. The end of the tunnel is getting distinctly lighter.

OCTOBER 14

BABY BULLETIN II

HOW'S THE LITTLE CRITTER DOING?

Much improved, thank you. She swallowed some methylene blue dye ten days ago, which promptly arrived in her stomach (and drained through a handy tube). This proved, for the first time, that at least part of her oesophagus is working, that there is some continuity of the pathway. The celebrations went on for days. The successful swallow averted a very unpleasant operation, which would have happened a week ago—I'm not going to go into the details of what it would have done.

SO WHEN'S NAOMI COMING HOME?

I can't see it happening in less than a fortnight, but it may not take much longer than that. She is growing stronger and healthier every day, more awake and more alert. There has been a suggestion that she will come home with a gastrostomy tube. We would feed her via a pump. That thought's a little weird, but we're dealing with it.

IS SHE BORED, STUCK IN THE HOSPITAL LIKE THAT?

Naomi is mostly just hungry. Stick a little finger near her face and she'll suck the skin off it. She has all the usual baby instincts (and can smell milk on Helen, which drives her half crazy). She's managing to focus her eyes most of the time, and clearly knows who we are. I don't think she's realised that she's missing 'The Simpsons' yet though.

It's true. You will suck the skin off a finger. You reduced both of my pinkies to prunes today. I can still feel your tiny mouth clamped around them.

You had a very restless time last night, with a lot of secretions making their way up as a result of all the shaking around yesterday. Dr Ian is still ecstatic after the success of the dilation. Helen tells him how strong your sucking motions are, how hungry you seem, and that you can smell her milk. He suggests that next Monday, if the dilation is successful again, we might try to give you a little milk through your mouth, just to see what happens. Your EBM intake is upped to 18 millilitres per hour today and will go up again tomorrow.

OCTOBER 16

Responding to the *Baby Bulletin*, your uncle Tim emails from San Francisco, where he's been since June (due back next month). Tim works in computers, but although he has made a career out of the machines, he is not their biggest advocate. 'Finally,' he says when he sees the baby photos that a friend has put on the Web for me, 'a use for the Internet!'

While leafing through your medical notes, I discover that you've actually lost 200 grams in the six days you've been out of intensive care. This is ridiculous. You're better than you have been. You're calm and comfortable. You should be gaining. Dr Barry said days ago that your EBM feed should be increased, but it hasn't happened. He is away at a seminar, his replacement hasn't been around, the dietitian can't authorise it on her own, etc., etc., etc.

So we complain loudly, insist on a meeting of all concerned, convince them that you are hungry as hell, and more than tolerating the amount of milk you are on. We even keep one of your dirty nappies to show them. Everyone gathers round to examine it. It's like that scene in *The Last Emperor* where the wizened old courtiers inspect the baby's output and solemnly declare, 'Not enough vegetables.' The result is that your EBM has gone up to 19 millilitres an hour, and has had Polyjoule, a calorie booster, added to it.

OCTOBER 17

You are away with the sleep fairies, quietly purring to yourself. I pick you up for a cuddle, but you stay firmly under throughout the morning, waking only momentarily during nappy changes and physiotherapy. We think the additional food has made you sleepy. You had the same reaction the first time they pumped milk into you. In the afternoon, you come around and keep us company for a while, stretching your arms and legs in your little towelling playsuit, adopting coquettish poses and making those facial contortions that we interpret as smiles. You put on another 100 grams, to take you back up beyond the 2.6 kilogram mark. It makes us feel a lot better about yesterday's tantrum.

OCTOBER 18

Peanut, it's so wrong that you're not here at home with us. I lie in bed with Helen and I'm constantly aware that something is missing. I have a sense of family, a physical sense, but no real experience of it yet. It's like owning a car I can't drive.

Meanwhile, we're entering the psychological zone one of the nurses warned us about a few weeks ago. When the hardest corner is turned, when parents feel they're through the worst of it, they get spacey and disconnected, drifting through the days. Now that you're putting on weight and looking better again, we both seem to have relaxed. Helen's quarrelsome chest is behaving itself and we're in some sort of thought-free groove.

As we get out and about, we keep running into people we know. We tramp through the routine, giving them the rundown of what has happened, accepting their sympathy and concern. Sooner or later, whoever we're talking to shakes their head and says, 'It's a pretty tough way to come into the world, isn't it?'

For some reason, it seems to surprise me whenever I hear it. I don't think like that. I think you were born a flawed gem. But isn't everyone? Other people's flaws may not be so easy to see. And maybe, if there's any sort of balance in life, what you're going through now means you won't have to face something later on. Maybe you'll be smarter than most. Maybe you'll be lucky in love. Maybe you'll be a hell of a cook. Maybe, while you're going through these tribulations, your karma bank is filling up every day.

All I know is that I don't feel unlucky as a parent. I would wish better for you, but I wouldn't call this the ordeal that it seems from the outside. There is so much on the credit side of the ledger. I have been able to watch you growing stronger every day, to feel your resilience, your strength of will, your calm, the power of your soul, for want of a better word. I am so proud to be your father, so full of love and admiration, so inspired by the last six weeks. I usually don't hold to the theory that whatever doesn't kill us makes us stronger, but in this case, I think we three—your mother, you and me—have all grown through this, have all received something special for our troubles.

If nothing else, we have learned valuable parenting skills from the nurses: how to swaddle you, how to calm you, when to get scared and when not to. Tonight we think we saw you suffering from reflux. Every few minutes you'd buck and kick and cry out (as much as your still open vocal cords would allow—they haven't recovered yet from the ventilator tube keeping them apart), before quietening down again. We have been warned all along that reflux will be a problem. We were glad to see it happen first in the ward. By the time we have to deal with it on our own, we'll be used to it.

OCTOBER 19
Sunday, six weeks

You have such serious, intent expressions. Vicki, who has been nursing you these past three afternoons, is convinced you are trying to tell us something, confused at your inability to communicate. And she's probably right—most of the time you look as if you're annoyed at not having the gift of speech. You look as if there are questions forming, things you'd like to ask, such as, 'Where am I and how the heck did I get here?' That thing they call a personality is slowly coalescing. It's like a sculpture—every morning there seems to be another chisel mark.

OCTOBER 20

Beach day at the ward. Over the weekend, the nurses worked double time to spruce the place up, painting seashore scenes on the windows, gluing shells to the doors, making a giant underwater scene for the desk and crafting a wave of blue balloons and cellophane next to the door. Today, they dress in lifesaver outfits with caps and zinc cream across their noses. You sit serenely in the middle of the chaos, surveying the scene from your bouncinette, in your red and yellow lifesaver hat.

For 24 hours, our ward represents Australia. ICU is Ireland, with its offices painted to resemble pubs and fish and chips shops, its equipment trolleys decorated as country cottages. It is ward against ward, competing for the Best Dressed prize (an upstairs Egypt ward wins, but I reckon they cheat).

Performers and celebrities wander the corridors, chatting with staff, patients and parents. And for a while at least, we all pretend we are somewhere else, living a more fabulous life. I watch as the nurses work twice as hard as usual to keep the good cheer happening. They will be exhausted tonight, but it will have been worth it.

Dr Ian comes past to see how you are (you're still putting on weight and still being bothered by reflux, usually around six in the evening). 'I'm predicting the leak has healed,' he says just before he leaves. 'We'll find out on Wednesday.' (The dilation has been put back.) It's the first time I have ever heard him say anything incautious. After two months of shrugs and silences and an overwhelming disinclination to predict any sort of outcome, he has finally let one through.

OCTOBER 21

I buy you two outfits today. The ladies in the kiddy fashion shop want to know everything, particularly when I explain that I need things which button up the front, to allow tubes to fit. (See, even now you're hard to shop for.) Helen has already warned me on a number of occasions about spoiling you. I reckon her odds of stopping it are pretty low. Still, maybe I'll discover some previously hidden reserves of restraint. And maybe you'll grow wings.

OCTOBER 22

Dilation. Keeping perfectly to hospital time, your 9 am appointment happens at 10.30, by which time we are all mightily bored with the radiology reception area. It's okay for you. You can just nod off and everyone cheers. When we do it, we're liable to be hauled off as unfit parents.

It's back into the lead jacket for me (so shapely, so flattering) as we hold you down on the table and Dr John pushes the guide wire down your throat. Strangely, you don't complain much, though when the tube is threaded over the top of the wire, you bring up floods of spit. Dr John fiddles with the wire, twisting and turning it, trying to find a way through the stricture. Some barium is pumped in to highlight a passage he can aim at. He is unsure if he can see a leak.

The balloon is inserted and inflated. I look up at the screen, still holding both your hands. (Are you getting sweaty palms or is it me?) The stricture has shrunk back a little from last week, but not as much as feared. After three dilations, the balloon is up to a diameter of 6 millimetres—last week he didn't take it further than four. I can hear Dr Ian from the other side of the room, excitedly talking to Helen. Dr John injects a little more barium and we watch it go straight down to the stomach. No leak at all. The cavity of air is still there, but much smaller.

You handle the whole process surprisingly well, with a composure that only deserts you in the really icky bits. Once or twice, you even nod off during the lulls, closing your eyes and drifting away.

After consultation with Dr Ian, Dr John returns to change the jejunal tube. The doctors want to try a bigger tube there, to keep the wound open while they have a special tube sent over from the USA. It will have two smaller tubes inside it, one going into the jejunum and one finishing in the stomach. With that in place, you could be fed into your intestine, your stomach, or both. You could have your stomach drained to control reflux. It would allow a lot of flexibility. Milk could slowly be introduced by your mouth, with most of your feed coming in down below. That way, the change would be gradual. But the hole in your abdominal wall must be kept open long enough to put the tube in when it arrives. So today's tube is a placemarker.

You recover quickly and well. Last week, you had 24 hours of discomfort. Today, you go out like a lamb the second we take you out of the radiology unit.

And for those doubters, like your grandfather, who think you really can't have mastered the smile muscles yet, well, this afternoon you prove them wrong. You beam up at us, your hands waving, your eyes wide and happy, your mouth curled in something that has not a trace of doubt about its description. Not a trace.

OCTOBER 23

10.30 pm. It's quiet in the study. All I can hear is the distant swoosh-swoosh, inhale–exhale of the breast pump and the occasional four letter word from Helen as she coaxes precious fluid from her argumentative mammaries.

Our main worry now is the reflux. Since you discovered it a few days ago, it seems to be getting worse, despite the fact that you're on two types of drugs to combat it. It wakes you during the day. You bob in and out of sleep like a boat on the ocean waves. Every few minutes you choke and flail and screw yourself up tight, and then just as suddenly, it passes, leaving your body flat and still and calm. Sometimes you threaten to bring something up, but it doesn't happen.

Dr Barry explains that he and Dr Ian have been discussing the concept of trying to test your oesophagus with a little milk. But they're not entirely in agreement. Dr Barry wants to be absolutely certain that the leak has healed before attempting it. He doesn't want to run the risk of infection in your chest. Dr Ian is feeling confident that the leak *has* healed. We figure that between the two of them, they will find a compromise.

Dr Barry tells us that he expects we will be in hospital for at least another four weeks. The gastrostomy tube has to be ordered and will take a fortnight to arrive. It may well be that by the time it gets here, we won't have much need for it.

He tells us that when you returned from radiology yesterday, the nurse found a louse crawling across you. Helen is shocked. No-one seems to know where it could have come from. It means they have to paint you with a treatment and leave it on for eight hours. While they are doing this, you finally get your action working and manage to vomit. It is mostly milk. At least getting rid of it seems to make you happier. You settle straight back to sleep and barely move or gurgle for the next three hours.

I pick up some photos on the way home. It's funny. When we got our first roll of film back, we were ecstatic about what we saw. We were grateful that the person was recognisable amongst all the machinery. But now, with no tubes, the pictures don't seem to do you justice. Part of the reason is that they've all been taken with the deadening flash. You're nearly seven weeks old and you've haven't been out in the air yet, except for the 5 metres from the hospital door to the transport van when you were two hours old. I wish we could just wrap you up and take you down to the beach.

October 24

The vomiting continues. You oblige by demonstrating the art shortly after I pick you up in the morning, your fifth expulsion since midnight. There is general agreement that it shouldn't be quite so regular and you are booked in for X-rays this afternoon. The theory is that the new tube had slipped and blocked the passage, stopping your stomach from emptying into the intestines.

I spend the morning tying to calm you and keep you asleep. At the X-ray, Dr John injects some contrast liquid into your system, which fails to get past the duodenum— there is a blockage. He takes the gastrostomy tube out. He says he suspects that the bigger tube may have caused an irritated swelling. With the tube out, the contrast goes through, but Dr John thinks you should have a few days without a jejunal tube, even a smaller one like before, to allow you to recover.

So you're back on TPN for three days, with Helen having to freeze or throw away the milk she's expressing. (As you might expect, she's not exactly happy about it.) Dr John put a gastrostomy tube into your stomach, held in place with a balloon, to drain your gastric juices and avoid them refluxing. You look like you did a few weeks ago. Two steps forward, one step back.

At a pre-auction showing of some modern furniture tonight (Helen's love), we run into various people we haven't seen for months. It feels odd to be out in public, away from the hospital universe. We see Andrew and Hannah, who is somewhere around the seventh month of her pregnancy. She says her masseuse told her today that she was the most relaxed pregnant woman she'd ever met.

October 25

Janina arrives for the weekend, to have her first cuddle. Helen bursts into tears, saying, 'I didn't want you to see her this way, I wanted you to see her at her best.' It's not that you're not gorgeous today, it's just that you're not happy. Your wide blue eyes are clouded.

A couple of hours later, the stoma bag begins to leak. The tube coming out of your stomach wound has to pass through the wall of the bag—it's hard to get the seal right. You have been impossible to settle all day and the leak is more than Helen, upset about you not getting milk, can bear. She insists that something be done and makes the registrar call Dr Ian, who says if the tube is giving us that much trouble, to take it out and let the wound drain into the bag on its own until Dr John can put a smaller tube back in.

OCTOBER 26
Sunday, seven weeks

I wake up in a foul and grumpy mood. I'm rude and surly to Helen and her mother. I behave like a total bastard and fail to apologise. I make myself a cup of tea and hide downstairs for an hour. Then, following time-honoured male tradition, I run away. I need some time on my own. I've always liked solitude and there's been precious little of it these past few months.

Dr Ian visits in the morning, but as he rises from his bed about an hour before the roosters stir, we miss him. According to the nurse, he is happy with the way the wound is draining, but annoyed about Dr Barry's insistence that you not be fed through the mouth. This is the first time that the two people in charge of your case have not agreed on direction, or at least, the first time we've been aware of it. We know they're both holding to their views based on a desire to offer the best and most appropriate treatment, but how are we meant to know who is right? One of the problems of hospital is that there are different people looking after different aspects of the care—there's no court of appeal when they disagree.

Dr Ian wrote very pointedly in your notes that in his opinion, your oesophagus should be tested. He insisted that you be given glucose and water, just a few millilitres. You have 5ml at 8 am, which causes you to cough and splutter. Not only do you have to learn to coordinate your mouth and throat muscles, but we're still pretty sure your vocal cords have not closed up yet (you open your mouth to cry and nothing comes out), so it's hard for you to stop fluids going down your windpipe. At midday, Nurse Pippa tries again, takes her time and manages to get 10ml down, most of which promptly leaks into the stoma bag. When I try at 5 pm, you take a few drops, then gag and choke.

OCTOBER 27

The speech pathologist puts her finger in your mouth, traces around your gumline, teases your lips and proclaims you to be in pretty good shape, with a strong sucking reflex for a girl who hasn't actually had a breast in her mouth. The nurses have been worried that you might need some help keeping your mouth sensitive and developing your muscles and abilities.

The pathologist tries to get you to drink some more glucose, carefully and slowly alternating the bottle with a dummy. She uses a one-way teat, which will only give fluid when you suck. You take a little on board, but grow distressed fairly quickly.

Dr Ian shows up in the late afternoon with his entourage of registrars and students (surgeons have disciples who hang off their every word). He immediately flips your notes over and begins to draw. As always. 'You know me. Just give me a pen and paper.' He thinks that the wound on your stomach is healing over so quickly that we shouldn't attempt to put any kind of tube in that way. He has spoken to Dr John and favours the idea of a naso-gastric tube, a tiny, thin tube which would go, as the name suggests, into one of your nostrils and then snake its way down into your stomach. Or, hopefully, your duodenum. That way, we could get you back onto mother's milk as soon as possible, and home in perhaps a shorter time than we've been led to expect.

You will have another dilation either tomorrow or Wednesday. The naso-gastric tube will go in at the same time. We're hoping it's tomorrow. We want you back on milk as quickly as possible.

Helen and her mother have been out buying picture frames. I grew up in a house without photos, in a family which had some kind of supernatural aversion to them. Now everywhere I look in the house, there are little pictures of you. In a way, they're like icons, objects of routine prayer.

OCTOBER 28

We spend the entire day trying to calm you, but you don't make it into the safe haven of sleep for more than a few minutes. The rest of the time, you are crying and screwing your face up. We think it is reflux. We think it is wind. We think it is a full nappy. We think it is Satan toying with us.

Dr Ian comes flapping in wearing his theatre gown at

4 pm, saying, 'Well, what happened?', apologising for not making the dilation. He's had, he says, a hell of an afternoon. So has the radiology department—its machines have broken down and the dilation has been rescheduled for tomorrow.

Dr Ian says he's spoken with Dr Barry. They have agreed that the best solution is to try to place a naso-gastric tube in such a way that it ends in your jejunum, where the last feeding tube was. If that isn't possible, it will finish in the stomach. You will be put on a continuous drip feed through it, instead of a bolus (meal) feed. They can't risk your stomach filling up and exacerbating the reflux problems. The drip feed will push through tiny amounts.

He says he is happy about the fact that you have taken some glucose on board, even though it hasn't been the smoothest of passages for the fluid. He suggests that Helen try offering you the breast, not as a way of feeding you, but to get you used to it, to let you taste milk. He says it in such an offhand, casual way that we could have been forgiven for missing the significance. But I look over at Helen and see she's gone white. She doesn't look ready, not so soon after watching you cough and gag and splutter about water. She isn't looking for that kind of rejection.

Dr Barry arrives a little later. He is still convinced that it's imperative for us to treat you as a severe reflux patient until proven otherwise. You're on two drugs to help: Cisapride, which makes the muscles push food through, and Ranitidine, which lowers the pH of your stomach so that whatever does make it back up is less acidic, less of a threat to your oesophagus.

Dr Barry explains that reflux happens because pressure in the stomach forces material back up the oesophagus. He makes it fairly clear that you will have this problem for some years. If it's serious, it may be many years. We have no way of knowing yet. This makes me realise how much we continue to focus on each day. People ask me what the long-term prognosis is and I just fob them off with something simple like, 'Well, we're going to have a pretty tough first year, an easier second one, an easier third one, and so on. By the time she's old enough to understand what has happened, it shouldn't be much of a problem.' Maybe that's true and maybe it isn't. To be honest, I really have little idea of what life will look like in three months' time, let alone in three years.

I come back from putting away the breast pump tonight to find Helen sitting with you in her lap, one of her nipples in your mouth. She didn't tell me she was going to do it. I'm not even sure she thought about it until the second of the decision. Thankfully, you don't choke, you don't splutter, you don't cry and you don't scream. You just aren't interested.

Meanwhile, unknown to Helen, I had run into Andrew in the foyer at lunchtime. I was surprised to see him (but not surprised enough to stop and think), slapped him on the shoulder and said, 'Andrew, what are you doing here?' He looked at me and said nothing for a few seconds and then, his voice trembling, 'The baby has died.' The floor fell away.

What could I say? Hannah became pregnant a few months after Helen. They were our only friends going through it at the same time. Their baby boy died yesterday, in his seventh month, in utero. When Andrew told me that they were inducing labour this afternoon, in the Women's Hospital next door, I realised that he couldn't believe the words were coming out of his mouth. He couldn't believe I was hearing them. I couldn't either. I put an arm around him, but he probably couldn't feel it.

I didn't tell Helen until we were on our way home in the evening. I didn't want to upset her any more—she was having a fairly tough day with you. I even reasoned to myself that I shouldn't tell her until she had finished most of her expressing for the day—tension and distress make her flow seize up. After I told her, we sat in the local Turkish pizza joint. 'I just never thought life would be this hard,' Helen said. She told me later that she felt as if her heart had been torn out.

OCTOBER 29

Helen leaves a card for Andrew and Hannah at the Women's Hospital. They're not taking visitors. Helen is still in shock—she's taken the news very hard. Her milk production froze last night, indexed, as usual, to her emotional state. She had a painful, difficult, badly disrupted night. A couple of times today I catch her with a tear in the corner of her eye.

After being miserable yesterday, you pull the angel card out of the deck. With the guidance of speech pathologist Denise, I get you to drink 11 millilitres of glucose and water, with just a little cough here and there, and no distress. We are all proud of ourselves.

In the afternoon, you cope remarkably well with another

dilation. Dr John slides the balloon tube into place easily. Your oesophagus is about 4 millimetres wide, a major improvement. He inflates the balloon four times, dilating it to 6mm each time. Next time, he says, he'll try the 8mm balloon. The oesophagus of a normal baby is about 10 millimetres at this age, but we're not pushing to make yours that big. Eight would be fabulous. And there is no leak at all.

After the dilation, Dr John threads a soft plastic tube through your nose, down your oesophagus and into your stomach. He tries to get it into your jejunum, but isn't sure exactly how successful he is. We'll know tomorrow sometime, when we take another X-ray. The tube doesn't upset you anywhere near as much as we thought it would (it doesn't affect your ability to swallow), and back at the ward, you are calm, awake and playful. I try giving you more glucose and this time you take almost 15ml. Helen gives you the last five of those. You are even better than this morning, taking big swallows, coordinating your sucking and swallowing.

OCTOBER 30

BABY BULLETIN III—Live Hard With A Vengeance
HAVE YOU GOT THE LITTLE CRITTER HOME YET?
Nope. Seven and a half weeks later and we're still indoors. Naomi's sitting there in her bouncinette in her own room, pretending to run the place. But she's looking really well—alert, smart as a whippet, putting on weight and wearing her own clothes.

WHAT'S BEEN HAPPENING?

Well, mostly what we've been concentrating on is dilating her oesophagus. So far, we've had three dilations and Naomi's been responding extremely well. Even the unpleasantness of the actual procedure (about half an hour) doesn't seem to linger with her any more. The doctors are 'thrilled'—her progress is much better than anticipated.

The tube that was feeding milk into her intestine came out a week ago. We replaced it, but her body basically rejected the new tube. So we've pulled all the tubes out of her stomach and we're letting the hole in her abdominal wall heal over, which is a relief for all of us—it had been taking a battering these past few weeks.

Now she has a soft tube which threads down her nasal passage, through her oesophagus and into the stomach. This morning we arrived at the hospital to find that the end of it had worked its way through the hole and was poking out of her stomach wound into the bag which is there to drain leakage. Weird. Glad I hadn't eaten breakfast. Anyway, it's back in place and she's being fed a small amount of breast milk, with a plan to increase it gradually.

WHAT DOES SHE GET FROM HER PARENTS?

She appears to have her mother's chin and her father's bowel movements. Helen can see all sorts of stuff, but I just nod when she points them out. I say, 'Yes, by golly, you're right,' but I can't see any of it. She looks like Naomi to me.

WHAT'S NEXT?

Well, it seems you swap one set of problems for another, decreasing in gravity each time. Our next major question mark is reflux. We're pretty certain, because of the effects on her pipes, that we will have a seriously vomiting baby on our hands once we start feeding her into her stomach. There are physical and chemical ways to help deal with that when and if it happens. We're just waiting to gauge the extent of it. If it surprises us all by not being bad, we may be allowed to all come home soon (with naso-gastric tube and feeding pump). That's a thought so odd that we're not really taking it seriously until it happens. If the reflux is bad, who knows?

WHEN WILL SHE FEED LIKE NORMAL?

Not for some weeks/months yet. But we have been working hard lately to teach her the suck–swallow reflex. We're trying her out with glucose and water out of a bottle with a special slow teat. She gets more proficient every day. Today she had two sessions and didn't even cough, let alone go through the whole gagging/spluttering/distress performance of a few days ago. Helen tried her out on the breast this morning, but collapsed in a fit of giggles when Naomi clamped down—Mum didn't think it would feel so strange.

While we're on the subject of feeding, I met a mother in the ward a few weeks ago whose baby, just under a year old, was heading home after having an operation on the valve in his stomach. He had been a really sweet and well-behaved kid in the ward and I said so to her. She said yes, but he was not so happy about having to take a dietary step backwards and return to mushy foods, to protect the recovering area. 'Oh,' I said facetiously, 'so no more hamburgers then?' 'No,' she replied, 'and he loves his McDonald's.'

YOU MUST BE LOOKING FORWARD TO GETTING HER HOME?
Yes, but we'll have to wean ourselves away from the hospital. I feel like we too have become institutionalised. I'm trying to train myself to stop reflexively looking at her monitors every time she complains.

OCTOBER 31
At Helen's insistence, I give myself a morning off the hospital routine. She calls to say you are fine. You have a bath and a nappy change, get on and off the scales (a nice little increase again; you'll hit the 3 kilo mark soon), and play with Mum. The nurses take your stoma bag away— anything coming out of the stomach wound is being soaked up by a gauze dressing. It's about time that bit of you got some air.

Dr Ian passes through, urging Helen to try feeding you milk from the bottle. We somehow have the feeling that we're almost being played off by the doctors.

In the afternoon, you grizzle and we call Dr Barry to ask if you could get a little more food. You're on 10ml of milk, 7ml of TPN and 1.4ml of lipids every hour. A fortnight ago you were on 20ml of milk. We think you might be hungry. As it turns out, you aren't. Your naso-gastric tube has clogged and is annoying you—perhaps it is sticking into you somewhere. Dr Barry decides to change it, which is most unpleasant for you, particularly as it takes three attempts to find the right spot.

The doctor says we can try feeding you a little milk orally. Ten millilitres here or there will not overtax your system. We are just about to give it a go when you fall asleep, exhausted after the tube procedure. We decide to give up for the day when you wake bright and playful. I slide a little finger into your mouth and you suck ferociously, so we prop you up on Helen's lap, retrieve the bottle with her milk in it and she tentatively gives you its teat. You grab it, suck and begin to swallow. In no time at all you've taken almost all of it. 'She really likes it,' says Helen, with not a little surprise in her voice and a tear in her eye. She has a smile you couldn't break with a hammer.

November

Helen is lying in bed. 'I want her home now,' she says. 'I want to chat to her. I want to tell her what I'm doing, what she's doing. I want her home now.' The truth is, it's getting close enough for us to smell it. I'd been thinking the idea would scare me, that getting you out of the hospital after so long would feel like freefall. It still might, but I don't care. I want to try it.

You have a littlish vomit at 9 am. Nobody seems too worried. After all, babies chuck. The alarm bells won't go off until you do it more often than most. The problem we do have is that the feeding tube keeps blocking. Because of your size and the delicacy of your system, they're using a special tube, so small and so soft that blockage is inevitable. We don't have to replace it today—the regular flushing with saline works—but it will probably have to be replaced during the week. Certainly, it's not dependable enough to consider bringing you home. A bigger, stronger tube will be needed.

I sit for an hour with you slumbering, radiating heat into my lap. Helen can tuck you into the crook of her elbow, her short arms keeping you straight, her breasts giving her something to lean you against. When I attempt the same position, it's much more awkward and ungainly. But my thigh is a great length to stretch you along. So I cross my legs, rest your head on my knee and tuck your feet into my belly.

That way, I can look down at you, keep track of the changing topography of your sleeping face. The veins, the tiny tributaries on the deltas of your eyelids. The flecks of dry skin on your forehead. The long, sensual curve of your eyelashes. The curls on your left temple, lifting away, defying gravity, heading for the sky. The double chin that arrives as you tuck your head down. The slight downward tilt of the corners of your mouth, which disappears the moment you wake ...

NOVEMBER 2
Sunday, eight weeks

Helen has been much calmer in the last couple of days. It's not just the fact that fewer stressful things are happening, that her breasts are behaving. 'I just feel a lot more confident about handling her,' she says when I ask. 'I understand what she's trying to say now. When she cries, I know why she's crying.'

Meanwhile, you've made it to 20 millilitres an hour. The TPN and lipids are gone. Your central line has been capped again and the only thing going into your body is milk. You yank the tube out of your nose this morning when the nurse isn't looking. It goes back in.

You absolutely grab at the bottle, taking 15 and then 20ml, as much as we are allowed to give you (a little bit more really—we cheat). It amazes me how quickly you've been able to pick this up; only a week ago people were telling us that stimulating your suck and swallow reflex might be a real difficulty. There must be something satisfying about being fed orally. Helen tries her nipple again a couple of times, but it seems to confuse and upset you. Dr Ian says you may never take the breast and that Helen should not think less of herself if that happens.

We visit Hannah and Andrew in the afternoon. They are showing remarkable spirit. They appear, from the outside at least, to be coping magnificently, helping each other, talking about it, making sure nothing gets bottled up and turned into bitterness. I could only wish for such grace in similar circumstances.

It makes me think about the luck we have. So many other fathers are back at work a few days after their child is born. I've spent the first eight weeks of your life beside you, watching all the tiny changes taking place. I've been able to see your courage, your strength. For most people, the all-important Firsts happen in a tumble of days. The first cuddle. The first feed. The first bath. With us, every one of those things has been longed for, yearned for, worked for and waited for. As each one happens, we celebrate. For many couples, these events are a blur, crashing one on top of the other. We have been forced to go slowly. And maybe, just maybe, the calibrations of our joy are a little finer because of that. Maybe we are stopping to smell every rose. Or maybe I'm fooling myself.

NOVEMBER 3

A big adventure. For the first time since the day of your birth, you feel the sun on your face and breathe air that hasn't arrived via the air-conditioning duct. Now that the gastrostomy wound is healing up, the chances of you spreading MRSA are much, much lower. So after weighing you (2.865kg) and washing you (you hate that) and feeding you (fun), we wrap you up, unplug your monitors and plonk you into the stroller. We only have to take Kangaroo

Pump, the machine that feeds you the milk in its gradual drip style (don't ask why it's named after the kangaroo— the only reason I can think of is that it does have a kind of pouch on the milk bag). So while I wheel that along on its wobbly stand, Helen pushes the stroller and we escape.

Down the corridor, into the lift, across the new café, through the glass door to the courtyard and fresh air. You squint at the light, even without the sun directly in your eyes. Tears form. You aren't really sure what is happening. Then a breeze blows up and the feeling of wind on your face startles you. We thought it might invigorate you, but you fall asleep almost immediately, having been wide awake indoors.

We sit and eat our sandwiches, trying to pretend we aren't just a little nervous about having you to ourselves. Twenty metres away, jackhammers break the ground for a new building. It doesn't bother you at all, which is perhaps just as well, because our neighbours have recently had plans go through council to renovate their house next year.

After half an hour, it's back inside and upstairs, to the ICU, where several nurses are there to say hello. They derive such obvious joy from seeing patients improve. It's a win-win-win situation. You get attention. We get reflected parental glory and the nurses get to see the results of their hard work.

November 4

There, in your medical notes, in the big red folder that sits out on the admin desk, are the words written in the scrawly hand of Dr Ian: 'No need for an oesophageal dilation this week. Central line out tomorrow. Plan for d/c this weekend.'

d/c?

I look at it twice, then a third time, before realising it means 'discharge'. They're seriously thinking of sending the three of us home. A few minutes later, sitting in a chair in your room, I look around. The pulse and blood oxygen monitor went yesterday. The pumps that supplied the drugs, TPN and lipids have gone, leaving only the Kangaroo. The central line, your last remaining surgical legacy, is due to come out. The naso-gastric tube may be invasive, but at least it follows the path that nature intended. So it really is down to you and the milk and the tube.

We'll have to take you home with the pump and a lot of complicated feeding schedules. We will have to be up in the middle of the night to give you medicine and add milk to the pump bag. We'll have to learn how to flush it when it is blocked. But these seem like small obstacles, like nothing.

We're taking more control of you as each day goes on, insisting on doing everything we can, from changing the pump bag to washing and weighing you. We take you down to the café again today, with the same response: 'What's this air stuff? I'm going to sleep.'

NOVEMBER 5

You pull out your tube again this morning, when the nurses have their backs turned. When Helen arrives at nine o'clock, it has been out for three hours. You take one look at her, poke your tongue out and smile a big cheeky smile. You're a minx.

Helen says it's just another example of you wanting to do it all yourself. Impatient. Pushy. Determined to get on with things. The nurses put another tube down. Helen feeds you twice from the bottle, 15 and 20ml. You have little catnaps (kitten naps) between each. When I arrive at lunchtime, the two of you are blissed out, staring at each other.

We wash and weigh you, take you out for a short stroll, then let you sleep for a couple of hours. It is agreed that we should try to give you more bottle feeds. The idea is to turn the continuous drip pump off for a while, then put a decent amount (a bolus) down your throat and see what happens. Overall, you're meant to be getting about 20ml per hour. So if we turn the machine off for two hours, we can give you 40ml in the middle of that period.

There are four basic reasons for reflux, as I learn from a convenient wall chart this afternoon: the length of the newborn oesophagus is short; the stomach has a low capacity; peristaltic function is not smooth or easily controlled; and the sphincter at the junction of the oesophagus and the stomach is immature. All four are exacerbated by your medical condition.

We try the 40ml feed at about 5 pm. You gulp and slurp and take all but a couple of millilitres, but your stomach has never been so full before and it makes you grizzly. Still, you keep it all down. In a week of feeding you into your stomach, you've vomited only once. No-one seems to be able to quite believe it. Even Dr Barry, who has acknowledged his cautiousness all along, laughingly says he might have been too hardline.

NOVEMBER 6

Today's task is to turn the pump off and see if I can get you to take 40ml feeds at two-hourly intervals. Your first feed is at eleven, an hour after the machine stops. You take 40ml. At 1, 3 and 5 pm, you take 35, 40 and 32ml. A two-hourly feed is exhausting for both of us. Because your stomach is so small, it fills up quickly. Feeding you 40ml can take almost an hour, which leaves half an hour to burp and settle you, keeping you carefully upright to ward off reflux. Then there's fifteen minutes to rest and fifteen minutes to prepare for the next round.

But everything stays down. I really expected that if we turned your pump off for eight hours and fed you in larger doses, you'd more than struggle with it. As it is, you have wind and occasionally cough, but hang onto the lot.

Dr Ian is so impressed that he urges us to take the naso-gastric tube out and keep bottle feeding. Sure. Two-hourly feeds around the clock. I don't think any of us is ready for that yet. When we get you up to three-hourly feeds, maybe, but not this early. Dr Ian is a dog straining at the leash. Dr Barry suggests we take it a little easier.

In a moment of peace in the late afternoon, while you are sleeping, your mother looks up from the bouncinette and says, 'You know, when I look at her I keep remembering the ultrasound pictures, the shape of her face, the half moon curve of her forehead.' When we get home, I dig the pictures out of one of the boxes we still haven't unpacked, and she's right. They always told us that ultrasound was a very inexact science, but the two pictures we have of your face are startling. They look so similar to the way you look now that they're almost spooky.

November 7

At 9 am you hook your finger in and jerk the tube out again. The nurse is actually holding you at the time, but you are so quick that she can't do anything to stop you. As they say in the tube-pulling business, you're good.

The removal spurs everyone—surgeons, paediatricians, dietitian, lactation consultant—to come up with a feeding plan that will hopefully move us slowly away from the tube and towards the bottle, without placing too much stress on your system. The plan involves giving you a bottle with 40ml, then following two hours later with 40ml via the tube (to give parents a break too), then a bottle two hours later and so on. For six hours in the middle of the night, you will go back to continuous feed, to give everyone, including you, a rest. This way, you'll be getting bolus feeds for eighteen hours, long enough for you to get used to them.

Of course, we have to run this program. The better you get, the more we take on a vaguely nursey role. I guess this is partly because they are beginning the transition too, trying to make sure we're capable of looking after you on our own. This has its up and down sides. On the one hand, it's good to have a feeding plan to work to. On the other, we're now almost nine weeks into the hospital trip, and the physical demands on us are increasing at a time when we're really feeling the exhaustion. Helen has what we think is a cold (and what we are praying is not the beginning of mastitis). I feel as if we could both do with a holiday before we get you home. But it wouldn't be a holiday without you, would it?

You're two months old today. We thought a cake would be useless, so we gave you something you actually needed, the newborn equivalent of a nice pair of socks—a pair of inoculations, one jab in each thigh.

November 8

This morning you have a bolus feed, 45ml down the tube, which leaks straight out the gastrostomy wound. We thought it had closed, but your nightie is green and sodden and your skin red from the acid. It completely throws me. I look at it and go instantly light-headed. Thoughts come tumbling in. Will it mean you can't feed? Will it mean you have to go back to the TPN? Is the end of the tube pushing against the wound from the inside, trying to get out again? Dr Anthony, the surgical registrar, tells us not to worry, that these things just happen. He says that wounds like this heal over at the surface, but take longer to effect a complete recovery. It's not uncommon for them to leak, particularly as we put more pressure on your stomach.

You cope with the feeding schedule, though your bottle limit is about 30ml before you get tired. We put any leftovers down the tube. Still, a week ago we were excited to get you to take 10 or 15ml. And tonight, Helen puts her nipple in your mouth before your feed is due, and you not only suck, but manage to get milk and swallow.

Another first, and one that has made a not insignificant contribution to the positive mood in this household.

The most interesting thing about the feeding change is that you now actually have time to get hungry. Because there was always milk in your system before, you were never quite hungry, never fully satiated. Now, when your stomach is empty, the milk hits your system like a freight train. There's a clear and obvious milk rush, your eyes rolling, your body relaxing. You look stoned.

NOVEMBER 9
Sunday, nine weeks

It's 1.13 am, which I guess makes it Monday, November 10, but I think you can give me a little leeway. I'm home so late because I went to see a Canadian singer, Ron Sexsmith. Ron's album, by the way, was playing in the car on the way to the hospital way back on July 11, when the haemorrhage happened and our world started its crazy axis tilt. His tangential relationship to you helped lessen the guilt about going out. And really, I had to go. Helen and I are starting to get cabin fever, trapped in the hospital. And before you complain that you have it much worse, you spent five weeks drugged to the gills on morphine. And anyway, the rest of the world could be one big hospital, as far as you know.

You sleep lightly and fretfully during the day, wake, then fight reflux for an hour in the evening before falling asleep in my arms. You won't be put on a bed or let me sit. I have to carry you, talking to you, distracting you with ward landmarks: the fish mobile in the playroom, the pot plants. What finally gets you into slumber is a gentle waltz as the shadows lengthen and the sun slides below the horizon. For a girl whose feet are still a metre and a half from the floor, you dance surprisingly well.

NOVEMBER 10

You lie there in your lemon print pyjamas, waving your arms. Conducting a silent symphony, your face a portrait of concentration. Practising karate moves, chopping left, then right. Impersonating a windmill. Clawing at the air. Who knows which it is?

It's a charming miniature ballet, this collection of seemingly choreographed movements. Until today, it's looked like nothing more than stretching, like you extending your limbs to see how it feels, pushing the muscles a little further each time, learning to use what you've been given. But this morning, when I hold a tiny silver rattle in front of you (sent back from Mexico by Shelli-Anne and another friend, Monique, it makes a magical tinkle, the kind of noise that should accompany the sprinkling of fairy dust), you grab it. You've reached over and touched a rattle in front of you before, but this time you get a firm grip, take it out of my hand and make it sing for you.

Meanwhile, there's a general feeling that the move to bottle and bolus feed is tiring you out, so we reduce the feeds, putting you back on the continuous drip for longer.

NOVEMBER 11

I meet a guy, tall, wiry, unshaven, nervous, on the fire escape stairs behind the ward. He is fidgeting his way through a quick cigarette, his five-year-old son inside awaiting surgery tomorrow to correct a stomach valve problem. It's not the same problem as yours, but it has similarities. This man had to cope with his baby being in ICU for a month at birth too. He tells me how much he hates it in the hospital, how every second he has to spend here is a bad second. He says he can't handle it, never has been able to. He went loco when his boy was in ICU, turned to drink and dope and tried to deny the whole thing was happening.

He looks scared and upset. I wonder if it's a male thing. We're just not taught to accept bodily weakness. We're so external, so in denial of the fact that we actually have bodily interiors, that maybe we find it hard to accept what can happen in there. We find it hard to cope with the concept of physical frailty. Maybe we just can't bear the thought of it all. And if so, why aren't I freaking out more?

Actually, I've noticed over the last few months that the emotional equilibrium of your parents' relationship has changed. When there was nothing to worry about, I was the worrier. Now, it's Helen. She was the calm one during the pregnancy. I have been the calm one since the birth. Friends sometimes ask why I have not lost control more. I don't feel I have the right to. I can't afford to fall apart or lose grip while there is so much still to be done. Coping is not a question of choice.

NOVEMBER 12

You've started to put on a little weight—2.925 kilograms (the cake and candles are still on hold for the 3 kilo mark).

You're not moving fast, and the hope of getting you off the pump is not coming much closer, but forward is forward. The central line is taken out today, another plus.

Another dilation this afternoon. I send Helen home because she is so exhausted—she had expressing troubles through the night and was on the machine at 4.30 am. The good news is that the balloon works well. The bad news is that in the two weeks since the last dilation, your oesophagus has shrunk back a long way. From the 6 millimetre stretch of last time, it is back to 2 millimetres. It is so tight that Dr John has trouble getting the tube through the strictured passage and into place.

Dr Ian comes to see you afterwards. He now feels he should put you under anaesthetic next week and try a different technique, a much stronger one. It's not an operation, more a procedure, but the idea marshals my dread. I hoped we were out of those woods. I thought you were responding to the dilations well enough we wouldn't have to take more drastic steps.

Perhaps it's just that the bigger you grow, the stronger your personality, the more I am able to empathise with your pain. The more you understand it yourself. When you were freshly minted, it didn't seem as if you had much of an awareness of what was going on. You still don't, but you have a lot more than you did then.

Meanwhile, talk of you coming home has resumed. It may be day leave at first. It may be for the weekend. That's about the limit. We could disappear for a couple of days, armed with a feeding schedule, but your condition has to be monitored and the schedule adjusted. If we didn't live so close to the hospital, they wouldn't be talking about it at all, I guess.

NOVEMBER 13

Helen wakes resolved to have you home, with the 'Enough is enough' determination of someone who won't be stopped. We decide that you should come with us for the weekend. We know how to work the pumps. We know how to handle the drugs. We know how to look after you, how to calm you, how to hold you when the reflux hits.

One by one we tell the hospital experts that it's time, for you and for us. The nurses think it is a good idea. The speech pathologist agrees. So too does the lactation sister. Dr Ian has thought so for a while now. The only nod we have yet to receive is that of Dr Garry, the paediatrician standing in while Dr Barry is away for a fortnight. I feel certain that won't be a problem. It was almost as if they have been waiting for us to insist, as if it's the requisite sign of confidence that makes them think it's okay.

So, weather and acts of God permitting, you are going to come home on Saturday morning (the day after tomorrow) and stay until Monday. We have a 48-hour limit. If we take you for longer than that we lose your bed; it counts as a discharge. It's not a complete release, but it's a start. A big start. I don't know if I can find the words to tell you how happy this will make us. I'm sure we'll be nervous, scared at having you on our own after almost eleven weeks of constant support, but the other side of the ledger completely outweighs those fears. I would wrestle alligators to get you out of this place. There's nothing wrong with the hospital—there's just something horribly wrong with the idea of you being here.

Today is dominated by your first short trip outside, in the stroller, up High Street to a sandwich bar. You are very excited, your eyes wide, trying to take everything in, wondering where the ceilings and walls have gone. Watching you so taken with new sights and sounds, and smells presumably, only strengthens our resolve to have you in your new house, in your own blankets, in your own cot, listening to the birds in the trees out back, cooking smells wafting from the kitchen. You're two months old and you haven't heard real music yet. There's so much to do.

November 14

As I type, I can hear the thin, distant tinkle of the musical mobile, the three bears parading in circles as the lullaby slows down. Your mother is standing downstairs, next to your cot, holding you in her arms, talking you back to the sleep you recently left to have your nappy changed. She is humming and swaying and grinning to herself, muttering sweet nonsense. She is in a state of nervous bliss.

We're at home. I might just write that again. We're at home. Damn that looks good! At around 6.30 pm on a day that is hot, humid and windy, you are carried past the frangipani and over the threshold. You are wearing a new, white outfit bought for the occasion by your mum. You sit in the baby capsule in the lounge room and feel the hot air on your face—it must be a shock after the air-conditioning. Your head swivels from side to side, your eyes wide, finally away from the godawful colour scheme of the hospital. You watch us as we watch you ... now what?

We get the final go ahead to bring you here from Dr Garry this morning. Then, during the day, the head nurse on the ward, another Helen, checks with Admissions and tells us we can bend the rules a little and take you for more than 48 hours. So instead of having to wait until tomorrow morning to pick you up, we liberate you today, bursting with excitement and adrenalin.

What a day. It starts out with you cracking 3 kilos. And not just half-heartedly either. You pork out overnight, tipping the scales at 3.025 kilograms. I walk around looking for nurses to share the good news. I must look like a silly, overproud dad, but I don't care. In the afternoon, a handful of the regulars are there. As promised, Nurse Vicki brings a passionfruit sponge cake in to celebrate. At 6 pm there is a spongey ceremony to acknowledge your landmark—half a dozen nurses shelve their diets for the occasion.

Sheila, the lactation sister, appears to be right. With each incremental weight gain, you seem to be gathering strength. You take to the bottle this morning with gusto. It strikes me, watching you on your mother's lap, just how hard you've been trying to get better all this time, how much you've been pulling us through all this. 'She's a good girl,' Helen says. 'She's a brave, good girl.' What will you be like, I wonder? Will you be fearless, after facing so much, so young? Will you take things in your stride that would stop others? Will you understand that everything is possible? That there will always be people there for you? How much good will come of this?

Helen thrusts a nipple into your mouth and instead of the usual mild dismissiveness, you begin to suck with concentration. She manages to keep the nipple in place and you have a few minutes of drinking success, locked to the breast and finally tasting it the way nature intended. Add to that our gate leave and the day seems impossibly bright.

Tonight is spent trying to hang the milk pump from curtain rods, doorways and whatever we can find as we move you from room to room, arguing about where you'll be the most comfortable. You would no doubt be more comfy if we just left you alone, but you have to grant us a few concessions on the first night home. We can't leave you alone.

You seem happy enough to contemplate your new surroundings before drifting into milk-enhanced slumber. It's after midnight as I type. I've just given you some medicine. In two hours, I'll get out of bed to add some more milk to your pump. In six hours, Helen will rise to feed you before pumping herself. Right now, she's hyper, wandering about the house with a book in her hand. Having coaxed you into sleep, she is trying the same trick on herself, with less success. I really ought to go and lie beside her, help her calm down. We're looking forward to tomorrow, a whole day with you here.

NOVEMBER 15

Like every other parent in the history of the species, we walk like zombies through a next-to-sleepless first night, falling in and out of bed. Not only have we finally become full-time parents, we have also become full-time nurses. In between the medical demands, we lie there listening to you snuffling away, stretching in your sleep, moaning, groaning, occasionally yelping to yourself. So many noises, Peanut. And in the silence of home, they sound magnified. I would swear your vocal strength has doubled in a day.

The pump misbehaves at 5.30 am. By the time we get the problem smoothed out—and it's amazing how dumb and clumsy two people can be at that time of day/night— we are all well and truly awake. By ten o'clock, it feels like afternoon to me.

We spend the day fidgeting, still trying you in different positions, in different places—pram, bouncinette, floor, cot—to see what exactly makes you comfortable. You seem amazed that the entire world is not dominated by a green, purple and blue colour scheme. You're not sure where you are, but you appear content to believe it's somewhere good. Seeing it through your eyes, I am surprised to note how much of the house is wood-brown or white. Your new best friend is the light fitting in the lounge room, which draws a broad smile from you every time it finds its way into your field of vision. I don't get it. It's a pretty nondescript light, but it gives you the jollies. There you are, laughing at our taste already.

When you are awake, you do the happy, playful angel routine, sitting in our laps and widening your eyes, smiling, playing with the rattling toy that is strapped to the pram. If I were the romantic sort, I'd believe you are perfectly happy to see us, your parents, every time you open your eyes, instead of the nurses and doctors. I call my parents. As it happens, my brothers are there, all preparing for a wedding later in the day. It feels good to be able to hold you up to the phone and let them hear you breathing, your blocked little snores. 'Sounds like you've given birth to a pug,' says Paul.

Later, you take milk from the breast again, lying on your side in Helen's lap and sucking away without complaint for five minutes or so. Mostly, however, you sleep. You pass out for more than two hours in the afternoon, wake long enough to be fed and have your nappy changed, and go out again. You're either exhausted from all the upheaval or contented to be here. Or both.

November 16
Sunday, 10 weeks

Things We found Out About You Today

• You appear to think the light fitting in the lounge room is some kind of higher being
• You're a social animal, excited by the presence of new people
• You can roll over
• You really have the hang of this breastfeeding thing, if only for very short periods
• You can clutch a tiny teddy bear to your chest for comfort
• The distance between happy and hysterical can be very short.

Things We Found Out About Us Today

• We find it very hard to concentrate enough on your

needs when there are other people around (distraction makes us clumsy)

• We're losing our language skills. I can't hear properly and Helen appears to have forgotten all nouns. 'Hand me the … ummm'

• Our urge to pick you up whenever you're unhappy is not always right

• We get frustrated when the feeding pump goes wonky, as it seems to do two or three times a day

• We have to be careful not to be too grumpy with each other when it happens.

Friends Pete and Kirsty drop in unannounced late morning, which is good until I take my eye off the ball long enough to pump an entire feed through the plastic tubing and onto the floor instead of into your tummy. Your mother is less than impressed at the waste of her milk. You snooze in Kirsty's lap, oblivious.

Then, having played Dr Jekyll for hours, you let Miss Hyde out of the closet, growing hungry and upset. Before we know it you are caterwauling about the shabby service at this hotel, asking to see the manager and threatening to report us to all the tourism guides. We try to put some milk down the tube, but that only seems to upset you more.

We begin to suspect there might be something wrong— perhaps the tube has somehow looped back up into your oesophagus and is delivering milk to an unintended destination. Like the good nurse I am, I take a sample of fluid from the end of the tube and test its pH on litmus paper, looking for the (appropriate) presence of stomach acids. The first three times, I get nothing. I call the ward and have one of the sisters talk me through the process of flushing the tube and aspirating it. After that, I get the right litmus result. In the meantime, you have calmed down and crashed out in Helen's arms, so we quietly turn the pump back on and finish the feeding.

In the late afternoon, just as we are zoning out, getting that I've-been-up-too-long spaciness, my friend David arrives. While he is here, Tim and Aleks turn up too, bearing armfuls of clothes purchased in the US. Aleks is hesitant about picking up someone so small, and prefers to watch from the lounge as your Uncle Tim cradles you in his lap for the first time. 'I could do this father thing,' he says as they leave.

NOVEMBER 17

You scare us this morning. The second your eleven o'clock bottle finishes, you start coughing and relocate the entire contents of your stomach to the outside of your chest. It's the first time we've seen so much come up so easily. I don't know who is more surprised, you or us. I pick you up to help keep down whatever might be left (not that there could be much). As I hoist you from the bouncinette, I feel and hear four loud bursts of activity in your nappy as well.

We are meant to have you back at the hospital before lunchtime, but neither of us is inclined to let you go easily. We dawdle and reason that you need the sleep, that we need to see whether the 1 pm feed will go down the tube all right (you don't even gurgle). I finally bundle you into the car at three o'clock and return to the ward to talk to the speech pathologist about the teat problem (it's not working well—she gives me another one to try), and to the lactation sister about the increasing success Helen is having breastfeeding (you sucked and swallowed for ten minutes this morning). The feeling at the hospital is that you look so good that you should be at home tonight too, though tomorrow we must bring you back so the doctors can check you over before Wednesday's procedure.

The nurses and doctors ask a series of questions about how we have coped with having you, continuing the delicate dance between staff and parents. For weeks now, they've been assessing us, monitoring our behaviour and our answers, trying to establish when we'll be ready to take you. We know they're watching us. And I think they know that we know that they're watching us.

Right now, you're asleep in the pram in the dining room, where you've been since 6.45 pm, silent except for the occasional moan and stretch. If I lean right in, putting my ear only centimetres away from your face, I can hear you breathing gently. Why are you so quiet now, when in six hours, you'll be howling and grunting and crying and keeping us awake, making us wonder what the hell each noise could possibly mean? When it happens, I feel like a ten-year-old boy camping in the woods, petrified at the odd breathing and scuffling noises of an animal rooting around outside the tent.

November 18

You play 'Love me, I'm gorgeous' games with us all morning, throw up a little, sleep for an hour, go to the hospital, come out for lunch (you spend the whole time moving your head from side to side, as if you are committing the scenery to memory, perhaps planning a future robbery of the café), drink some more, complain about life for a while, sleep, wake up full of smiles, have a bath, drink, go back to sleep. You may be discharged as early as the day after tomorrow, depending on how well tomorrow's procedure goes.

November 19

BABY BULLETIN IV

WHAT'S HAPPENING TO NAOMI?

Today was kind of weird. She had a procedure under anaesthetic this morning. We had been hoping that we had made it past the operating theatre stage of our hospital experience, but the balloon dilations just weren't working well enough. After the last balloon trick, we left things for two weeks and in that time, Naomi's oesophagus closed back up again, almost as tight as it had been at the start. So it was decided to try something more serious. This morning's procedure involved positioning a conical rubber rod in her throat and pushing it through the tight part, narrow end first. That way, the further you push, the more it stretches. The surgeon said afterwards he was very happy with the way it went. Her pipe is now stretched to about a centimetre. We'll find out how it's fared in a couple of weeks' time.

Meanwhile, it gave the little critter a pretty miserable day, with a sore throat and no food. The wider pipe has also made it easier for her to bring things up, and three times today, she vomited up the soft tube that usually feeds her into her stomach. This was not smart. I have been trying to teach her the concept of cause and effect, but she just doesn't understand—if you expel your tube because it annoys you, the nurses or doctors will just put it in again and it will then hurt more. Come on, Naomi, it's not that hard to get.

HOW ARE HER SPIRITS?

I know I'm a dad, but she's just great. She's such a happy, bouncy little thing. When she's awake, she's very alert. She smiles her broad, gummy, cheeky smile whenever she sees Helen or me. She's easily transfixed by rattles and toys and her Goldilocks and the Three Bears mobile (just how bizarre is that story when you stop to think about it—little blonde cow steals food, messes bed, is rewarded).

WHAT ABOUT THE NIPPLE?

Oh, okay, I guess I should tell you. Every day we let Naomi spend a little quality time with Helen's nipples, which, let's face it, is more than I get. In the last week, she has twigged to the fact that sucking on them actually produces something. (See, I *am* getting somewhere with this cause and effect stuff.) Yesterday she spent five to ten minutes on each side, with results! It's still early days, but the signs are good. We thought for some time that breastfeeding might never be an option, that by the time Naomi was ready, Helen would have lost the ability. Not the case.

I GET THE FEELING YOU'RE STILL WITHOLDING
SOMETHING . . .

You're right. The big news is that, if Naomi's recovery
from this morning's effort goes according to plan, she
could be discharged from hospital on Friday. Yep, day
after tomorrow. Nearly eleven weeks later . . .

ARE YOU SCARED?

No, because (I'm cheating by leaving all this stuff out
of my explanations) we actually had gate leave last
weekend. We packed her into the car on Friday afternoon
and didn't have to take her back until Monday. The
whole experience was frightening and joyous and
wonderful.

We did all the new parent stuff (not sleeping at
all the first night, lying there listening to her snuffling
away in the next room like a warthog with bronchitis).
The only hassle is that we are full-time nurses as well
as full-time parents. Even if Naomi doesn't want to
wake us up three times in the night, we still have
to get up to top up the pump or give her medicines.
And for Helen, it means a day which is nothing but
tending to her own milk machine or Naomi's milk
machine. The sooner we cut out the middle machines,
the better.

So, we're pretty much aware of what we're in for. If
we can get some routines and schedules in place, it will
only be very tiring. And that's just fine by us. We're
looking forward to giving it a shot.

NOVEMBER 20

I can't believe I told everyone you're coming home. It's not like me to count a chicken before it's hatched. You repay me this morning by giving us the biggest fright we've had in weeks. You have a bottle at seven o'clock, but don't seem to want it much. Another 40ml goes down the tube at 9 am. At 11 am, we try the bottle again. You take 10ml, then splutter and gag. It is obvious to all of us that your throat is giving you a lot of pain after the procedure. Trying to drink is no fun at all.

I keep you on my lap as we slowly put the remaining 30ml of the bottle down your tube. But almost the second we finish, you gurgle and bring the lot up, all over yourself, the bunny rug and me. We've seen you vomit before, so we aren't too perturbed, but this time, you don't stop. You keep on retching, bringing up every drop in your stomach. After ten minutes it still hasn't stopped. Helen is holding you carefully on the bed, keeping you tilted on your side so anything that comes up will have easy access to the world.

I try to get nurses and doctors to have a look. We both get scared when the liquid coming up begins to turn green. And still you can't go more than ten or fifteen seconds without coughing, hacking and contracting. With everything in your stomach out, what is coming up is pure bile. The look on your face is one of terror.

Ruth has just arrived for a visit when you begin your display. She goes suitably ashen. Her news, by the way, is that she's ten weeks pregnant. But ssshhhh! We're not allowed to tell anyone yet. I'm sure seeing a baby going through your kinds of motions really helps to convince her that fertilisation was a terrific idea.

About 20 minutes after the vomiting begins, you calm down, drifting into exhausted sleep. We consult Dr Anthony, who says it happened because your stomach is full and your whole system is irritated after the procedure. And the other truth, as Dr Ian has pointed out to us, is that your stricture has until now helped prevent vomiting by keeping the passageway tight. I guess we can start expecting to see your meals encored more often.

NOVEMBER 21

When I was in fifth grade, I was deeply in love, for about twelve minutes, with a girl called Tracy, whose birthday was on 21 November. She left that year, moved away without much more than a wave at the end of school. Every year, on this day, a memory of a blue dress and blonde curls comes back to me. I have no idea why. It didn't mean much. I'm sure it was all of a week before I found someone else to have a crush on.

Now I have a better reason to remember the date. Now we are three in the house again, me typing, Helen on the couch attached to the damn pump and you in the bouncer, wrapped up tight and snoozing. I have been on the verge of tears for the whole day. Even though we've had you here before, even though you're nowhere near being recovered, there is something so strong and so powerful about the idea of home, about officially leaving the hospital. I never thought I could find the word 'discharge' so attractive.

We arrive this morning to find you're back on continuous feed because of the vomiting. Dr Anthony advises that, given your reactions in the last day or two, you should be left to recover through the weekend. Not only has your throat taken a beating, he says, but your stomach has been traumatised. Helen and I reason that we're as capable of monitoring your progress as the hospital staff, so the fact that you've gone backwards shouldn't stop us bringing you home.

You sleep most of the day, helped by the satiety of constant milk flow into your stomach, with a hint of Panadol here and there to smooth the edges. When you are awake, you want to be picked up and held. Every so often (five seconds ago) you bark loud and sharp, three or four times, as if to bring milk up, but mostly, you keep it down.

Because it is your last day, we have flowers delivered to both the ward and the intensive care unit. And I write cards. There are very few times in life when we get to think about what we'd like to say to people before we have to say it. This is one of those lucky occasions. After having the thoughts in the back of my head for the last week, this is what I scrawl:

To everyone at ICU,

Here's to a day we would never have had without you. If we've learned anything since Naomi's birth, it's that life is a team effort. And we couldn't have found ourselves in a better team. After two and a half months in this hospital, it seems to us parents that great care is as much about the tiny, human details as the big, surgical picture. When we look back, we remember the unscripted, daily kindnesses—Mary-Rose ringing Helen at King George V the morning after Naomi's first operation, Caroline snapping the perfect Polaroid of our daughter attempting to remove her ventilator tube. These are just two examples—there are so many others. And this is not about singling anyone out. There were times when we thought you moved beyond mere professionalism and into the realms of magic. For a couple of natural born cynics (come on, we're journalists—it's our job), that's saying something. Given that you do what you do 24 hours a day, 365 days a year, your compassion, dedication, and above all, heart, still amaze us. Thanks for making such a difficult time so easy, for baby, for mother and father. Whatever Naomi makes of her life will be at least partly a tribute to all of you.

Finally, after eleven weeks, we pack up our meagre belongings, take down the Three Bears mobile, dig the frozen milk out of the ward freezer and prepare to leave. Before making our stage left exit, we take you for a walk up the corridor to visit the folk in ICU. By coincidence, we pick an odd moment to do it. We enter the unit to see that the couple whose baby boy was next to you when you first arrived, the couple who, we later found out, had to make the decision to turn the machines off, are also there. They have come back to say thank you to the staff, and to present them with a gift. I can't help thinking how brave of them it is to return to a site of such trauma, how strong and generous to offer their thanks. How strange that we two couples, with such different stories, should cross paths again.

We slink by as discreetly as possible and make for the back of the room, where the nurses gather to coo and cluck and insist that we visit occasionally, so they can see you grow. Then it is back to the ward to repeat the goodbyes, before leaving at exactly 4 pm.

Home. It's hard to believe the hospital saga is finally over. I know we'll be back in and out, with dilations and tests and paediatric appointments, but you now live somewhere. How do I feel about leaving the hospital? Disconnected. Like something has just been cut off. Hmmm. Ask me tomorrow.

Downstairs on Helen's pillow there's a little Tiffany's bag with a ring in it, the third ring, the one with the tiny diamond that I bought so soon after you were born, hoping that your homecoming would have been so long ago. The card says: *'To mother and daughter, who have already been through so much, something else to share.'* Soon, Helen will put the machine away for the night, stow the milk in the fridge, to be used tomorrow, and pad off on her tired little feet to bed . . .

NOVEMBER 22

According to Helen, I shouldn't be writing this. 'But nothing happened today,' she insists, as I head to the study, leaving her on the couch. For the (short) record then, here's what did happen:

You grumble in your sleep all night, growling and stretching and keeping us awake. You spend most of the day defiantly awake. I suspect this is because you slept for much of yesterday, and because you are a touch over-excited to be out of hospital again. This morning, while Helen is at stretch class at the gym (don't worry, it'll never happen again), I sit on the edge of the table and talk to you. You lie in your bouncer, looking beatific and inscrutable, like some miniature Dalai Lama. You get reflux around lunch, but manage to keep everything down. In the afternoon, Helen takes you for a walk to the park around the corner. Later, while she naps, I calm you by holding you on my lap, your head tucked under my collarbone, your spine lying along my forearm, my hand underneath you.

NOVEMBER 23
Sunday, 11 weeks

We can tell, each day, that your throat is less sore, but it's still bothering you. We experiment with small bolus feeds with moderate success. Otherwise, today is restful. You are awake most of the time, sitting around banging on whatever rattly thing we can put within your reach, grabbing at decorations and toys, talking to us, making us compete for your smiles and favours. I never knew a baby could be such a spur for competition. We sit on the lounge together, you asleep in my lap as the last day of the cricket against New Zealand unfolds. I can't believe my luck. All my life I've been looking for good excuses to sit around and watch Test matches.

NOVEMBER 24

You see me naked. The gown just seems to open of its own accord, okay! I think this is worth noting because I feel sure that in 28 years' time, when you're paying a psychiatrist to unravel your life, this will be a Repressed Memory you might choose to recall. So here, officially, it is recorded. Now sue me.

NOVEMBER 25

A well-meaning friend commends Helen and me for our strength, for the way we've handled the problems that have come our way in the last few months. She says when you grow up, you will learn from having such strong parents. I reckon it's the other way around. You have taught us resilience, put up with so much, set such an example. If you're not complaining, what right have we? We are not the strong ones.

Did I mention, by the way, that your mother is wearing the ring I gave you both on the ring finger of her left hand? What does that mean?

NOVEMBER 26

Summer arrives in all its heaving, sweaty glory, and you're trying to cope with what has happened to the air. It used to be thin and breathable. Now it's thick and clotted and doesn't seem to want to go down. It's 11 pm and the temperature is somewhere in the mid-twenties. You're lying downstairs in the bassinette in a singlet, perspiring ever so delicately.

Finally, you're back to where you were before the dilation a week ago. You're still not taking more than 20ml at a time from the bottle, but perhaps that could be solved with a different teat. We might experiment, now that we're sure you're pretty much recovered. And tomorrow, when no-one is looking, we might get cocky and try to put 50ml down the tube to see if your stomach will handle it.

NOVEMBER 27

First, an apology of sorts. I was going to compose a poem in your honour today, but nothing rhymes with 'mucus'. Sorry.

No problem with the jump to 50ml. We take you in to the hospital to be weighed (3.31 kilograms) and discuss your progress with the lactation consultant and dietitian. Everyone agrees you're in good shape, though it would be nice to see you put on a little more weight. Helen was sure you were going to be 3.5. Most babies your age have broken the 5 kilo mark.

Your overall milk target is put up to 25ml per hour. This sounds great until we realise that it means we have to get your stomach to take 75ml at once before we can go to three-hourly feeds and pull the wretched naso-gastric tube out.

Three times today, you fall asleep in my lap during the tube feed. Your breathing is so quiet it scares me and I sit frozen, not wanting to move lest I startle you awake or somehow alter what is such a beautiful feeling. Every time it happens, I find myself fixating on something different, such as the downy hair on your arms, where your biceps must be. Or your crooked little finger.

Feeding you is so complex, so mathematical. We spend half the day planning and discussing it, and the other half doing it, sitting there with a watch in one hand and the syringe in the other, trying to squeeze each millilitre smoothly and cleanly down the tube.

NOVEMBER 28

So anyway, have I told you yet how happy I am about this fatherhood thing? I am forever creeping over to where you're snoring and stretching in the corner, leaning down to push a hair away from your forehead (you still have a full head of it), or plant a little kiss somewhere, on your cheek, on the little dimple in your chin, on your right eyebrow, with its ginger strands pointing in all directions. To me, it feels like psychic refuelling. You just fill me up. You should be charging for this.

As all parents should be, Helen and I are totally smitten. We forgive you everything. Even when you woke up at midnight last night and decided it was time to play. You looked up at me so happily, with smiles so enthusiastic, that it felt like an honour to sit there and make faces back at you, to clutch your baby hand. Even when you threw up on us this morning, then again on the outfit I changed you into the second I put it on ...

The trick of yours that I'm most enamoured with involves your hair. You can't see what's on the top of your head, though you did manage to get some milk up there this morning—I haven't quite worked out how. Anyway, you can't see what's up there, but you've been looking at my hair flopping about since you were born, clearly wondering what it is. In the last few days you've been able to get your own hands up. Now every time I look down, you have a handful of your hair and you're giving it a good tug. I don't like to be an over-protective father and tell you what to do (though when you go to the beach when you're sixteen, you're going in overalls), but I suspect that if you manage to pull your hair out, you might actually miss it one day.

November 29

2 am. I've been in bed for an hour and a half when the alarm on the pump goes off, warning me to add more milk to it. You've been sleeping like the proverbial. But for some reason, you decide to move from quiet, deep sleep into noisy light sleep, offering us a symphony of howls and grunts and weird glottal gurgles and wails, each of which pierces the night air at exactly the moment we are sliding back into dreams.

For three hours, I am in and out of bed every fifteen minutes, trying you in new positions, switching you from bouncer to bassinette, swaddling you, unswaddling you. Nothing, absolutely nothing, works. It gets to the point where I don't even bother going back to bed. I just sit in the corner of your room with my head in my hands, thinking the kind of thoughts that went through Jack Nicholson's head in *The Shining*.

At five o'clock you tire of the small tortures and finally manage to hook a finger into the exposed part of the tube and yank it out. Ah, how did we know it would be at 5 am? For weeks, we have discussed the possibility of you pulling it out at home. We have always said, 'and if she does it at 5 am ...' Normally, parents would put a tube like yours back in themselves, but because of your operation, we have to return to the hospital. It's standard procedure for you to have an X-ray too, to ensure the placement is right.

Helen and I stick to our plan. We pull the tube out completely, then put you back to sleep for an hour. (Now, you go quiet!) Helen gets up at six o'clock to give you medicines—it's a long time since the Ranitidine has had to go in orally and you still hate the taste, though the Cisapride isn't a problem. Then she gives you a bottle.

I take you to Emergency at 9.30, where a nurse puts a new tube in as quickly as she can. We shoot off to X-ray to confirm its position. You cry and cry and cry until we are both exhausted from it. Back at home, you sleep for most of the day. Just to add the extra element of fun, you return some of every feed, small amounts, but enough to go through a pile of outfits and bunny rugs. The washing mounts.

Being at home is not quite playing out as expected. It's strange, but now that you're out of the hospital, out of someone else's world and into ours, it's easier to see that you're still a sick, fragile baby. We were so enthusiastic about getting you here, and I remain overjoyed that we have, but there is also a feeling of anticlimax starting to creep in as we realise the workload confronting all three of us.

What's hardest is the unpredictability. We can't make assumptions about how each day will unfold—there are too many variables. We can't lie you down—we can't let you stretch out flat. We can't change your nappy without considering how far from the last feed it is, how much milk is in your stomach. We can't throw you in the car and visit friends—the schedule is too tight. In many ways, we have swapped one prison for another. We can't relax. There's never a point where you're fed, sated and in safe territory. Reflux strikes when it feels like it. It's almost inevitable after feeding, but it can arrive at any time.

We also realise how unprepared we were for your arrival. After all this time with you in the world, we still had not organised ourselves to set up a nursery, to create a personal space for you here. We couldn't do it until we had you under the roof.

November 30
Sunday, 12 weeks

Another month ends. I thought, when I began writing this, that the story would have told itself by the end of September, that an ending would lurch into view, saving me from all this late-night typing, my brain beginning to see double. I thought I would be able to bundle up a nice little sheaf of papers and give it to you on your 21st birthday. Maybe 10,000 words all up. It would be a sweet, short ode to your being. Nothing, as we have learned from you so clearly, goes exactly to plan.

I thought, even when events took their abrupt turn towards the abnormal, that I could stop when you got out of hospital, but I know now that it wouldn't feel right. Whatever this experience is, we're still in the thick of it. We've just shifted venues and priorities. The tube reminds me constantly that medical science is a bigger part of our lives than I want it to be. Perhaps the day to stop typing will be the day we consign it to the bin forever. Perhaps this ain't over until the fat baby sings, or at least until there's a fat baby. Whatever, we're getting closer, but we're not there yet. Not yet.

You are on your best possible behaviour today, which is handy, because you have visits from John and Dee and their daughter Paloma, and Steve and his daughter Isabella. They all arrive as Helen is trying, with reasonable success, to get you to breastfeed. You've gone right off the idea of the bottles. Helen thinks we should abandon them. There is a lovely moment when everyone is here, with all five women on the couch at once: you in Helen's lap, Dee beside her, and the two girls perched wherever they can fit, all touching and stroking and staring. Little girls and babies—what is it? For me, what is special is the feeling of normality it brings. The only people who have seen you and touched you have been adults. It's something else again to have kids come and play with you, even if it is gently and cautiously. I was a little concerned about how they'd cope, but the two girls aren't worried about your tube at all. They just see a baby. You.

December

There's a frangipani flower by the screen in front of me. White at the edges of its curling petals, deepening to yellow as the folds wrap around each other in the centre. A scent that is delicate, fleeting, oddly cool, like water spray. This particular flower fell off the tree this morning. Helen brought it in while I was out, left it here for me to find.

The tree, which stands outside the front door of this house, your home, was one of the reasons I wanted to live here. Not one of the big, sensible reasons, but one of the small, quirky details that sway you, like the colour of a skirting board or the curve of a wall. When we moved in, the tree was bare, its knobbly branches nude and stunted. A week or two after you were born, the green leaves began to sprout. Now, in the week after your homecoming, it has finally started to bloom.

As you do. I marvel at how much you're growing. Perhaps I concentrate too much, measuring you in my mind all the time. The legacy of this beginning is that we are obsessed with feeding you. We wish the weight onto you. Look, we say, Naomi has finally added some bulk to her calves. Your thighs, by the way, were the part of you to thicken first—perhaps it will be the story of your life.

Each day you seem to be adding more fleshy deposits. Your ribs could do with a little more covering, and your upper arms are slow to get on the train, but mostly, you're filling out. Which is a serious relief. I had been harbouring fears that we would fail you at home, that you would go backwards. But we can do this.

Today I see the first signs of a sense of humour. I hide my face from you, then bring it back into your line of vision. You smile. I do it again. You smile again. I move in and out of view. You grin that broad grin at me, your whole face breaking open. Wow, you understand a running gag. Now, who's on first ...

DECEMBER 2

So what are you thinking? Lying there all day, looking up at the world, taking in the patterns and people and objects. Do you have the vocabulary to think? What shape do those thoughts take? Do you wonder? Do you connect? Or do you just want us to change the channel?

When I look at you, the questions that seem to be crossing your face are, 'What's this thing taped into my nose?' and 'Who are these weird people making faces at me?' The other thing crossing your face is your hand, your fingers constantly scraping, pulling and clawing at the tape and the tube. You whip it out again this morning. I have just stepped out of your room and into the kitchen to put the kettle on. Helen is downstairs. Less than five seconds after I take my eyes off you, I hear a yelp and a cry of surprise. By the time I get back to the bassinette, you are holding the tube, with the tape still attached to it, waving it triumphantly. You look up, catch the shock on my face and break into a big smile.

We try feeding you, in the hope that we can get enough milk down to avoid going to the hospital until the afternoon, when we have a scheduled appointment with Dr Barry, who has agreed to go on seeing you as a paediatric outpatient. You won't take enough, so it's back in the car and off to

Emergency. A new tube is put in, always a howling wrestle, and an X-ray done to check its position. I ask the nurse to tape the tube down very carefully, bringing the tape in as close to your nose as possible, so there's less tube for you to grab at. It's still not close enough, I reckon.

In Outpatients for the meeting with Dr Barry, Helen is handed your notes, which have been brought back from Medical Records. The two folders are more than 10 centimetres thick. We weigh them before we weigh you. Your notes are 3.8 kilograms. You are 3.44.

You are measured at 54.9 centimetres, up from 51 at birth. Dr Barry checks your head circumference and shows us your growth plotted on a chart. You began below the accepted normal range and you're still below it, but over time, the gap is slowly ('almost imperceptibly', as Helen so optimistically puts it) closing.

December 3

The dilation goes reasonably well, I guess. Dr John slides a balloon tube through your nasal passage (I won't be surprised if you hate balloons when you grow up) and pushes your oesophagus out to 8 millimetres. He says afterwards that the stricture is much softer than it was before, much easier to stretch out. We're booked in to repeat the process in two weeks.

Dr Ian watches proceedings from behind the screen with Helen. He can see how upset she is and asks why she comes into the room, why she doesn't just sit outside until it is over. Helen says that even though it hurts to see you in distress, not seeing it would hurt more.

Always keen to encourage us and push things forward, he tells her we should take the tube out and get on with it. We try to explain that the most you'll take via the bottle is 25ml and you're meant to be getting 25ml every hour. If we fed you every hour, you'd lose so much sleep you'd be too tired to suck. And we'd be insane within a week. He says we should try you on solids, with that 'why not?' shrug of his. Swallowing them would help keep the stricture open.

Dr Ian assures Helen that if she gets pregnant again, we won't have to go through all this, that TOF is a statistical, rather than genetic, event. A second pregnancy. Now there's a question we haven't really broached yet. If I'm honest, I would say that at the moment, I don't see it. I don't rule out the possibility of you having a brother or sister, but I can't quite get my brain around it. There's too far to go with you before we think of that.

At home, you spend most of the afternoon emptying your stomach over yourself, three outfits, four bunny rugs, Helen and me. Your sharp, savage retching comes in bursts every few minutes, and is heart-rending.

DECEMBER 5

After a terrible morning of hysteria and screaming (and that's just your mother and me), we give up trying to fill your stomach and put you onto continuous feed. Your system is so upset from the dilation that it seems wise not to tax it. The continuous feed helps, insofar as you stop crying and bringing the milk back up, but even its flow is hard for you. You're limp and unhappy. Three times during the afternoon you wake up with reflux pain. We find these days so dispiriting. It seems we have a dilation every fortnight, spend a week getting you back on track, and then have only one week to move forward again.

December 6

Today is less of a battle, but really only because we know what to expect and how to beat a hasty retreat. We leave you on continuous feed after a lunchtime experiment with a bolus feed is met with half an hour of retching instead of cheery thanks. When you're awake, at least, you don't seem bothered by your sore throat. You hang out happily in the bassinette, thwacking the little plastic toys strung across it, gurgling and chatting to yourself. I swear I even get a chortle out of you. A friend of Helen's, Carolyn, turns up in the afternoon and you go straight into seduction mode again. You twinkle whenever there are new faces around. You seem excited by the floating voices. An audience of two obviously isn't enough for you.

December 7
Sunday, 13 weeks

I've been sitting by the bassinette in the dark, listening to you breathe, watching you move your hands in your sleep, leaning right in to smell you. For a long time, weeks, months, you didn't have a smell. Well, okay, you did, but I could never quite pick it up—it was always masked by the antiseptic smells of the hospital, the glue smells of the tapes, the body lotion and hand creams of the nurses rubbing off on you. It's only been recently, when I move in close to your skin, that I can get a soft, musky sweetness. There's a hint of vanilla in it, and something else I can't put my nasal finger on.

I'm smelling you for the same reason as I've been watching you today, trying to suck you in through my eyeballs, trying extra hard to imprint you on myself, to get your picture on the insides of my eyelids, the feel of your skin on my fingertips, the scent of your cheek in my nostrils. I am a condemned man. Tomorrow I get up and go back to work, to the rest of my life, a place I don't feel much like visiting. You're not ready. I'm not ready. I'd be lying if I said I'm not worried about how Helen will handle you and the damn breast pump. Worried about you. Worried about how I'll handle being away from the two of you.

So I'm here, and I'm typing, and I'm wishing that I had more to say. I don't want to go to bed. I don't want to go to sleep. Because when that short sleep finishes, I have to leave.

December 8

I rise early so Helen can go for a swim—it will give her strength and help keep her sane. I spend the day at the office quietly nervous, but don't ring; Helen will call if there is a problem.

When I arrive home at six o'clock, both you and your mother look well and happy. In fact, you look better than you have for days. Helen has been able to keep the feeding regime up and though you obliged with the occasional chuck, it was not of the high-distress, bile and mucous type we've been seeing lately. You took the breast three times and were apparently more than happy on each occasion. We are now phasing out the bottle. You prefer the breast. (Who said you'd never get there?) It will make it harder to measure your intake, but I think you're getting robust enough, slowly, to be your own judge—you'll tell us if you need more.

DECEMBER 9

A day without vomit. Hallelujah. You are almost, almost over this last dilation completely. It's been a tough week. Two days into her solo flight, Helen is coping well, though I pour her into bed at 9.30 tonight, utterly exhausted. This could be partly because you decided to wake us up and demand attention for an hour and a half at 3 am. Given the 10 pm medicine, midnight medicine, 2 am pump change and 6 am pump change, that doesn't leave us with a lot of uninterrupted shut-eye. You sleep amazingly peacefully from about 7 pm until midnight, but after that, it's a lottery.

I spend another day at work feeling vaguely empty, as if I should be elsewhere (mind you, I suspect I used to feel like that even before you came along). Everything is starting to wind down for Christmas, so there's not much adrenalin in the place. There's not much of me there at all. My body is present, but ...

DECEMBER 10

You tip the scale at 3.56 kilograms. Which is up, but not high enough. You're not going backwards, but your forward motion is not at a rate acceptable to the medical fraternity. We're going to try to up the Polyjoule added to the breast milk. We're also going to up the breast milk. To be fair, it's been a pretty hard week and I'm surprised and pleased that you even managed to put on 100 grams—so much of what has gone in has come straight out again.

Excuse me, it's 12.20 am. What are you doing up? I am sitting here typing in silence and then suddenly hear all these little groans and growls, the sounds of a stretching baby. By the time I walk into the next room, you are kicking off the bunny rug and stretching your arms above your head like a heavyweight boxer who has just won inside two rounds. It must be that three-hour sleep you had this afternoon. I have to lie on the carpet next to the bassinette, stroke your hair, take your little hands away from your mouth and fold them over your chest, so that you won't start waving them about and startle yourself fully awake.

DECEMBER 11

Four days into the week and Helen is cactus. She's history. It's just too hard looking after you and keeping up with the breast milk provision. In any two-hour period, there's 20 minutes of trying to get you interested in the breast, half an hour of syringing milk into you and half an hour of keeping you upright to minimise the reflux. If, at that point, you're asleep, you can be carefully put down into the bassinette, which leaves Helen all of about 35 minutes to pump before the next feeding cycle starts.

And of course, that's only when the plan works. Today she had fifteen minutes when she wasn't either on the breast pump or attending to you. By 4 pm, she says, she was half asleep and half in tears. By the time I got home at 7.30, after being held back by a five o'clock meeting, she was not so much hysterical as in another headspace completely, talking to herself like a madwoman. The hysteria came when I dropped a full container of hard-earned breast milk onto the floor, losing more than 100 millilitres of the precious stuff.

You are throwing up occasionally, still bringing up the green and unpleasant stomach juices more than a week after a dilation. This worries us. We thought it would go away. It always has before.

December 12

Helen kicks the bedroom door in at 7.28 am, demanding I get up. You've been howling for an hour. She is halfway through expressing and can't quieten you down. We feed you and watch you vomit seven times in the next half hour. You shift from lap to lap, hacking and spluttering, the tears running down your face, your eyes filled with confusion and pain.

Enough is enough. Helen gets in touch with Dr Barry, who suggests there may be a problem of some sort at the duodenum. There may be too much bile heading upwards from that point, instead of down. He suggests we feed you 30ml an hour for 20 hours of the day, leaving four breaks of an hour where we need them. He's happy as long as you're getting 600ml.

You take the nipple enthusiastically (it still surprises us that you can suck and swallow so easily with the tube in place), but you're not interested in the bottle, and every time we bring a dummy near your mouth you gag and spit. As I am pushing the last 30ml feed down the tube, I put a little finger near your mouth. You pounce on it, sucking furiously. By the end, you've clamped both hands onto the finger and you're manoeuvring it to suit you. You've really been concentrating on grabbing and touching in the last few days—as I am singing to you tonight, you reach out and put your hand in my mouth, trying to catch the words.

DECEMBER 13

A little better. Sure, you do the reverse meal trick on a couple of occasions. Sure, you are periodically upset and let us know about it. But really, it is your best day of the week. Dr Barry's hourly-feed idea seems to be taking the pressure off your system. It's easier for us too. It takes fifteen minutes to feed you and five to ten to settle you afterwards. The two-hourly feed was taking at least half an hour, with anything up to 45 minutes to settle you.

You still won't entertain the bottle, but you give Helen's nipples a workout. In between, when you aren't catching a few dozen winks, you are back to being happy and chuckly and taking in the world around you.

Today's big step forward is in the bath area (you've been complaining about the water since you were born). I fill up the downstairs bath, strip myself off and drag you in with me. At first I curl up tight with you curled up tighter against me, so you can get used to the temperature of the water. Then I slowly unwind, with you floating a little more freely all the time. I lay your spine along my stomach, with the back of your head resting against my collarbone. You kick a little, let your arms spread in the water. I tuck my hands under your armpits and lift you off, holding you out in the open water, keeping your head above, but letting you feel the warm wetness surround your body. You seem quite happy to be there, kicking away, even smiling at me, and at Helen, looking on from above. It is only when we wet your hair that you start to cry. We finish the bath and hustle you into the soft towels. You calm down immediately, then look up with one of those expressions that says, That was a great—can I have another go?

December 14
Sunday, 14 weeks

We have a picnic today, you and I. A pic-a-nic, Booboo. A long glass of orange cordial for me, a syringe of breast milk for you. We sit in the deckchair on the front porch and watch the weather change, the wind rustling the frangipani leaves, the rain clouds rolling in, coagulating, threatening, but never actually breaking into rain. Your mother is at the pool. You and I have nothing better to do and it is hot and humid in the house. I point out the plants, the sky, the telephone wires, the cars, the house across the street having second-storey renovations. You wave your arms, push your feet into me for support and stare intently at everything, only occasionally making any sound or showing any inclination to offer an opinion.

December 15

There I am, at 2.43 am, staggering around in the dark as usual, trying not to trip over the chairs that always seem to leap out at my legs in the wee hours, holding the milk in one hand and the penlight torch in the other. My intention is, as quietly as possible (I do *not* want to wake you up at this time of night), to top up the pump and get back to bed. I have been upstairs in the kitchen, measuring milk and warming it in the microwave, a task that takes up way too many brain cells—no-one should have to do maths at 2.30 am. With the right amount in the bottle, I creep downstairs and into your room.

And as I am about to pour the milk into the pump bag, completing my nightly mission, I notice a dark patch on your chest. Yes, it is what I thought, the tape from the tube, which has wrapped itself twice around your arm. I dim the torch by holding my thumb over the end and move the light closer to your face. Your clean face. Your pristine face. Your unmarked, untaped, untubed face. And is it just me or is there a look of silent satisfaction on it?

Helen rises first as usual, calmly feeds you from the nipple and wakes me in time to be at the hospital by 9.30 am. You seem to want a little more food in the Emergency waiting room, so she hauls out her breast and feeds you there for a few minutes.

The rest of the day proceeds without incident. You take milk happily from the breast and down the tube without difficulty. At 6 pm, you spend 35 minutes sucking furiously, an unheard of amount of time. You howl whenever she tries to switch breasts or move you away.

So here's what we're thinking: maybe the tube was positioned badly after the last dilation. Maybe it was sitting right at the top of your duodenum, irritating the area. Dr John had a quick look while we were in X-ray this morning, pumped some contrast down, and he couldn't see anything wrong with the area. Of course, you've been getting much better these last few days, so whatever the irritation was, it must have been disappearing. But Dr John said that you wouldn't have been experiencing the bilious vomit unless the region was upset.

December 16

Helen says you've been doing it for a while now, first thing in the morning, but today is the first time I see it. Or should I say, hear it. Your voice. Today we have a conversation. It isn't much of a conversation, frankly, and I think I hold up my end better than you do yours, but it is a start. I am talking to you during a feeding, telling you about the day and the world and why you should never vote for the conservatives, and every time I leave a pause in the conversation (which, as people frequently remind me, is not often enough), you chime in with a comment. Always the same comment. Something along the lines of 'Aahh!'

I think for a while that you have decided to speak English and rather than the usual 'mama' or 'dadda', have begun with the indefinite article. If the next detectable noise you make is 'the', then my theory will be proven correct. I expect after that you will go to conjunctions, and then, perhaps, a crazy lateral jump to pronouns.

Anyway, 3.74 kilograms and boy, is everyone happy about that. You're really taking to the nipple now. They always said that as you put on weight you would get stronger and be able to make more demands. Now you seem to want to suck every hour or two. I have to leave a little finger in your mouth for a whole tube feed tonight—it is the only way to keep you calm as the food goes down the tube. Dr Barry recommends we stay on one-hourly feeds for a few days longer, particularly given the dilation that is due tomorrow and the possible after effects of that.

December 17

Well, this won't be a long entry. The night is like glue. Sitting here at the keyboard, the sweat is rolling off me, trickling into places I really don't want to talk about. So let's concentrate on the good news. The dilation went as well as these things can go. Except for the usual screaming and the distress on your part, and the two-hour wait in X-ray, it was quick and textbook-simple.

Dr John used an 8 millimetre tube and dilated easily up to its full possible diameter. He said afterwards that your oesophagus was softer, and we could see on the screen that the balloon inflated easily. So we are still moving forward. Now we're booked in for another dilation on 31 December. Fingers crossed, it might be our last for a while.

December 19

BABY BULLETIN V—The Goodbye Girl
This is it. Last bulletin. As I type, sitting here in my den on this sticky Friday night in Sydney, there's a little

wheezing, gurgling package beside me, wrapped up in the lightest of sheets, sleeping the sleep of the just and mucus-filled.

SO YOU DID GET OUT THEN?

Yep. We've been out four weeks today. I've been meaning to write for a while now, but it never felt quite right. You always think that your journey back to hospital is just around the corner, that if you write and say, 'We're home', the next morning you won't be. In the end, we liberated Naomi from the Big House because it was, in the word of Gough Whitlam, time. We could have stayed longer. She could still be there. But ultimately, we knew all three of us would fare better at home, and that we would have to take the plunge. She still requires medication seven times a day, and still feeds mostly through a tube going into her stomach via her nasal passage, but this is a much better deal. We're nursing full time as well as parenting, and if she doesn't get us up in the middle of the night on her own, her nursing regime will, but we wouldn't trade. It's pretty special to wake up and know she's here.

SO WHAT'S BEEN HAPPENING? YOU DON'T WRITE, YOU DON'T CALL ...

We're housebound. At the moment, she has to be fed hourly, which doesn't leave a lot of time for a social life. She has been on two-hourly feeds before, and we're hoping to get her back to that point in the next few days. But that won't provide us with a licence to spend the night doing the bossa nova in some dingy coffee-stained bar either. Three-hourly feeds remain the goal.

Meanwhile, we just hang out and watch the days come and go. She keeps us busy. I've been teaching her the joys of cricket and trying to speak to her in words of no fewer than three syllables. I want her first word to be something like 'Philanthropist'. She has begun to talk in her own odd way, but so far, only animals seem to understand her. This week's impersonation: the crow. 'Arrrk! Arrrrk!'

IS ALL THE SURGERY OVER?
We hope so. We've been taking her back in for fortnightly oesophageal dilations, the process where they put a balloon down her throat and inflate it. The last one was the day before yesterday. She seems to have recovered from it beautifully, which is a great relief, because the one before left us with ten days of constant vomiting of bile, milk and mucus, and a lot of pain. Our surgeon rang this morning and said that the dilation we have booked for December 31 has been cancelled. He wants to wait another couple of weeks. That's great by us. We're hoping the dilations will be able to be monthly now. This is how we will mark progress. Monthly, two monthly, three monthly, six monthly . . .

WHAT ABOUT THE REST OF THE MEDICAL STUFF?
Well, it splits into surgical and paediatric. The surgical is concerned with making the oesophagus work better. The paediatric is about feeding and growing. Unfortunately, progress in the former tends to restrict the latter. If you dilate her throat, she's more likely to have trouble feeding. It's not a terrible problem, but

it contributes to the slowness of this whole thing.

Naomi is gradually closing in on the acceptable weight range for a baby of her age. We weigh her at the hospital every week and the weight is plotted on a graph. If you look really closely, you can see the gap between her weight and the normal range closing ever so slowly (if she lives to 120, she might even get fat). She left hospital at 3 kilos and is now 3.74. She's three and a half months old. Still, we're very happy with the way she's stacking it on. She has thighs.

AND THE FEEDING?
She won't touch plastic. She won't take anything from a teat and she won't suck the dummy. But she has taken to the breast in a major way in the last week. It's very heartening for all of us. She's probably taking about a third of her milk directly from the source. The rest goes down the tube, pushed in slowly by syringe.

HOW'S NAOMI'S STATE OF MIND AFTER EVERYTHING SHE'S BEEN THROUGH?
She's just great. I can't tell you what a relief it is to find that she's so alert, so social (loves people, won't go to sleep when there are visitors). She smiles all the time, understands running gags and stupid facial expressions and seems to think pretty much everything is funny.

AND WHAT ABOUT YOU TWO?
Oh, we're as fine as we could be. Tired, tired and then a little extra tired, but getting there. Helen goes to bed early and gets up early. I go to bed late and get up late.

We rub shoulders in the middle of the night for a couple of hours and somehow manage to get around five hours' sleep all up, baby permitting. (Man, can she make some weird noises at 4 am! The whole barnyard!)

IS THAT REALLY IT?

Progress is slow and steady. The worst is well and truly behind us. We're at home and I'm back at work. Some semblance of normality has returned, whatever that means. Life is beginning to be just that, life.

DECEMBER 20

As I type, I'm just back from another game of 'What sort of present has Naomi left for Dad in her nappy?' I've had another lovely Saturday with you. By spending the day looking after you, I give Helen a break to gather her thoughts and look after herself, but really, I'd jump at it even if it didn't have such positive side effects.

Today we sit outside again, the summer sun dappling the enclosed porch, me in the deckchair and you in your bouncer, raised on a table so you can see out into the garden and the world. I read the paper and you rock yourself, checking out the passers-by, watching the flowers fall from the tree every time the wind picks up.

The day started at 2.23 am with a familiar cough. One that says, 'Hi, I'm in the other room pulling the tube out right now.' We had both been expecting the tube to come free fairly soon. The humid weather makes the duoderm tape lift from your face. It was only going to take the slightest of tugs to break it from its moorings.

We come back from the hospital zonked, hardly able to make polite conversation with the visiting Michelle and Maxine. Helen hates watching the tube being put in and becomes quite upset, especially when the tube has to be repositioned after the X-ray comes back. You go to sleep almost immediately and stay under for three hours. I'm always glad when you sleep after a hospital visit. It tends to mean that you wake up well, as if the yuckiness of earlier in the day was some other time, some other place.

December 21
Sunday, 15 weeks

Naomi's List of Reasons Why the Tube Has to Go

1. I don't like it
2. I really don't like it
3. You're not listening, are you?
4. How many ways can I say this?
5. The tape holding it in place is brown. And brown is so last year.

I go to the kitchen this morning to make myself a glass of cordial and of course, that is just long enough. A minute, maybe two, and you greet me with the tube in your hand, waving it gently. This one took 24 hours to get out—your personal record. Helen tries putting you on the breast, hoping you will miraculously start taking enough to justify leaving the tube out. No luck. You suck enough to kill your hunger, but not as much as you need.

I leave Helen to express and take a nap, while you and I head off to the hospital. It's the weekend before Christmas, so Emergency is full of parents and kids, sick from the heat or injuries sustained in school holiday games. We have to wait for more than an hour before another tube can be put in. For my sins, I get to watch the second half of Disney's *Snow White and the Seven Dwarfs*. What a strange film. At the end, Snow White dies and is put in a glass coffin. And she doesn't decompose. Then a prince arrives, kisses her and she comes back to life. I know there's meant to be something in there about the power of redemptive love, but let's face it, the dwarfs loved her more (the prince had never even met her), and they couldn't bring her back to life. And what's with the dwarfs? Seven guys, living together, all wearing the same clothes. Helloooo?

It's tough getting the tube in. I tell the nurse that the duoderm is lifting because of the humidity, so she tapes the tube in a different way, using a lot more tape and covering your nose. I go into mild shock. The sight of you with so much tape takes me straight back to ICU. My reaction is as if the ventilator tube had been put back in. I start to cry and take a few deep breaths to stop. I know it doesn't make any sense, but the minimal taping makes me feel as if we're moving forward, makes the tube easier to accept. The more tape, the more it looks as if we're back somewhere else. Reactions are not always rational.

December 23

4.04 kilograms! You finally make it past those notes. That's a 300-gram gain in one week, almost twice as big as any you've had before. There have been a few days where we have sworn we could see you putting on weight between morning and night. We dismissed it as a trick of the light and our weary eyes, but perhaps we were right. Maybe if you watch closely enough, you can see someone grow. Now I'm going to go watch a kettle and see if it boils.

DECEMBER 24

Somewhere in the last week you've moved from being a baby to being a tiny person. I know that sounds like a daft distinction to make, but it's true. You seem to have accumulated enough facial expressions, enough moods, enough strange habits (pulling on your hair). Your personality is forming.

You've affected our personalities too. We speak to you in a strange procession of voices, singsong tones, constant questioning: 'Do you really think that? And what else happened to you today?' Helen noticed last week that she has begun to remember Polish words that her mother must have spoken to her as a baby, terms of endearment, names that she couldn't have heard for 35 years. They're all rolling off her tongue, little surprises each of them, no doubt to you as well. Helen's also trying to speak French to you here and there, to get you prepared for languages. (I have none—I'm still wrestling with English.) I'm sure you'll work it all out in the end.

DECEMBER 25

Well, for what it's worth, this is your first Christmas. Actually, it is probably worth quite a bit, given the mound of presents with your name on them, toys and clothes from the visiting Paul, a baby monitor and some more toys from my mother and father. All in all, you do pretty well for a Jew at Yuletide.

My parents couldn't make it and Helen's side of the family (and therefore, technically, yours in religious terms) don't do Christmas. My mother has said she would like to have a proper family Christmas next year. This year, with you requiring such attention, didn't seem like the right time. We're not capable of travelling and not really inclined towards having our house taken over by a crowd of people either.

In the morning, we go to drinks at Hannah and Andrew's. It feels like a major production and takes about two hours to get ready to go for an hour. Dressing, expressing, feeding, preparing, worrying, etc., etc., etc.

It's good to see them again, both looking well, coping okay with all the attention that a baby (you) receives in that kind of group surroundings. You are tired and sit in the corner watching everybody, a serene expression on your face. After a while, you shut your eyes. I speak to the father of one of Hannah's oldest friends. Before his retirement, he had been a cardiac surgeon. He carefully and quietly enquires about what has happened to you, how it has been handled and who has taken care of you. Later, before he leaves, he shakes my hand, clasps my arm and tells me that sometimes, babies like you are the sweetest ones, the ones who have been through an ordeal and have knowledge, perspective on the world. He tells me they grow up into the best people. And I don't care if some, maybe all, of what he is saying is just residual bedside manner, I almost cry.

December 26

Another day, another tube removal. I can't say we are too upset to see the tape come off. I have been finding it very difficult to deal with so much of you being covered up, and though she hasn't said anything, I know Helen has too. So when you casually rip the tape and tube loose this morning, neither of us moans. I feel a bit guilty about that. Having the tube put in is no fun for anyone. And wanting to improve the way you look, wanting to put you through distress for aesthetic reasons, is pretty selfish. But tonight, seeing you again with just a little tape on your cheek, and your sweet nose exposed, well, I can't hate myself for it. And I can rationalise—we didn't take the tube out, you did. We just silently willed you to.

I take Paul to the hospital for moral support, company and, I suppose, because I think someone else in the family should see what happens when the tube goes in. He is quiet. When you really start suffering, when you are crying and bringing up mouthfuls of spit and the nurse and I are frantically trying to keep you upright and suctioned, I see him go pale. A couple of minutes later, when I am able to pick you up to comfort you, he has dropped to his haunches.

Having him there might be unfair, but it means I can see the event through someone else's eyes. It is good for me to realise how shocking it is, this thing you (and we) go through almost routinely now. I say, 'Bet that makes you feel like parenting.' He replies that it must be tough. I say, 'Heartbreaking,' and turn away because the tears are starting to come. It *is* heartbreaking. It's terrible seeing what you go through, having to hold you down as you sweat and scream and beg for it not to happen. If only you understood why it is.

DECEMBER 27

1.42 am. A cough. A wail. A shower of sobbing. A familiar story. You with your hand wrapped around a coil, tape off your face, tube three-quarters of the way out. I can't push it back in, so I gingerly extract the rest, trying to do it smoothly to avoid aggravating you any further. I turn the milk pump off, rock you back in the direction of sleep, and head off to bed. Fourteen hours. And I thought your one-day record was impressive.

Helen rings Dr Barry at 9 am to ask if there is anything that can be done, or if we have to keep going through this routine of heading back to hospital with you every two or three (or one) days. He says that if worst comes to worst, we could talk about a gastrostomy. I don't think so.

Then Dr Barry goes lateral on us. He says maybe we should just leave the tube out for 48 hours. As an experiment. Yes, you would lose weight, but perhaps it's time to gauge where you're up to. As he points out, you haven't really understood the concept of hunger. So maybe, if we go to a program of breastfeeding and you're not being constantly sated thanks to a tube feed, you'll start to take more from the nipple. Maybe.

The idea is that Helen should take you to the hospital to be weighed (4.084 kilograms) and then take you back after 48 hours, to see exactly what the loss is. Actually, I am against the idea. I know Helen needs something else to happen, that the hospital trips and the suffering are getting to her. I also know that Dr Barry is responding to that need in her to break this routine. But I think it is too early. We've only just had a good week with you, a big, confident weight gain. I think it is too much of a risk. (I guess the doctor's job is to take educated risks.) As soon as Helen tells me what Dr Barry has said, I have the immediate picture of us on Monday morning, weighing you in and being depressed.

But I could be wrong. So, it's onto the nipple every two hours, with the yummy medicine squirted in via syringe as needed. You feed five times today. The rest of the night will be the test. I have to wake you up and give you medicine at ten, then bring you downstairs to Helen at eleven, then give you medicine at twelve, then Helen will feed you at 1.30 am (all this presuming you'll play ball) and then, to give ourselves a break, we'll sleep until you wake us up, or 6 o'clock, whichever comes first. By the end of 48 hours of this, I expect Helen to be a wreck, but if, somehow, it works, then it will have been worth it. I'm not a betting man, but I think the odds are about the same for me being eaten by ants.

DECEMBER 28
Sunday, 16 weeks

To call us nervous would be an understatement. We think about taking you back to the hospital to have a tube put in, but Dr Barry dissuades us. He says we should finish the experiment. We ring because your bowel movements have changed consistency and your urine is forming small, clear crystals, like sugar grains. He says it's not anything to be worried about and asks how you look. I say you are fine, but a little lethargic, and that the weight is already falling off, particularly on your torso. Helen thinks she can see the loss on your face as well. Your hunger is unpredictable, sometimes surfacing after an hour, sometimes taking three hours. Having been on such tight, military schedules for so long, it's a little weird for us. Tonight you demand to be fed at exactly the time dinner hits the table. So we have our first family meal, you in Helen's lap, tugging away at her breast. I cut Helen's chicken into pieces so she can stab it with her fork.

DECEMBER 29

We put you on the scales. The figure is 4.05 kilograms, a loss of only 30 grams in two days. Dr Barry says we should continue the experiment for another 48 hours. He listens to our descriptions of the last couple of days and says he thinks the loss will have stimulated your hunger. Helen says she thinks you're not taking anywhere near enough milk, that at most you are spending 10 minutes on the breast, sometimes only three or four. Dr Barry replies that 80 per cent of the milk is taken in the first five minutes, so you may be getting more than we think.

The bonuses of this situation are that you're less irritated, your breathing is better and the mucus in your throat is almost non-existent. You're so quiet when you sleep now that it's unnerving. The drawbacks are that you seem a little less energetic. And the weight thing.

Though we should both be exhausted, it's actually not

too bad. For me at least, it's much better. I'm not in and out of bed doing medicines and machinery changes, measuring amounts of milk and priming pumps. When Helen wakes up to feed you every two hours, I wake up too, but we both fall asleep when it's over. So in a way, it's less stressful. The natural, human normality of it makes it easier too. No machines to be dealt with.

December 31

Nothing turns out the way we expect it. That's the truth, so you might as well embrace it, respect it, learn to live with it. We thought we'd get a normal pregnancy. We expected you to be born without fuss. We hoped we'd bring you home from hospital in a few days. We believed you'd come home more or less fixed, righted, on track. None of these expectations made it out of the trench into the open. But the realities have not been so bad. Expectations, hopes and goals are worth having, but it's also good to see them dissolve sometimes.

The readout on the scales says 4.09 kilograms. In two days, you've recovered the weight you lost and even started to creep a little forward. Dr Barry takes one look at you and says, 'Another two days.' We are beginning to let ourselves hope that the tube may be gone, or if not gone, then on the way out. We feel the significance of walking into a new year with no tube, of starting as we mean to go on, as we mean to finish.

It's actually strange how much more confidence it gives us. It shouldn't have such a profound effect. It's only a tube. But we look at you and wonder if you're not in control again, dictating. Maybe, in just pulling and pulling the tubes out, you were saying, 'Enough. I can do this on my own. Just give me a try.' You've been doing it all your short life.

It's now 1.32 am. I keep thinking I should be writing something profound here, something to tie the year up, to square it all away. But I can't. I don't have the strength. And life for us is not about being profound or smart. It's about getting through one day and into the next. It's about eating, sleeping and trying to have the best possible time while awake.

January

JANUARY 1

How many kisses have already been offered to those cheeks, still recovering from constant taping? How many kisses can a girl have in her life? You're starting to find them funny now, the wet squeaky sound, the pucker of flesh against your face. One day soon, you'll kiss back and no doubt frighten the hell out of both of us.

JANUARY 2

4.02 kilograms. We wait for half an hour in Emergency to talk to Dr Barry. Helen feeds you and we both sit quietly, partly tired and partly in fear of what weight loss means. Eventually, the nurses get hold of him on the phone and while Helen talks, I weigh you again to see if the short suck has made any difference. 4.04 kilograms. Better, but still a disappointment.

Helen explains that you had a grizzly day yesterday, with a lot of mucus rattling in your throat. Dr Barry says to go another 48 hours. He ups both the Cisapride and the Ranitidine, which seems to improve things a little as the afternoon goes on, but you still aren't taking very much milk at any one time.

You are, however, clearly happier, and play with strength and commitment for a couple of hours. We pull you up by your arms. It's one of those things we can do over and over again. You smile and laugh and gurgle and have a whale of a time. You're increasingly enjoying physical things, being held up in the air, being supported on your wobbly legs, having your limbs moved. You like to kick and push against things, to feel pressure, to feel the development of muscles.

I add the best shots from the recent rolls of film to the photo album. I take it to Helen and show her one of the early pictures, of you in ICU with tubes and tape like a spaghetti junction on your chest. 'How the hell did any of us survive that?' I ask. We stare and stare and stare, but there's no answer.

JANUARY 3

The problem with medical experiments is that we never get the controlled conditions we need. Here we are trying to get enough food into you via the nipple so you can grow. You're not particularly keen to help us, preferring to take a little at a time. Then there's the mucus problem. Now, one of Helen's breasts has started giving her grief. You've been clamping down hard and it's sore and swollen. It stings unbearably even if she leaves it out in the open air—wearing clothes is too much. Which puts us in the interesting situation of trying to get you to take enough milk from one breast.

Meanwhile, you become more mobile, more portable every day. Until now, taking you out hasn't really been an option, thanks to the regime of feeding and expressing. But even though the regime is still here, we feel more confident. Losing the tube gives us the desire to continue the normalisation process. One of the problems of taking a tubed baby out is that, while most people are fine about it, you still end up constantly talking about the problems, receiving the well-meaning but unwanted looks of concern and compassion. Some people are great at seeing the baby, but some just see the medical situation. And that's not fair on you or us. Do I sound like I'm rationalising here?

JANUARY 4
Sunday, 17 weeks

3.995 kilograms. Down again. And still no tube, though this reprieve is only for 24 hours. Helen reasons with Dr Barry that her breast problems have meant you aren't getting enough milk. She tells him this morning that she hopes she'll be able to fully feed you by the afternoon. He asks about the bottle and we explain that you won't take it. He says that if you are hungry enough, you will. That's fine for him to say, he doesn't have to try.

At home, I decide to try feeding you another way. You suck medicine from a syringe, so why not milk? You mount a pretty vocal argument against the idea, but after 20 minutes of wrestling, I get almost 30 millilitres in. It's exhausting, and you don't like it, but it does work. It does, at least, give us another option. It's 11 pm and neither of Helen's breasts is up to it yet. I've syringed eight times so far today. I'm waiting to do it again at 12.30, then Helen will try the nipple at 2.30, 4.30 and 6.30. If she can't do it, at least we know we have a fallback position. And if we have to go through it to keep the tube out, then so be it. Who needs sleep?

JANUARY 5

4.01 kilograms. Another stay of tube execution. You made it through the night and morning on the breast, for which I was extremely grateful, because it meant that I got some sleep. Helen, on the other hand, was wrecked by the time I got up and we had one of those 'You don't do enough– I do my share' arguments, the pointless and irrational blow-ups that spring from exhaustion. In some illogical way, neither of us had the energy to stop the fight. Maybe we need to be angry sometimes, to vent the frustration and tiredness we feel.

Dr Barry says to give it another 48 hours. Today is the tenth day without the tube in (if you count the first as the one when you ripped it out at 2 am). That's an achievement. You're still with us. You've only lost a total of 70 grams. You look pretty well. And it's still a lot better than the alternative.

JANUARY 6

Someone asks me today if I feel my life has changed drastically since you arrived. I say I'm really too busy to know. Maybe. Maybe not. I don't feel as if I've had any epiphanies. Perhaps I get more simple joy out of each day, though they do seem to be rushing by a heck of a lot faster.

JANUARY 7

Four months old and you continue to surprise us. 4.13 kilograms. That's 120 grams in two days. Now if you could just keep adding weight for another few days, another couple of weigh-ins, I might be able to stop breathing so shallowly.

It's amazing how a positive report card changes the mood in the house. There's a lightness to Helen that I haven't seen since well before you last yanked the tube. I think she knows now that she and her breasts can do it. They can feed you. The two of you, four of you, can get through this together.

JANUARY 8

Helen calls me into the darkness of your room. You're spread across her lap, mouth clamped to nipple, gently sucking. In the quiet, I can hear your tiny, clucking swallows. Either that or the crickets that live outside the window are making some weird noises.

'Look at her arm,' says Helen. She's smiling, entranced. You're carving the air with the limb in question. Conducting again. Cutting smooth arcs with your palm. 'She's so graceful,' says Helen, brushing her fingers against yours as they swish past.

Another tough day, full of upset throats, feeding complaints and general exhaustion on all fronts. Helen and I raise voices at each other during the worst of it, when you've been howling for almost an hour, complaining about the blockage inside you. We hate ourselves for doing it in front of you, kicking ourselves even as we hear it. We have this picture of ourselves as parents, as people who will never argue in front of a child, who will never show the worst emotions. It's just not possible. Not for human beings.

JANUARY 9

The thing that keeps surprising me is what a normal baby you look like. When I see you now, there's nothing to alert me to all of your travails, not unless you're doing your usual trick of pulling up your shirt to show everyone your scars (you do it because you love to bring fabric to your mouth). The tube has gone. The hospital that used to frame my vision of you is somewhere else. If I met you in the street, I'd think you were a little small, a little delicate, but I'd just presume you were premature. Then I'd turn you over to the cops—a girl of your age should not be out in the street on her own, talking to strange men.

Even the look in your eyes seems to be changing. I pin up a few photos at the office, and Mike, one of the guys I work with, says he thinks you've lost the haunted, intense look you had in earlier shots. I almost double take. I'm so used to seeing reminders of your fragility. I'm so used to thinking of you as a sick baby that it's hard to start thinking of you as a well baby. Of course, the tube could go back in tomorrow. But you know what? I don't think it will. I believe we're on the road.

JANUARY 10

4.11 kilograms. You're not listening to us. Up is the direction, not down. You have a bad morning, clogging up and screaming every time we try to get you to drink, so we aren't really surprised about the weight loss. Dr Barry decides, to our surprise, to keep going *sans* tube, with two changes to the current program. First, he suspects from Helen's description that the problem is heartburn and that the Ranitidine is not doing its job. So we've bumped up the dosage and also invested in some Mylanta. Second, he thinks we should start trying to put some solids into you, so we buy some rice cereal. Helen tries the cereal tonight. The results are inconclusive. You don't seem to hate it, but you don't keep much in your mouth.

JANUARY 11
Sunday, 18 weeks

He was right. The Ranitidine is not working. It's odd. For weeks and weeks it seemed to be doing the job. Now all of a sudden it's having little effect. Three times this afternoon I have to give you Mylanta, squirt a quick millilitre down your throat. A few minutes later, you calm down again. But it only masks the problem, it doesn't take it away.

Dr Barry has another drug in mind, Losec, but it can only be administered with solids. Helen mixes up some cereal again this morning and pushes the end of a spoon over your lower lip. It's not that you hate the taste. It's more that you have this look on your face of, What the hell do you expect me to do with this? Maybe you're swallowing a little, but if you are, it's not much. Most of it you just push straight back out again.

JANUARY 12

4.19 kilograms. So now you're just toying with us. Up one time, down the next. Truth is, I'm ecstatic. This is the heaviest you've ever been. The gain is substantial. And we both feel like we've been doing okay these past few days, getting our acts together.

The only blot on the landscape is the question of the extent to which your throat is tightening again. Swallowing is gradually becoming tougher for you. As the stricture closes, the milk can't get through fast enough, so it banks up until it hits the larynx and makes you splutter. You were due for a dilation this week, but Dr John is away.

We're away next week, heading off to Melbourne for a wedding and the chance to see your grandmother, aunts, uncles and cousins. This is our first trip away from home, our first real effort to behave like a normal family. It will be a chance to see what we're capable of.

JANUARY 13

Dr Ian's solution is obvious, but as usual it has somehow failed to occur to either of us. He says he doesn't want to put you in the hands of anyone new, so he'll do the dilation himself, not the balloon, but the rod again, under anaesthetic. Tomorrow morning. Helen calls at about three in the afternoon, telling me she is taking you to the hospital to be checked over by the anaesthetist. A bed has been booked for you in good old C1 South Ward.

You, according to Helen, are none too pleased to be back in the hospital, even if a few of the faces are familiar. She says you sit quietly, with your bottom lip trembling. If Helen moves away, you start to cry. We decide to take you home again. If you have to be ready to go by 6.45 am for an 8.30 procedure, that's not such a problem. You and Helen are up by then anyway.

We're a bit thrown by the idea of the rod, but at least you'll have five days to recover before Melbourne. And maybe it will mean that we can leave a longer time in between procedures again. We know you can't make another fortnight without something being done, so this is the best option. We can almost *hear* your throat closing at the moment.

JANUARY 14

I wake at 8.30 to find an empty house. Helen calls to say that you are heading off to theatre. She tells me not to bother coming yet, since you'll be in prep, theatre and recovery for quite some time. At eleven, I can't wait any more. I find you asleep in the ward bed, with Helen reading a book beside you. Dr Ian says your throat expanded easily under the rod. It had closed significantly—he couldn't get a 4 millimetre dilator through the stricture—but it was easy to push out. The look on your face is one of blissful peace.

You spend the afternoon in the ward, with Helen trying to feed you every couple of hours. We expected that you might be so sore that a tube would have to go back into place, but nobody else seems to think so. You suck carefully, taking small amounts. You throw up a few times as the day winds on, nothing too worrying.

It is odd being back in the ward. Nice to see all the familiar faces, good to watch the nurses making a fuss about what a big and healthy girl you are. What shocks me, in this context, is how far you've come. You don't look like these babies any more. You look much too well to be here.

JANUARY 16

11.40 pm. I've just crept back upstairs, cradling you in my arms, after another feed. Helen propped up on the pillow, you snuffling away, sucking and swallowing in your sleep. This is my nightly routine, staying up to give you medicine, then ferrying you up and downstairs for feeds, giving Helen a chance to get some sleep in between. Most nights

I'm here typing as the date changes, waiting to give you Cisapride or to make sure it stays down.

I almost have you standing today. We play a game where I put my hands under your armpits and lift you. Then I let you fall far enough so that your feet hit the ground and you can feel your weight. You smile and laugh and let your legs buckle. Today you snap your knees back and stand, assisted, for a few seconds. Twice. It is lovely to see you, looking up at me with your big blues and an expression of, Hey, what's happening down there?

You're also holding your head more upright. Now, when I sit you up, I don't have to assist you. It bobbles a bit—you look like a Thunderbird puppet. But it stays upright instead of lolling away. And you get to move and turn and look at what you want.

JANUARY 17

You really do have a way of bringing us back to Earth. The scales refuse to go any higher than 4.180 kilograms, down 10 grams in the last few days. We were both banking on a sizeable increase. Helen, who has had a tough few days since the dilation, takes it very badly, the tears immediate.

Our depression is compounded by the fact that you have your worst day for a long time. Who knows why it happens, but you don't have a single feed between dawn and dusk. Every time you try to eat, it comes rocketing back up your oesophagus, mixed with stomach acid, and hits the irritated area at the stricture. You cry and scream and cough, and that's the end of the feeding and the start of half an hour of trying to bring you back down again. You never get enough food to lose the feeling of hunger, so you can't sleep long enough to help with the healing process. The Ranitidine is now having absolutely no effect on you. What used to be reflux is now stinging, painful heartburn.

JANUARY 18
Sunday, 19 weeks

You have a quick regurgitation, first thing in the morning, and seem to get some annoying green stuff out of your system. Then you are right as rain for the rest of the day, which we spend playing, hoisting you up and making you laugh as Flying Baby, bouncing you up and down as Trampoline Baby and just sitting you on my lap and talking or singing to you. You have this new game, that Helen started, of putting your hand into any open mouth you can get to, having a good feel and then laughing to yourself. Yes, us weird people have teeth.

You have also developed a particular strain of humour. You think any word that starts with the letter 'b' is funny. Bus. Bear. Ball. Bureaucracy. Bum. (Note to self: one of those words actually is funny.) What a complex, absurdist way to divide things up into funny and not funny. Imagine if you still felt the same way as an adult. 'Robin Williams is not funny. Spike Milligan is not funny. But the chapter of the dictionary between A and C is hilarious.'

JANUARY 19

4.12 kilograms. Helen is worried that your lack of demand for milk is making her breasts smaller, shutting down the production line. She fears it won't start again when you are able to take more. Dr Barry still seems to think we're on an acceptable path, especially given the problems exacerbated by the dilation. I wonder how much longer we can do this. It's been 23 days since we started this tubeless experiment and you've put on less than 100 grams. There must come a point where we have to stop ourselves falling further behind. Other babies would usually put on about half a kilo in this time. You started life small (in the bottom 3 per cent) and you're not going forward. It's not a prescription for our comfort.

Tomorrow, you and your mother go to Melbourne. I follow the next day.

January 20

10.15 pm and here I am, padding about the house, standing in doorways, looking into empty rooms. I hate the fact that you're not here, that Helen is not here. I suspected it would feel strange, but not this strange. I feel disembodied by the lack of you. There's a ghost in this house and it's me.

You're sleeping in your grandmother's apartment in Melbourne. Helen rang a couple of hours ago to fill me in on the trip and let you hiccup down the phone at me. So far, so good. I knew everything would be fine. I knew she'd handle the flight as long as there wasn't an act of God to derail her. No matter how hard this trip is, it will be good for us. We have to get out of this house. We have to make a life.

JANUARY 22

You aren't as happy to see me as I am to see you. Or as Helen and I are to see each other. No, you are asleep. The good news is that, with your grandmother's help, Helen has managed to get some cereal and Losec into your system. The trick, apparently, is violence. Shovel the stuff in quickly, so you have to swallow at least some of it. Then, take a teddy bear and hold a gun to its head.

You scream at 10 pm when I give you the Ranitidine. You've never liked it, but you really, really hate it this time. It isn't like a tantrum, just fifteen inconsolable minutes. There is no obvious swallowing pain. Presumably, it's only heartburn. How long will it take us to get Losec into you regularly?

You sleep a couple of hours in the morning, cry at your cousins when they arrive, twinkle at your mother's friend Sheryl, and go to sleep to the sound of a new toy that plays (*plink plink plink*) 'Rock a Bye Baby' while projecting psychedelic light patterns onto the ceiling. Why are all kid's stories so bizarre? I can accept that putting a baby in a tree might be handy in a part of the world where people spend a lot of time outdoors and there are predators, but why a falling, presumably injured baby should make us feel all drifty sleepy is another thing.

JANUARY 23

Your mum and dad go out this evening, for the first time since you came home. Having managed to convince you at seven o'clock that sleep would be a good thing (why is it that we have to have this conversation every day?), Helen and I borrow the mobile phone, leave a watchful grand-mother in her armchair and exit the building. The café is not far. Around the corner. But it might as well be Uzbekhistan. It's as far as our world allows. We feel strange and loopy, like astronauts outside the ship, tethered by wires.

January 24

We're on the road, in our hire car, slicing through the Victorian countryside towards Beechworth for Malcolm and Wenona's wedding, the official reason for this trip. It's January dry, the crackling grass looking like it could go up any second. How will you cope with this excursion? We have no idea. Really, it's what we're here to find out. You're in the back in the baby seat, making the occasional noise, but mostly sleeping. When you're with us, you sit and stare out the window at the sky and the passing trees. We pull in to a roadside resting place, have a steak sandwich from the handy caravan and feed you under the gum trees, the dry grass and dust beneath us. I take a photo of you and your mother out in the elements.

Beechworth is an oasis of green. We dress you in a new outfit (with a slightly silly pixie cap—you can look at the photo twenty years from now and hate us), and take you to the wedding, in the grounds of what used to be a mental asylum and is now a university campus. You behave perfectly for the entire hour, 5 to 6 pm, that the bride spends being late, then start to howl the second she turns up. Perhaps it's her outfit. Such a critic. So I miss the vows while I wander around trying to calm you. This, I fear, is a glimpse of my life to be. You will start howling at every crucial moment: the last minute of close football games, the point of murder mysteries where the killer's identity is revealed, the moment when gossip conversations turn really juicy. I will spend my life craning to hear something I can't quite make out.

JANUARY 26
Monday, 20 weeks and one day

Back in Melbourne after a gentle, easy trip yesterday. Up at six o'clock. I feed you cereal, which you eat half-heartedly, sitting there with the stuff plastered all over your face—at least it's going in now, along with the Losec. I go back to sleep for an hour at 8 am, when Helen surfaces. You and I try visiting Tim and Aleks, but after 30 minutes you're hungry, so I take you back to your grandmother's apartment. Family dinner. Three small cousins running riot. It's such a shock to see it, to realise how quiet our life is. When they leave I find myself wondering if we should have more than one. Helen's mum insists that we should. I have doubts.

As we see more people, I find myself constantly answering the question, 'What will it be like when you grow up?' Well, hopefully by the time you're old enough to read this diary, most of the difficulties will be well into the past tense. You will have to eat smaller meals more often (grazing is what they call it, another supermodel behaviour). You will have to keep something to drink on hand to avoid food getting stuck on the way down (I suggest beer). You will always have to avoid foods likely to give you heartburn. And you should avoid eating meals too close to bedtime, just to be safe. These small legacies aside, you should lead a remarkably normal life, well, as normal a life as you can hope for with us as your parents. (Hmm, on reflection, I may have been writing about the wrong problems.) Perhaps every year or two or five, you'll have to have your throat dilated, but on balance, touch wood, it won't be something that gets in your way.

January 27

Fwooooooooooooooh! How do you spell a long, slow exhalation? I'm not sure. All I know is that the slumping breath is what I hear coming out of myself tonight. I just don't get it. 4.05 kilograms. Much as we no longer bother to take anything for granted, I really did suspect that the worst we could expect after such a reasonable week would be the status quo, not a decline. Back home, back to the familiar worries.

The thing is, as everybody has kept saying to us over and over, you look so well. You have colour in your cheeks. You look bigger. And as a little human being, it's as if you've come out of your shell during the trip. It's done so much good to see people and places, to get out and expand your horizons. And rather than being anxious, we were actually quite relaxed for much of the time. We hoped this would rub off onto you. You've been feeding regularly and the change of drugs seems to have had a positive effect. You took solids three times today.

Dr Barry leaves a message to tell us to persevere. We should come back in on Friday. He says we've had an odd week and shouldn't be too worried. But they're *all* odd weeks. It's been four and a half of them now without weight gain. How long is this experiment meant to go on? We feel as if we don't really understand what we're trying to achieve any more.

JANUARY 28

Helen takes you down to the beach today—you go out into the world and sing to nature. You love being outside. (You can't possibly be my daughter—summer, to me, is an excuse to stay indoors and grumble about the hot weather.) Helen says that until now, she has been a little too scared to enjoy you, too aware, too constantly, of how fragile you still are. With the trip under our belt, and you so bouncy and bright, it's much easier for her to relax.

She has become convinced that your throat has tightened up again and is making it hard for you to eat. She rings Dr Ian and asks if that could be what's happening. He says yes. She says we were hoping the last procedure would give us more room than a fortnight. He says nothing. Helen can hear the familiar shrug through the phone, the one that says, 'Don't ask me for an answer to that because there isn't one.'

So, you're booked in on Friday for a long hospital day: a weigh-in, a consultation with Dr Barry, a visit to Out-patients for immunisations, and a familiar journey to radiology, where Dr John will give you a barium swallow so we can see what's going on in your oesophagus. And if it is closing, then he'll dilate it again.

The other thing Helen says to me tonight, as she comes

back up the stairs after feeding you, is, 'You have a very beautiful daughter.'

January 30

4.01 kilograms. You go for a barium swallow and a dilation this afternoon. Dr John says the stricture has tightened, but not as far as previously. Your throat is still open to about 4mm. He dilates it up to 10mm and says it expands easily. So now we have a situation that confuses us. We're just not sure why you're not putting on weight. And neither is Dr Barry. Helen is almost despondent about the state of affairs. Feeding is such a personal, physical thing for her. She thinks she's failing you.

January 31

Feeling better, though things have not actually improved. Helen says she was turning it over during the night (when you're up at 11, 1, 3 and 5 ...) and decided that if the tube has to go back in, then so be it. As my mother says on the phone today, we have to think of the whole experiment as a victory. We only thought we were going to keep it out for a couple of days—it's been five weeks now. And if it goes back in, it won't be the prime feeding route. We will control the tube more than it controls us.

Today isn't bad, for a day after a dilation. You sleep for most of it, still weary after the procedure. You throw up a couple of times, once fairly violently and once just the daintiest of dollops. Overall, you eat well, with a major achievement late in the afternoon. We feed you rice cereal and Losec, and a fair quantity at that, but you still look a little hungry. So Helen opens a bottle of strained apple baby food and offers you a few spoonfuls, which you suck into your mouth, turn over with your tongue and then swallow. You might take more, but she isn't keen to put too much fruit into such a sensitive digestive system. We'll build up to it. You also take some milk to wash it down, all in all the most we've ever seen you eat.

We are buoyed enough by this to go for a long walk to the beach, you in the stroller with your blue bonnet on, staring at the trees in bloom and the dogs on leashes and kids on skateboards and cars rushing by and people showering and other babies in prams and I don't know what else. Having a world to look at tires you out. We sit on the steps and watch the waves roll lazily over as you sleep between us.

February

Monday, 21 weeks and one day

Helen takes you in to be weighed. This is it, crunch time. So much has been going right lately. The only lingering unease (and what an unease) is your weight. And Dr Barry, who has pushed this experiment so hard, has made it clear that the window of opportunity is finally closing. Either we see some improvement or El Tubo is back.

Naomi, the Universe has a black sense of humour. When Helen gets to the hospital, she finds out that the scales in Emergency, the ones that have been depressing us for a month, the ones that seem to specialise in bad news, are broken. And how long have they been broken for? No-one is sure, but probably for some time. According to the shiny, new replacement scales, you're 4.37 kilograms. You've been gaining weight, not losing it. Not wanting to believe it, Helen tries standing on the adult scales, first without you and then with you, to measure the difference. They suggest you might be as much as 4.4 kilos.

Our eyes haven't been lying. You *are* getting bigger. It's achingly slow, but there is progress. The dilations seem to be working, and the weight is gradually accumulating on your bones. The tube is not coming back. The tough times are not over (even today, you have to be fed every hour because you are so clogged up and phlegmy), but more and more, the road we're on feels familiar. And we're pointed in the right direction. We have a pretty good idea of what we're in for now, of what constitutes our daily life, with all its ups and downs. We have achieved some sort of normality, whatever that is.

There are still causes for concern. The doctors have flagged another possible operation, perhaps when you're eighteen months old, to build a valve at the junction of your oesophagus and your stomach. This would help fight the reflux. Whether it's needed is up to you and how well you handle life. If you thrive, you may postpone it forever. If you thrive, we may be able to start phasing the drugs out as you become stronger and more able to manage the situation yourself. Sitting up will help keep the food down. Walking will help it even more. Time, patience and good fortune are all we need.

Our parental priority is to help you to gain weight, to help you get to the point where you can help yourself. We've been told that your growth will be slow for a year or two. Then, hopefully, you will begin the catch-up. Then, hopefully, we will get some sleep.

In the meantime, if we start feeling sorry for ourselves, we just have to look at you to be reminded of what this is all about. Sometimes, my fingertips trace along your scars at night. I survey the warm roughness, the thick, rubbery touch of the healing tissue, and I'm reminded of where we've been. But in the light of day, I see the remembered redness of those same scars slowly dying to the softest of healthy pinks, and I know where we're going.

So I feel that this is where I should stop, that this is the day I've been expecting and hoping would come. It's been a long, strange year, a journey to all kinds of places I never imagined I'd go. The constants have been Helen, the thought (and reality) of you, and this diary. Each, in its own way, has kept me moving forwards. Helen has brought me love and support, you have brought me strength and joy, and this diary has given me therapy, exorcism and the chance to explain to myself what was really going on.

I once said I'd finish on the first day of pure happiness that came our way. Today is not a day of pure anything, though if I had to nominate, I'd say it was a day of relief. Mine was a foolish, romantic thought. Life is not pure, Naomi. It doesn't work that way. Pure happiness passes in seconds or minutes or, if you're very lucky, hours. Days are a bit much to ask for, unless you have access to strong antidepressants. And the pursuit of pure happiness is pointless anyway. Life is not about a single state or emotion. It's about balance in the face of chaos, about finding a way forward through good and bad. It's about realising there is sorrow and there is joy and which one we choose to emphasise is up to us.

As your father I hope with every drop of my blood that the worst of the adversity is over for you. In my rational moments, I know it probably isn't, that there will be other times of pain, other travails, other suffering in your life. But it's not my job as a father to be that rational. It's my job to love you, to dream of the best for you, to do what I can to help you find it. I have faith that you will. I have faith that your strength and resilience will see you right. I have faith.

Naomi, the way you have come into this life has been harder than some and easier than others. If I can squeeze in one more thought, it's that what has happened to you makes you different, but it doesn't make you special. Everyone has a tale to tell. What makes you special is a million other things. What makes you special is you. What makes you special is how much you mean to Helen and me. Your story isn't over—it's only just crossed the starting line. But I can't help feeling, as I take in your sleeping face, that your life is becoming more and more your own, and that it's time to get out of the way and let you do the writing yourself.

POSTSCRIPT

The tube never went back in and other than our regular breezy visits to Emergency to check her weight, Naomi has stayed out of hospital. She's picked up her share of bugs and viruses, but she's fought them all herself. Touch wood, it has been a year since her last dilation and she's not showing signs of needing one soon.

Our main problem has been getting food in and keeping it there. (Note to parents with reflux babies: buy a good washing machine and a carpet cleaner and forget about sleep.) In weight terms, Naomi started out in the bottom 3 per cent of babies. She has now made it past the 10 per cent mark. Progress is slow, but we are ahead of expectations. We are still lucky.

Naomi never crawled, because we couldn't really let her spend time on her stomach, but she got herself around with a bum shuffle much like the one I developed at her age. She walked late, at seventeen months, but only because she was determined to wait until she mastered the skill before showing it to the world. We caught her walking sometimes when she thought we weren't looking.

This book will be published a few weeks before her second birthday. When people ask me what the last couple of years have been like, I tend to say 'the longest decade of our life—and the best.' Naomi is feisty, flirtatious and fearless. She's as stubborn as her parents, but much cheekier. Now that she's on her feet, she's made friends with all the kids and pets in the neighbourhood, and spends as much time as she can out in the street looking for adventure. She still makes us cry occasionally, but she makes us laugh every day.

ACKNOWLEDGEMENTS

Thanks to our family and friends (those who are mentioned in this book and those who aren't, but were there). Thanks to Andrew Korda, Barry Duffy, Ian Kern, John Pereira and the staff of King George V, Sydney Children's Hospital Intensive Care Unit, C1 South Ward and Emergency. Thanks to John Alexander, John Lyons, Anthony Dennis and the *Sydney Morning Herald* staff, particularly the Web team, for their support. Thanks to Sophie Cunningham, Fiona Inglis, Emma Cotter, Bernadette Foley, Ruth Grüner and Caroline Baum, for their help with this book.